TRAINING ACTORS'

Contemporary actor training in the US and UK has become increasingly multicultural and multilinguistic. Border-crossing, cross-cultural exchange in contemporary theatre practices, and the rise of the intercultural actor has meant that actor training today has been shaped by multiple modes of training and differing worldviews. How might mainstream Anglo-American voice training for actors address the needs of students who bring multiple worldviews into the training studio? When several vocal training traditions are learned simultaneously, how does this shift the way actors think, talk, and perform? How does this change the way actors understand what a voice is? What it can/should do? How it can/should do it?

Using adaptations of a traditional Korean vocal art, *p'ansori*, with adaptations of the "natural" or "free" voice approach, Tara McAllister-Viel offers an alternative approach to training actors' voices by (re)considering the materials of training: breath, sound, "presence," and text. This work contributes to ongoing discussions about the future of voice pedagogy in theatre, for those practitioners and scholars interested in performance studies, ethnomusicology, voice studies, and intercultural theories and practices.

Tara McAllister-Viel is Head of Voice and Speech at East 15 Acting School, UK.

Routledge Voice Studies

Series editors: Konstantinos Thomaidis and Ben Macpherson

https://www.routledge.com/Routledge-Voice-Studies/book-series/RVS

The Routledge Voice Studies series offers a platform for rigorous discussion of voice across disciplines, practices and areas of interest. This series aims to facilitate the dissemination and cross-fertilisation of voice-related research to effectively generate new knowledge and fresh critical insights on voice, vocality, and voicing.

Composing for Voice
A Guide for Composers, Singers, and Teachers
Paul Barker

Voice Studies
Critical Approaches to Process, Performance and Experience
By Konstantinos Thomaidis and Ben Macpherson

Training Actors' Voices
Towards an Intercultural/Interdisciplinary Approach
Tara McAllister-Viel

TRAINING ACTORS' VOICES

Towards an Intercultural/
Interdisciplinary Approach

Tara McAllister-Viel

Routledge
Taylor & Francis Group

LONDON AND NEW YORK

First published 2019
by Routledge
2 Park Square, Milton Park, Abingdon, Oxon OX14 4RN

and by Routledge
711 Third Avenue, New York, NY 10017

Routledge is an imprint of the Taylor & Francis Group, an informa business

British Library Cataloguing-in-Publication Data
A catalogue record for this book is available from the British Library

Library of Congress Cataloging-in-Publication Data
Names: McAllister-Viel, Tara, author.
Title: Training actors' voices: towards an intercultural/interdisciplinary
approach.
Description: Abingdon, Oxon; New York, NY: Routledge, 2018. |
Includes bibliographical references and index.
Identifiers: LCCN 2018008811| ISBN 9781138088689
(hardback: alk. paper) | ISBN 9781138088696 (paperback: alk. paper) |
ISBN 9781315109718 (ebook)
Subjects: LCSH: Voice culture. | Voice culture–Korea (South) | P'ansori.
Classification: LCC PN2071.S65 M45 2003 | DDC 792.028–dc23
LC record available at https://lccn.loc.gov/2018008811

ISBN: 978 1 138 08868 9 (hbk)
ISBN: 978-1-138-08869-6 (pbk)
ISBN: 978-1-315-10971-8 (ebk)

Typeset in Bembo
by Sunrise Setting Ltd, Brixham, UK

This book is lovingly dedicated to my children
Tilly, Plen, and Mae
Mi vida, mi alma, mi corazón.

CONTENTS

ACKNOWLEDGEMENTS

I would like to gratefully acknowledge those who gave of their time and talents to make the work documented here possible.

First, this monograph was written with the generous support of the International Research Center, "Interweaving Performance Cultures," Freie Universität-Berlin, Germany, Research Fellowship 2015–2016. Thank you to Erika Fischer-Lichte, Gabriele Brandstetter, Matthias Warstat, and Christel Weiler for inviting me to the IRC and for your invaluable feedback during the writing of this monograph. Thank you to Torsten Jost for our conversations that shaped Chapter Five and for your practical support throughout my time in Berlin. Thank you to Holgar Hartung for your support and attention to every detail.

To my students in South Korea and Great Britain: Thank you for your patience, kindness, and trust. Your hard work and honest feedback have shaped this research and guided me as a teacher.

To my teachers: I am particularly grateful to Phillip Zarrilli for your continued support over the past 30 years. To Karen Ryker, for nurturing my work well beyond graduate school. To the loving memory of my first p'ansori teacher, Han Nongsŏn, who treated me with such kindness. I have been humbled by the patience, support, and generosity of my second p'ansori sonsaengnim, Sŏng Uhyang. I am also deeply indebted to Bae Il-dong and Seo Suk-Ja, who helped me learn when I struggled most. To Chan Park, who graciously took me into her home to teach me and whose research and writing have guided my own work from the beginning.

I would also like to thank the master teachers who graciously welcomed me into their classrooms and gave me the gift of their knowledge in training and interviews: Ahn Sook-son, Chong Hoi Suk, Choi Yoon-Cho, Choi Young-Ai, Cicely Berry, Kristin Linklater, and Patsy Rodenburg. I would also like to thank Moon Seung-Jae for his shared enthusiasm for this work. I am guided by the ethnographic research of Um Hae-kyung and Heather Willoughby, whose work as practitioners, scholars, and researchers have directed my focus and whose supportive e-mails have encouraged me.

My tremendous appreciation for translation assistance: To my friend and in-class translator of four years at KNUA, the talented Park Mi-kyung, who taught me to look behind the mountain. To my friend, colleague, and in-class translator at KNUA in 2001, Lee Yu-Kyung, who was never too busy to offer the gift of her time. To my good friend and colleague, Hwang Ha-Young, an incredible scholar, and her brother Hwang Il-Suk, for onsite translation at Namdaemun Market, and the loving support of their parents. To my good friend and colleague, Yoo Jeung-Sook, for support as in-class translator for the 2003 Summer workshop at KNUA and for the pleasure of working together at East 15. To my friend Ahreum Han for helping me decipher dialects through street noise on audio samples. And Park Young Hoon for translation during conference lectures and workshops, chasing permissions, and your support over the course of 18 years.

To my colleagues at The Korean National University of Arts, School of Drama, especially the love and support of my long-time friend, Professor Kim Soogi, who trained with me under Phillip Zarrilli so many years ago at the Asian/Experimental Theatre Program, University of Wisconsin-Madison.

To my friends and colleagues at The Royal Central School of Speech and Drama and East 15 Acting School for your support and feedback while developing voice curriculum for both institutions.

To Eva Marie Gauss for your invaluable feedback reading an early draft of this monograph. And to the series editors of Voice Studies for their patience and support.

Finally to my family for their continued support and my best friend, Amanda Ward Prince, for your fierce belief in me.

INTRODUCTION

Training actor's voices: Towards an intercultural/ interdisciplinary approach

In the January 2010 special issue of *American Theatre* magazine,[1] five master voice trainers were singled out for special attention as "pillars of voice work": Arthur Lessac, Cicely Berry, Kristin Linklater, Patsy Rodenburg, and Catherine Fitzmaurice were described as "the great lions of the field of voice work" and "visionary innovators in the craft" in which "there can be hardly any actor, singer or voice specialist who has not been touched directly or indirectly by the five individuals" (Gener 2010: 33). These eminent teachers are responsible for establishing the predominate mainstream principles and practices currently found in most voice programs in US and UK acting conservatoires and university theatre departments, specifically helping to create a strong trans-Atlantic link between Anglo-American voice pedagogies.[2]

They have also had significant influence outside of the US and UK, shaping contemporary voice pedagogy globally through their books, workshops, teacher training certification programs and participation in university and drama school teacher training courses that attract international students.[3] As evidenced in their writings of practice, overseas teaching experiences have, at times, affected the way they think and talk about the voice. For instance, in Berry's *Text in Action* (2001), she explored the cultural differences in sound, specifically detailing her experiences teaching voice workshops in Seoul, South Korea. Berry wrote, "And this poses questions about how much the sound pattern is intrinsic to the nature of the culture and to what extent the sound pattern influences the way we think" (59). Their practice has a global focus and sometimes integrates principles and practices that are considered "non-Western." As Erika Fischer-Lichte pointed out, cultural exchanges in the theatre change the sphere they enter as well as the sphere they leave behind (Fischer-Lichte 1997: 1, 133–134).

The international scope of contemporary mainstream Anglo-American voice pedagogy parallels other forms of the "global phenomenon" in theatre practice (Fischer-Lichte, Riley, and Gissenwehrer, 1990: introduction). Apart from these five influential master trainers, institutional developments seem to signal an increased interest in border-crossing: The Center for Performance Research (CPR) based in Aberystwyth, Wales and Falmouth, England, has been hosting the bi-annual Giving Voice conference since 1990, bringing to the UK internationally recognized voice trainers and practitioners from around the world. Their 2016 conference was co-hosted with The Grotowski Institute in Wroclaw, Poland alongside the Institute's VoicEncounters festival (Centre for Performance Research 2017). The Royal Central School of Speech and Drama (RCSSD) (re)opened the International Center for Voice in 2000, and the Voice and Speech Trainers Association (VASTA) had their first international conference in Glasgow, Scotland, August 2005, titled "Breaking Boundaries: Crossing the Cultural Divide."

This monograph steps into this trend to both reflect on current practice as well as devise another training possibility through the development of an explicit inter-cultural approach to training actors' voices. Here, I investigate the integration of a branch of Anglo-American voice training, that I call the "natural" or "free" voice approach, based on the work of Berry, Linklater, and Rodenburg, with adaptations of a traditional Korean vocal art form called *p'ansori*. The premise of this mono-graph is that cross-cultural influence has been integral to developing current Anglo-American voice practice and will continue to be influential to its future development. If there is an "increasing interest in cross-cultural exchange" (Berry 2001: 63) in the new millennium, what does this mean for the future of voice training? When the actor's voice is trained through different models of experience, what sort of actor emerges? When the actor changes, what sort of theatre emerges? How might intercultural voice training suggest new ways of creating theatre? One aim of this monograph is to add to ongoing discussions between practitioners and scholars about the future of voice training for actors in a global community.

Underlying this book and informing it are my own experiences teaching and studying voice outside of the US. In 2000, I moved from Chicago, USA, to Seoul, South Korea, in order to accept a two-year Visiting Professorship in Voice at the Korean National University of Arts (KNUA 2000), School of Drama. I taught full-time for the first two years, part-time for another two years and guest taught for a fifth year while completing my PhD in Performance Practice (Voice) in England. Directly thereafter (2005), I accepted a permanent full-time post, Lecturer-Voice, at the Royal Central School of Speech and Drama (RCSSD) in London, England. I continued to return to Seoul periodically over the next ten years to guest teach and lecture.

Active border-crossing has influenced my teaching practice over time, espe-cially when designing intercultural curriculum for the educational aims of the insti-tutions with which I have worked. Keeping a permanent residence in England for ten years allowed me to become an American/British dual national and member of the EU. This brought other employment and artistic possibilities; I began teaching freelance workshops and lectured at acting conservatoires in Spain and Germany. In 2011, I accepted a post as Head of Voice and Speech at East 15 Acting School, London, England, UK, a position I sought, in part, because of the school's large international student population and the privilege to teach with a prestigious international staff.

In this monograph, I use my voice classrooms at KNUA 2004 as a case study with additional examples from my classrooms at the Royal Central School of Speech and Drama (RCSSD) and East 15 Acting School (E15), to document and critically reflect on how 'going global' changes the most fundamental principles and practices of Anglo-American voice pedagogy. I begin with autobiographical material as one departure point for exploring larger intercultural training contexts and the issues that arise from those contexts.

My experiences creating intercultural training opportunities, both within and outside of my voice classrooms, are not unique to me or to the institutions I work/ have worked for, nor does such interest in cross-cultural curriculum emerge from isolated, recent developments. My ability to develop an intercultural approach to training actors' voices would have been impossible without the cosmopolitan educational communities already in place where I taught, the government funding and work permits I received by both Korean and British governments, the granting organizations that funded my work, the resources available at the Korean and British universities who employed me, the surrounding theatre communities who were also interested in active border-crossing, and a history of cultural exchange in theatre already in progress that nurtured me both as a student and a teacher.

For instance, the year I arrived at The Royal Central School of Speech and Drama (2005), I was placed in charge of two of the three voice programs within the undergraduate acting conservatoire: the BA(hon) Collaborative and Devised Theatre and BA(hon) Music Theatre.[4] I participated in training students to be "active cultural border crossers" (Tatinge Nascimento 2009: 61). I created a three-year relationship between CDT and The Grotowski Institute in Wroclaw, Poland, offering my students training opportunities in the Institute's Forest base in Brzezinka and visits to the Year of Grotowski (2009) international festivals and symposium in Wroclaw.[5] Reciprocally, I set up training workshops by Teatr ZAR, The Grotowski Institute's in-house company, at RCSSD and co-curated Theatre Noise international conference.[6] Training, performance, and research outcomes included, among others, an original, devised public performance, *The Runners*, by CDT students at Shunt Vaults, London, a companion roundtable "Song, Memory, Emotion,"[7] and a publication of collected essays (Kendrick and Roesner 2011). Partial funding was provided by the Polish Cultural Institute in London, the Teaching Quality Enhancement Fund (TQEF), and RCSSD's Centre for Excellence, in which staff were encouraged to create international ties with European training institutions.

My interest in cross-cultural exchange and ability to develop intercultural curriculum was grounded in my own training through the well-established educational institutions I chose to attend. Like many undergraduate students, I took advantage of study abroad programs that linked US universities with other institutions outside of the US. I traveled to the Soviet Union and Europe while studying towards my BA theatre and music degrees. These experiences provoked me to seek out additional intercultural training, specifically as an MFA Acting student at the Asian/Experimental Theatre program at the University of Wisconsin-Madison, Department of Theatre and Drama,[8] which had been training actors since 1964, the "nucleus of a newly established International Theatre Program." It had been established as a "result of an increased concentration on International Studies within the university as a whole. Initial support for development of the program was provided by grants from the Rockefeller Foundation and the Ford Foundation" (Zarrilli et al. 2009: 215).[9] At UW Madison, I trained intensively through various traditions simultaneously, specifically taiqiquan, kathakali, kalarippatyattu, and hatha yoga, as well as popular mainstream approaches to voice training including Berry, Linklater, Lessac, and Rodenburg.

I had spent the majority of my professional acting career integrating these specific modes of training into performance. My training was tested predominately in front of mainstream US audiences and within conventional employment markets. I apprenticed at the Milwaukee Repertory Theatre in order to earn my Equity card, acquired an agent, and freelanced for national recognized repertory companies, Shakespearian festivals, film, and television. My training also allowed me to produce my own work within a Chicago-based theatre company I helped to establish. In this way, my training "worked" for me; it was a set of skills that allowed me to do what I wanted to do artistically, it paid my rent, and it offered me job opportunities outside of the US.[10] My training at the Asian/Experimental Theatre Program was one reason I was specifically hired by KNUA to design their voice curriculum for both the undergraduate and postgraduate acting programs.

The Korean National University of Arts, School of Drama: Case study

KNUA, now called K-Arts, is a government-sponsored academy founded in 1993 with the opening of its first school, the School of Music. The School of Drama opened in 1994. From 1995 to 1997, three more schools opened: the School of Film, the School of Dance, and the School of Visual Arts. The last of the Schools opened in 1998, the School of Korean Traditional Arts, two years before I arrived at KNUA. With the opening of this final school, the Korean government mandated that actors-in-training at the School of Drama should add two years of traditional Korean singing, primarily *p'ansori*, to their required drama training (KNUA 2004, prospectus).

P'ansori is a traditional Korean vocal art form in which a single vocalist performing on a straw mat [*p'an*] tells a story using sung passages [*ch'ang*] and spoken passages [*aniri*], along with dramatic gestures [*pallim*].[11] The single vocalist is accompanied by a seated drummer playing a double-barreled drum [*puk*]. At certain points during the performance, the drummer and/or the audience will shout calls of encouragement [*ch'uimsae*] to the storyteller, which is vital to the energy and spirit of the performance. One traditional *p'ansori* story may take several hours to perform with the storyteller embodying multiple characters and character voices. Vocal endurance, strength and flexibility is paramount to the *p'ansori* performer, as is the unique sound [*sŏngŭm*]. These elements are directly related to breathing from the lower *dahnjeon*, located two inches below the navel and two inches inside the body. Within the School of Drama at KNUA, breathing from the *dahnjeon* was one of several *p'ansori* techniques considered beneficial to Korean actor training.

The actor training at this conservatory included an "integration of fusion techniques" in "both external and indigenous methods and traditions," in order to develop "a contemporary national culture and Korean artistic 'voice'" (KNUA 2000).[12] The "integration" of techniques included "[Kristin] Linklater voice technique, Alexander movement, Asian martial arts . . . and traditional Korean singing" (KNUA 2000: 14). To this mix, I added the approaches of Cicely Berry and Patsy Rodenburg because the similarities of their training approaches create a significant branch of training useful to my students.

The particular combination of approaches to training actors' voices were chosen for several reasons. The choice to train actors' voices through *p'ansori* training comes from a larger history of integrating *p'ansori* with Western theatre aesthetics over the past 100 years, from the beginnings of *ch'anggeuk* theatre in the 1900s to the Korean avant-garde in the 1960s and 1970s, to Korean postmodern performers today. However, the study of *p'ansori* and other Korean traditional arts within education was mandated by the Korean government as part of a larger support scheme first implemented during the 1960s to preserve indigenous art forms.

In 1963, the Korean Government implemented the Intangible Cultural Property scheme and aligned the performing arts, namely, *p'ansori* (Intangible Cultural Property Number 5), with nation building (Um 1999). At this same time, Korea was undergoing tremendous change after the Korean War (1950–1953).

> As it entered the 1960's [*sic*], the Korean government endeavored to establish a growing industrial economy. This was particularly true as the incoming regime of Pak Chung-hee introduced a series of five-year development plans. Western culture became dominant as one result of this policy and indigenous traditions continued to fade.
>
> *(Han 1990: 36)*

KNUA's founding mission can be understood within this wider socio-historical context. It read,

> The launch of the Korean National University of Arts has also served as a much needed catalyst to recapture, after many years of heavy western influence at the expense of traditional Korean artistry, a contemporary national culture and Korean artistic "voice" composed of both external and indigenous methods and traditions.
>
> *(KNUA 2000: 8)*

The KNUA curriculum was designed not simply to train the literal voice of the actor, but as an institutional vehicle for "voicing" Korean "contemporary national culture." For a country struggling with issues of national identity through a politically turbulent 20th century, "nationalism," or an understanding of what it means to be "Korean" within an ever-shifting landscape, became a main issue. KNUA, in partnership with the Korean government, chose to use pedagogical structure as one means of strengthening a cultural voice.

The particular Anglo-American voice approaches were chosen in part because they were internationally recognized. The founders of these approaches, Linklater, Berry, and Rodenburg, had been teaching overseas extensively throughout their careers. Seven months after arriving at KNUA, I would take my MFA Acting students with me to complete a five-day voice training intensive with Cicely Berry in Seoul, as a part of the 2000 Seoul International Theatre Festival. Also, KNUA wanted their voice curriculum based on dominant mainstream methods taught in US and UK acting training programs because familiarity with these approaches would be necessary when KNUA students participated in travel abroad programs and/or accepted work in the US or the UK. Finally, all of KNUA's acting faculty in the School of Drama had trained in the US and Europe, and used their overseas educational experiences to aid in the design of the new KNUA training curriculum.

As a result of training in two unique traditions simultaneously, with the intent to "integrate" methods, my students and I altered the way we thought and talked about voice and this in turn affected the way I taught the voice exercises I brought with me from the US.

The origins of this approach

This research began by trying to find practical solutions for certain curriculum problems. My first problem at KNUA was adapting the voice curriculum I brought with me from the US to the cultural context of KNUA and the needs of Korean actors-in-training by way of English/Korean in-class translation. The second problem arose when attempting to integrate two unique vocal training traditions simultaneously, adaptations of *p'ansori* and an Anglo-American branch of training I call the "natural" or "free" voice approach. My third curriculum problem arose when I attempted to transfer my KNUA-based curriculum to the very different cultural context of London-based acting conservatoires. Eventually, I developed a research strategy from these experiences and asked, can the curriculum I created to train my US students be adapted to train KNUA students? Then, can the emerging intercultural approach I designed for KNUA be adapted to train my UK students? A larger question emerged over the years, could the developing intercultural/interdisciplinary training provide an alternative paradigm for training the actor's voice or was each adaptation too context-specific and tied to my personal way of working as a teacher? In answering this question, I turned to Lo and Gilbert's idea of creating "strategic way[s] of rethinking the local and context-specific through the global and vice versa" (Lo and Gilbert 2002: 48–49).

Just as I arrived at KNUA's School of Drama to design and implement voice curriculums specifically beginning with Linklater's first book, *Freeing the Natural Voice* (Linklater 1976),[13] *American Theatre* magazine (January 2000) published an article entitled "Far horizons," in which Linklater had been interviewed as one of eight professionals responding to the question, "Can American artists benefit from leaving the comfort of US training traditions and studying theatre in, or through the lens of, another culture?" (Wren 2000: 38–39). Linklater's reply sparked a very public debate between herself and SITI founder Anne Bogart,[14] subsequently published in various issues of *American Theatre* and culminating in an eight-page special insert in the magazine the following year—a discussion between Linklater and Bogart mediated by David Diamond with a Q&A from select theatre professionals (Bogart 2000: 3; Diamond 2001: 32–38; Linklater 2000: 3).

In the article that began the debate, Linklater wrote:

> Young actors are too easily tempted to taste the appetizers and desserts of butoh, kathakali, kabuki, Suzuki, Balinese dancing, t'ai chi and the tao of voice instead of getting deep nourishment from the meat and potatoes of our own European-based, verbal traditions. Good actors are inherently versatile— they can pick up ideas from all over the place—but they should be wary of becoming whores with low self-esteem. They and their teachers sell themselves short when they bow down to foreign gods.
>
> *(Wren 2000: 38)*

What interested me about her comments was her focus on Eastern practices and what appeared to be an adversarial relationship created in her comparison between Eastern and Western (European) verbal traditions. Earlier in her career, Linklater appeared to advocate certain Eastern modes of training, specifically "t'ai chi and yoga," for "ridding the body of habitual tensions" as part of the necessary preparatory work for developing the actor's voice (Linklater 1976: 4). By 2006, Linklater's work had elements that were explicitly interwoven with Eastern training modes:

> I must acknowledge that very few of the physical exercises were created by me; I have appropriated and absorbed them from many different sources . . . Yoga floor exercises have been customized for specific vocal purposes and may be almost unrecognizable as Yoga.
>
> *(2006: 3)*

The binary created between East and West in Linklater's response to the "Far horizons" question is problematic, in part, because traditions considered "Western" may have already "appropriated and absorbed" non-Western practice.[15] Also, this question, asked by a leading US theatre publication at the turn of the new millennium, seemed out of step with developments in contemporary US theatre and actor training. A decade before this discussion, I had graduated from UW-Madison. I did not have to leave "the comfort of US training traditions" in order to "study theatre in, or through the lens of, another culture" (Wren 2000: 38). Finally, Linklater's comments in relation to "verbal arts traditions" (Wren 2000: 38) were of particular interest because of the job that lay ahead of me designing voice curriculum at KNUA.[16]

Unlike Linklater's insistence that American actors "get [their] roots deep enough into this tradition" before they "have earned the right to meet other, international ones" (Diamond 2001: 32–33), the curriculum at KNUA offered simultaneous study of different traditions throughout the students' time at the school. This was similar to my experience as a student at Madison. The KNUA curriculum model, and to some degree the UW-Madison training model, seemed to suggest that there was no linear hierarchy in which the student must first learn one tradition before learning others. This is not to say that the power relationship between traditions in the studio or the process of interweaving traditions is easily managed. In fact, such interactions are controversial.

Linklater warned, "If we come to them [non-Western training modes] as if we're going to the street fair—to see what we can pick up to decorate our living rooms—then we're in trouble" (Diamond 2001: 32–33). Bogart agreed: "'boutiquing' is dangerous [. . .]. The word I look for in actor training is rigor" (Diamond 2001: 34, original emphasis). The way p'ansori and Anglo-American voice training interacted at KNUA was rigorous. Frequently, my students would finish two hours of p'ansori training and come directly to my class for another two hours of voice training. However, "rigor" was only one part of structuring this interaction. Integration strategies were needed, as well as ways to avoid reducing art forms to a series of training techniques that "decorated" the emerging approach.

Korean scholar Choi Sun Hee has suggested one can avoid reducing an art to a "mere technique" by placing it back into its historical and cultural context (Choi 2000: 61). Many of my KNUA drama students had not been familiar with p'ansori training and culture, but through the School of Traditional Korean Arts, they were exposed to one understanding of p'ansori culture in a classroom setting, along with the instructor's personal understanding of p'ansori history. This provided some cultural and historical context for the p'ansori vocal training. Likewise, Anglo-American voice training also needed to be placed in a historical-cultural context. KNUA was one of the first schools in Korea to offer voice training as a separate module within actor training. One of the first questions I fielded from students on my first day of teaching was, "What is 'voice' training and why has it been separated from the acting classes?"

Many of the freshman students had never heard of voice training before and the mainstream voice texts I brought with me from the US did not necessarily help to define and describe the discipline for them. The content of the texts exemplified the information the authors considered important, but my students had other considerations not addressed in these texts. I noticed more than ever before the degree to which US and British culture influenced pedagogy and discipline-specific language with phrases like "voice beautiful" and "outside inwards" (Linklater 1976: 3). Although several authors tried to make the discipline more accessible by targeting the layperson within the books' readership (Linklater 1976: 1; Rodenburg 1992: ix), the reader would need to be a cultural "insider" to put the work into an understandable context. My Korean students would also need to be fluent in English, with a working vocabulary of the specific teaching languages used in voice texts. At that time, no voice texts had been translated into Korean, although the Head of Acting was in e-mail contact with Linklater to authorize a Korean translation of *Freeing the Natural Voice*.[17]

The basic assumption that the voice can be trained as a separate discipline from acting training and that one can write down that training in a text for others to teach and learn is a particular kind of pedagogical philosophy. Linklater wrote, "In the following chapters I have tried to capture the work that Iris Warren said should never be written down" (Linklater 1976: 4).

Freeing the Natural Voice is also designed to fit a certain kind of curriculum, which trains actors for a particular kind of theatre. In the back of our class text, Linklater suggested a "Hypothetical four-year actor-training program" (Linklater 1976: 202–207).[18] Although her approach would fit well with such a proposed four-year acting training program, it would have to be considerably adapted for the specific curriculum design already in place at KNUA. Linklater suggested that the first year is an "un-doing process" intended to "break down physical and vocal habits." The second year focuses on placing the training within the context of Stanislavsky-style approaches to building a character, "answers to questions such as 'Who am I?' [. . .] 'What do I want?'" In the third year, "singing classes begin now, speech classes (dialects to be lost or acquired, problem [*sic*] diction etc), dance [. . .] fighting (fencing, wrestling and whatever is 'in' in Oriental fighting arts)." In the fourth year, "as many plays as possible are done before audiences" (Linklater 1976: 202–206).

The singing component suggested in Linklater's curriculum was *p'ansori* and traditional Korean singing at KNUA.[19] I could not teach the "speech" material as a voice and speech teacher because I did not speak Korean at that time and my students usually did not speak English. I taught through in-class Korean/English translators.[20] KNUA students received Korean speech training from a Korean professor in another class. My KNUA students also did not need the English language accent/dialect materials I usually taught in my US voice classrooms. Linklater's comment about using whichever "Oriental fighting arts" were in fashion to train actors, sounded a bit dismissive. Asian martial arts training was a rigorous and serious training component at KNUA and manifested itself in the bodies I taught in my voice class, a factor that would shape my curriculum design.

I am not alone in attempting to adapt voice training outside of the cultural context in which it was first developed or to integrate principles and practices of voice training with Asian practices. Within the UK and US, there have been both implicit and explicit integrations of Asian modes of training in mainstream voice pedagogy. Current master teachers include, but are not limited to:

• Catherine Fitzmaurice who, in 1972, began practicing and adapting yoga, along with bioenergetics and shiatsu, with the "traditional European breathing techniques" she learned as a student at London's Royal Central School of Speech and Drama (RCSSD), London, UK (www.fitzmauricevoice.com 2017).

- Kristin Linklater, author of *Freeing the Natural Voice* (Linklater 1976), *Freeing Shakespeare's Voice* (Linklater 1992) and *Freeing the Natural Voice revised and expanded* (Linklater 2006), founded in her work with Iris Warren at the London Academy of Music and Dramatic Art (LAMDA), London, UK, adapts yoga into her practice (2006: 3).
- Patsy Rodenburg, author of *The Right to Speak* (Rodenburg 1992), *The Need for Words* (Rodenburg 1993), *The Actor Speaks* (Rodenburg 2000), *Speaking Shakespeare* (Rodenburg 2002) and *Presence* (Rodenburg 2007), who also graduated from RCSSD and worked alongside Berry for nine years at the Royal Shakespeare Company, includes yoga positions, such as "child's pose" in her breath exercises (2007: 74).
- Barbara Houseman, who trained as a voice teacher at RCSSD and worked alongside Berry for six years at the RSC, author of *Finding your Voice* (Houseman 2002) and *Tackling Text* (Houseman 2008) includes shiatsu and tai chi in her approach (2007: 20, 40; www.barbarahouseman.com/#!about/c202h).
- David Carey, graduated with a diploma in Speech and Drama at the Royal Scottish Academy of Music and Drama (RSAMD), Glasgow, Scotland, UK, is current resident voice and text director at the Oregon Shakespeare Festival (2017) and former Senior voice tutor at RADA and principle lecturer in Voice Studies at RSCCD and also worked alongside Berry at the RSC, and Rebecca Clark Carey, graduated as a voice trainer MA Voice Studies from RCSSD and is current Head of Voice and Text at OSF and former voice tutor at RADA, have both co-authored *Vocal Arts Workbook and DVD* (2008) and *The Verbal Arts Workbook* (Carey & Clark Carey 2010) and make explicit their use of a voice practice "developed from within the Western tradition of theatre training" combined with "Chi Kung" and "Yoga" (2008: xvi, 4; www.osfashland. org/en/about/osf-company/artistic/resident-artists.aspx).

Some popular approaches could be characterized as particular "intercultural" integrations and include, but are not limited to:

- Stephen Chun-Tao Cheng's *Tao of Voice*, which attempts to unify "the best of Western vocal technique and ancient Chinese philosophy and breathing practices" in order to offer "improvement of tonal quality and power and extension of vocal range and dynamics" (Chun-Tao Cheng 1991: 2–3).
- For voice trainer Michael Morgan the question whether "such an intercultural foundation provides the actor with more expressive capacity for a multi-textured, emotionally, intellectually and spiritually enriched voice" became part of his investigation into the Fitzmaurice Voicework approach, along with an interest in "reaching diverse student populations through blending East/West disciplines" (2008: 1).

Like Morgan, some voice trainers seeking to reach student populations within multicultural, multilinguistic environments, feel that this demographic is not being satisfactorily addressed in mainstream voice practice (Brown 2000: 17, Brown 2001: 124–128; Burke 1997 in Hampton and Acker: 58, 61–62; Ginther 2015 in VSR: 41–60; Klemp et al. 2015 in VSR: 82–90). A roundtable at The Voice and Speech Trainer's Association 2013 annual conference focused on "working with international acting students for whom English is not the first language" and raised the concern that "at best we [voice trainers] were using and adapting techniques and creating performing opportunities. At worst, these problems were being ignored or minimized by colleagues." (VSR 2015: 82). Carey and Clark Carey acknowledge,

> This [Western] training culturally assumed that it was acceptable, for example to require students to wear specific types of clothing, to work in bare feet, to touch each other, to sight-read, or to work only with texts from the Western canon. However in our contemporary context of multiculturalism and diversity, many of these practices are rightly being questioned.
>
> *(Carey and Clark Carey 2008: xvi)*

Debates in *New Theatre Quarterly* highlight problems in mainstream contemporary voice training and the cultural assumptions about the body/voice embedded within the practice (Werner 1996: 249–258; 49, Werner 1997: 48–52, 183, 248–254). During this debate, Jane Boston wrote,

> The time is now right for the teaching methodologies of voice practitioners to be viewed, along with those of their counterparts in other artistic disciplines, as both socially transparent and analytically traceable—and thus as developmentally answerable to both the academy and the conservatoire.
>
> *(NTQ 51, Boston 1997: 254)*

From an intracultural[21] perspective within the US, voice trainers Micha Espinosa and Antonio Ocampo-Guzman criticized,

> Very few actor-training programs are able or willing to understand the complex navigation of identity—an integral part of the Latino experience in the U.S. As a result, these programs measure their Latino students against rigid, old-fashioned and unexamined Eurocentric values.
>
> *(Espinosa and Ocampo-Guzman 2010: 150)*

Espinosa and Ocampo-Guzman also point out the wide spectrum of ways students relate to English as the primary teaching language found in professional actor-training programs and the "complex relationship most Latinos have to the physical body" (2010: 151).[22] Although their focus is on Latino experiences within the US, their larger concern about the "complex navigation of identity" when training the actor, specifically addressing issues of language and body, apply to intercultural training contexts as well. There is an interdependent relationship between intra-cultural and intercultural aspects of practice (Tatinge Nascimento 2009: 61, 132;

Zarrilli, Sasitharan, and Kapur 2016: 335). In this book, I focus on the intersection between "international" and "intercultural," although the concerns addressed here overlap at times with intracultural concerns in many US and UK voice classrooms.

Voice training, in the context addressed in this book, is situated inside the larger learning objectives of actor training. With the rise of the intercultural actor (Tatinge Nascimento 2009: 1–23; Zarrilli et al. 2013: 262–267), intercultural voice training is not a niche approach but will become, I suspect, a required mandate for many acting conservatoires, like KNUA. The special issue of *Theatre, Dance and Performance Training* (2016, issue 7.3) asserted

> In the twenty-first century, contemporary theatre practices and modes of actor/performer training are being shaped within the crucible of a global, (largely) urban, cosmopolitan context, which is inherently multi-, inter-and/or intra-cultural. . . . Therefore, any consideration of both acting/performance and training today must address our global, urban, multi-, inter-, intra-cultural realities as *the norm* rather than the exception.
>
> *(Zarrilli, Sasitharan, and Kapur 2016: introduction, italics in original)*

If the intercultural actor is "the norm rather than the exception" and the training is inherently "intercultural," then this asks larger questions about the very "materials" of training, such as the actor's body and voice, and how they are understood through multiple worldviews.

When I create intercultural curriculum, I am often addressing larger underlying questions of what is voice? What is body? What is breath, "energy," sound? What can/should these materials do and how can they do "it"? In my experiences, I found it necessary to (re)consider not only how to adapt the techniques from the source traditions I use but also negotiate the belief systems that underpin the practice.

In this monograph, I investigate ways of interweaving two traditions, specifically adaptations of the "natural" or "free" voice approach and adaptations of Korean *p'ansori*. I apply practice-as-research, ethnographic research, and interculturalism as a "way of working" (Marranca and Dasgupta 1991: 11) and traditional print materials research as my methodological tools to critically analyze current voice practice and suggest a possible alternative paradigm for training actors' voices.[23] Throughout my methodological framework, I not only examine current literature but also certain key conversations that helped shape the choices I made. Chapter one addresses specific conversations that influenced my practice and suggested methodological approaches to researching practice. Throughout the monograph, I include autoethnographic material to contextualize my approach and situate my position as a performer, teacher, and researcher. Both *p'ansori* scholarly literature and Anglo-American voice training texts insert autoethnographic material and "oral histories" as integral to understanding their different "traditions." The inclusion of this material aims to explain how oral art forms and training are passed down from one generation to the next, or offers an understanding of the location of the ethnographic researcher in her field experience, or understanding the complex territory of teaching and learning from a personal perspective.

I critically analyze "what is a voice?" within both the "natural/free" voice approach based on my experiences in training Berry, Linklater, and Rodenburg methods as well as their writings of practice, and within adaptations of Korean *p'ansori* based on my experiences in training with Human Cultural Treasures Han Nongsŏn and Sŏng Uhyang and briefly with Chan Park, as well as scholarly writings on this practice. Chapter Two investigates what is a "natural" or "free" voice? Through a comparative analysis of the three master trainer's practice and writings of practice, I argue that the "natural/free" voice, as a branch of training, is founded on certain key principles and practices, which I detail with reference to both the master teacher's training texts and recorded studio practices. Chapter Three investigates what is *p'ansori sŏngŭm*? Focusing on *sŏngŭm* [trans. "voice/sound"] and the vocal dynamics of the spoken and sung voice passages of this storytelling form; the chapter describes some of the ways body/voice is treated during training, particularly during *sankongbu* [lit. "mountain study"] in which performers regularly lose their voices. It discusses why this training approach is important in cultivating the particular sound of *p'ansori sŏngŭm* as well as the cultural and performance representation of *han*. Using recordings of my *p'ansori* lessons, field recordings, interviews, and scholarly material from *p'ansori* practitioners and ethnomusicologists, it details one understanding of how the *sori* is trained in *p'ansori*. These two chapters offer an understanding of the source traditions in preparation for later interactions.

Through comparative analysis in the remaining chapters, I investigate "what can a voice do?" Through interweaving these two different traditions, I ask, "How can/should a voice do 'it'?" Chapter Four embeds these questions within an investigation of the role of breath and consciousness. Chapter Five builds on understandings of breath and voice to investigate how "energy" and "presence" function conceptually and practically in both traditions. Chapter Six looks at how different understandings of sound link listening and voicing within both training traditions and investigates the role of text and "vocal text" in both script-based approaches and in oral forms within a series of practice-as-research, site-specific projects called The Namdaemun Market Projects.

I argue that a continuum of training that teaches various ways of perceiving and doing places different traditions in a polar relationship. What a voice "is" and what it "does" is understood in reference to each other; each tradition becomes an embodied context for learning the practice of another tradition. Through trial and error as well as strategically designed interactions, the different trainings inside of the trainee's body can interface. These combinations create different body knowledges from which the trainee is able to develop alternative methods and models for training the voice. I also argue that an intercultural approach that offers a different way of working may or may not offer a different "sound." The video samples of student performances from the Namdaemun Market projects do not "look" or "sound" like *p'ansori* performances, nor would a theatre audience necessarily know that these pieces were based on ideas adapted from *p'ansori* training and perform-ance principles. The objective is not to mimic or reproduce *p'ansori* aesthetics as a piece of vocal theatre, but instead to discover the many ways the two source trad-itions can interact, and in doing so, what outcomes they might produce. Depending on the objectives of the training, intercultural practice can offer what Ben Spatz calls the "direct and indirect uses of technique . . . that is, between what actors reliably do and what audiences reliably perceive" (Spatz 2015: 125).

The benefit of training in two different traditions simultaneously and placing them along a continuum of training means the student can call upon different training techniques depending on the performance task. The student can think and talk about "voice," "body," "breath," "energy," "sound," and "text" using different concepts and different vocabularies. In my experience, having multiple worldviews in the voice studio enriches the experience of training and designing interactions between worldviews helps address the many ways my students understand their bodies and voices and the potential of voice as it is trained. Through a sustained critique of current practices, this monograph also offers an alternative understand-ing of key principles and practices of training voice that could benefit the ways voice trainers and scholars think, talk about, and train actors in the 21st century.

Reflecting on the issues raised at the beginning of my tenure at KNUA, I focused on three areas, which eventually developed into a research methodology: issues surrounding embodiment in voice training, interculturalism as a way of working, and researching through practice(s). The next chapter will examine key conversations that helped guide the development of my curriculum in relation to these three areas.

Notes

1 *American Theatre Magazine* is a highly read publication within the US and internationally.
2 Rodenburg is Head of Voice at Guildhall School of Music and Drama, London, UK and has had a long-time association with Michael Howard Studios in New York, NY, USA in which she recently established The Patsy Rodenburg Centre for Voice and Speech offering The Rodenburg Master Teacher Certification Program; Cicely Berry maintains her post as Voice Director of The Royal Shakespeare Company (UK) while working extensively with Theatre for New Audiences in NYC (USA); Kristin Linklater is Professor Emeritus at Columbia University, NYC (USA) and established the Linklater Voice and Speech Centre, NYC (USA) offering a teaching certification program in Linklater technique, but also lives and works within the UK, specifically in Orkney, Scotland (UK), where she has recently opened the Linklater Voice Centre.
3 Arthur Lessac founded The Lessac Training and Research Institute® that offers training certification as Lessac Practitioners and Lessac Certified Trainers: http://lessacinstitute. org/about/certification-opportunities/. In 1970, Lessac joined SUNY-Binghamton where, according to Alfred Brooks, chair of the Department of Theatre, "there is now a nation-wide and to some degree, international, group using his method and text in many schools and universities. Here at SUNY-Binghamton, teacher training workshops are held each summer—three will be conducted in 1973 (Special Preface to the 1973 edition of Lessac's The Use and Training of the Human Voice)." At the time of his death, "Mr. Lessac was creating a new drama department, teaching at the University of Rijeka in Croatia" (Lessac Institute. org 2017). Catherine Fitzmaurice founded the Fitzmaurice

Institute which offers training certification in Fitzmaurice Voicework®. Certified trainers are found "mainly in the United States but now also in permanent residence on six continents" (www.fitzmauricevoice.com/about.htm).

4 BA(hon) Visual and Physical Theatre, later renamed Collaborative and Devised Theatre (CDT) under Catherine Alexander, associate director Theatre Complicite, and BA(hon) Music Theatre under Dr. Bruce Kirle, until his untimely death.

5 My CDT students attended lectures and performances by special presenters including Peter Brook, Richard Schechner, Jenna Kumiega, Goerges Banu, Else Marie Laukyik, Ludwik Flaszen, and Mario Biagini from the Work Centre, Pontedera, Italy.

6 Invited presenters included specialists in voice and sound: Grotowski Institute director Jaroslaw Fret, Catherine Fitzmaurice, Cicely Berry (Keynote), Alice Lagaay, Liz Mills, and Eva Maria Gauss.

7 With special guest Piotr Borowski, one of Poland's leading experimental directors and founder for Studium Teatraine.

8 My experiences include training in hatha yoga, *taijichuan* (Wu form), and a South Indian martial art called *kalarippayattu* under Phillip Zarrilli for three years as part of my MFA Acting degree from the Asian/Experimental Theatre Program, University of Wisconsin–Madison. Years later, I returned to study again under Zarrilli for four years during my doctoral studies at the University of Exeter, England. For a better understanding of the way I learned taijichuan as adapted for acting training, see the writings of A. C. Scott, founder of the Asian/Experimental Theatre Program at the University of Wisconsin–Madison, specifically his *Actors Are Madmen* (Scott 1982). For an understanding of the way I trained in kalarippayattu as part of my acting training, see the writings of Zarrilli, specifically his *When the Body Becomes All Eyes: Paradigms, Discourses and Practices of Power in Kalarippayattu, a South Indian Martial Art* (Zarrilli 1998) and *From Kalarippayattu to Beckett* (video) (Zarrilli 1999).

9 A.C. Scott founded the Asian/Experimental Program and served as its director until his retirement when Phillip Zarrilli took over the direction of the program, working alongside Scott during the transition of leadership (1979–1980).

10 In Seoul, I was a cast member for the EBS television show, 영어 회화 yeong-eo hoehwa [lit. English conversation], an educational show that taught English to Koreans. I also worked for KBS television as an English-language voice over artist for commercials and for KBS news.

11 Practitioners and scholars define *p'ansori* in a variety of ways. (Also refer to Chung 1998: introduction; Jang 2014: xv–xvi; Kim 1980: introduction; Park 2003: 2–3; Pihl 1994: 3; Um 1992: introduction; Um 2013: 11–16.)

12 KNUA is not the only Korean school to develop a curriculum based on combinations of indigenous arts with Western actor training, nor is this way of working isolated to Korea. For instance, the Theatre Training and Research Program in Singapore trains performers in voice, movement and acting through combinations of Western acting training with Japanese noh, Indian kutiyattam, and Beijing Opera.

13 An expanded edition was published in 2006 titled *Freeing the Natural Voice: Imagery and Art in the Practice of Voice and Language*.

14 SITI (Saratoga International Theatre Institute) was co-founded in 1992 by Anne Bogart and Tadashi Suzuki to "redefine and revitalize contemporary theatre in the United States through an emphasis on international cultural exchange and collaboration" (http://siti.org/content/about-us).

15 The larger question here, which intercultural discourse periodically problematizes, is: "What is understood as 'Eastern tradition' and 'Western tradition?'" (refer Zarrilli et al. 2006). Here, I attempt to define what I mean by Eastern and Western modes of training within the particular contexts of the actor training institutions in which I was a student and teacher: KNUA, UW–Madison and my current position as Head of Voice at East 15 Acting School (UK).

16 For further reflections on ways I adapted Linklater's first book to the learning context at KNUA's School of Drama, see McAllister-Viel (2001).

17 Later, an official Korean translation of the book was completed by Haerry Kim, a former student of Linklater's at Columbia University (www.thelinklatercenter.com/designated-linklater-teachers/designated-teacher-bios/haerry-kim).

18 US universities usually offer four-year undergraduate training courses, but English universities usually offer three-year undergraduate courses. KNUA offered a four-year undergraduate BFA acting training course.

19 Since 2003, KNUA provides a Musical Theatre course, which offers students Western-style singing as part of their acting training.

20 There are larger issues here about how intercultural exchange is mediated through language choice and translation. See Lo and Gilbert (2002).

21 In Chapter One, I examine definitions of "intercultural" versus "intracultural."

22 Also refer the way Venus Opal Reese (2010) defines "embodiment" in "Keeping in Real Without Selling Out," in Margolis and Tyler Renaud (2010). Later I will problematize the relationship between bodies and voices in voice pedagogy through the use of a Western biomedical model as the basis by which exercises cross culture.

23 By "practice as research" I mean using the experiences of the body/voice to critically analyze voice pedagogy. This form of "empirical research," or knowledge gathering conducted through embodied practice and first-hand experience, establishes a primary relationship to voice training and performance. I also simultaneously establish secondary relationships to practice through more traditional scholarly research.

References

Berry, C. (2001). *Text in Action*. London: Virgin.

Bogart, A. (2000). "Culture Shock," *American Theatre*, April 3.

Boston, J. (1997). "Voice: The Practitioners, Their Practices, and Their Critics," *New Theatre Quarterly*, 51, 248–254.

Brown, S. (2000). "The Cultural Voice," *The Voice and Speech Review: Standard Speech*, 1, 17–18.

Brown, S. (2001). "The Cultural Voice: An Interview with Danny Hoch," *The Voice and Speech Review: The Voice in Violence*, 2, 124–128.

Burke, K. (1997). "On Training and Pluralism," in Acker, B. and Hampton, M. (eds.) *Vocal Vision: Views on Voice by 24 Leading Teachers, Coaches and Directors*. New York: Applause, 57–62.

Carey, D., Clark Carey, R. (2008). *The Vocal Arts Workbook: A Practical Course for Developing the Expressive Range of Your Voice*. London: Methuen Drama.

Carey, D., Clark Carey, R. (2010). *The Verbal Arts Workbook: A Practical Course for Speaking Text*. London: Methuen Drama.

Centre for Performance Research (2017). http://thecpr.org.uk/giving-voice-2016-wroclaw-poland. Accessed 30 March 2017.

Choi, S.H. (2000). "Questions for Dr. Zarrilli," 2000 Seoul International Theatre Festival Special Lecture Series— *Interculturalism in Staging*, booklet, Seoul: Munye Theatre, 61.

Chun-Tao Cheng, S. (1991). *Tao of Voice: A New East-West Approach to Transforming the Singing and Speaking Voice*. Rochester, VT: Destiny Books.

Chung, S.S.Y. (1998). *The Impact of Yin and Yang Ideology in the Art of Korean P'ansori tradition: An Analytical Study Based on the Late Mme. Pak Nok-Ju Version of P'ansori Hungbo-ga*. Unpublished PhD in Ethnomusicology at University of California-Santa Barbara.

Diamond, D. (2001). "Balancing acts," *American Theatre*, January 32–38.

Espinosa, M., Ocampo-Guzman, A. (2010). "Identity Politics and the Training of Latino Actors," in Margolis, E. and Tyler Renaud, L. (ed.) *Politics of American Actor Training*. London: Routledge, 150–161.

Fischer-Lichte, E. (1997). *The Show and Gaze of the Theatre: A European Perspective*. Iowa City: University of Iowa Press.

Fischer-Lichte, E., Riley, J., Gissenwehrer, M. (1990). *The Dramatic Touch of Difference: Theatre Own and Foreign*. Tubingen: Narr.

Fitzmauricevoice.com. (2017). www.fitzmauricevoice.com/about.htm. Accessed 30 March 2017.

Gener, R. (2010). "Pillars of Voice Work," in "Special Section: Approaches to Theatre Training," *American Theatre*, 27 (1), 33.

Ginther, A. (2015). "Dysconscious racism in mainstream British voice pedagogy and its potential effects on students from pluralistic backgrounds in UK Drama Conservatoires," *Voice and Speech Review*, 9 (1), 41–60.

Han, M.Y. (1990). *Kugak: Studies in Korean Traditional Music*, trans. I. Peak and K. Howard (eds.). Seoul: Tamgu-Dang Publishing.

Houseman, B. (2002). *Finding Your Voice: A Complete Voice Training Manual for Actors*. London: Nick Hern.

Houseman, B. (2008). *Tackling Text (and Subtext): A Step-by-Step Guide for Actors*. London: Nick Hern.

Jang, Y. (2014). *Korean P'ansori Singing Tradition*. Toronto: The Scarecrow Press.

Kendrick, L., Roesner, D. (2011). *Theatre Noise: The Sound of Performance*. Newcastle upon Tyne: Cambridge Scholars Publishing.

Kim, W.O. (1980). *P'ansori: An Indigenous Theater of Korea*. Unpublished PhD in Theatre at New York University.

Klemp, S., Ginther, A., Battles, J., Shane, L. (2015). "We've only just begun: reflections and insights 'Giving Voice to International Students' roundtable from the 2013 VASTA Conference in Minneapolis," *Voice and Speech Review*, 9 (1), 82–90.

KNUA (Korean National University of Arts). (2000). *School of Drama Prospectus*. Seoul: KNUA.

KNUA (Korean National University of Arts). (2004). *Prospectus*. Seoul: KNUA.

KNUA (Korean National University of Arts). (2015). http://eng.karts.ac.kr:8090. Accessed 9 December 2015.

Lessac Institute.org. (2017). http://lessacinstitute.org/about/certification-opportunities/. Accessed 30 March 2017.

Linklater, K. (1976). *Freeing the Natural Voice*. New York: Drama Book Publishers.

Linklater, K. (1992). *Freeing Shakespeare's Voice*. New York: Theatre Communications.

Linklater, K. (2000). "Kristin Linklater Responds," *American Theatre*, April 3.

Linklater, K. (2006). *Freeing the Natural Voice: Imagery and Art in the Practice of Voice and Language, Revised and Expanded*. London: Nick Hern.

Lo, J., Gilbert, H. (2002). "Toward a topography of cross-cultural theatre praxis," *The Drama Review*, 46 (3), 31–53.

Marranca, B., Dasgupta, G. (eds.) (1991). *Interculturalism and Performance*. New York: PAJ Publications.

McAllister-Viel, T. (2001). "Adapting Kristen Linklater's *Freeing the Natural Voice* to KNUA's acting training program," in *K. Linklater's Voice Training and the Materials of Narrative Skill*. Seoul: KNUA Press, 224–232.

Margolis, E., and Tyler Renaud, L. (eds.) *The Politics of American Actor Training*. London and New York: Routledge.

Morgan, M. (2008). *Constructing the Holistic Actor: Fitzmaurice Voicework*. Saarbrücken: Verlag.

Oregon Shakespeare Festival (2017). www.osfashland.org/en/about/osf-company/artistic/resident-artists.aspx. Accessed 30 March 2017.

Park, C. (2003). *Voices from the Strawmat*. Honolulu: University of Hawai'i Press.

Pihl, M. (1994). *The Korean Singer of Tales*. Cambridge: Harvard University Press.

Reese, V. (2010). "Keeping It Real Without Selling Out: Toward Confronting and Triumphing Over Racially-Specific Barriers in American Actor Training," in Margolis, E., and Tyler Renaud, L. (eds.) *The Politics of American Actor Training*. London and New York: Routledge, 162–176.

Rodenburg, P. (1992). *The Right to Speak*. New York: Routledge.

Rodenburg, P. (1993). *The Need for Words*. London: Methuen.

Rodenburg, P. (2000). *The Actor Speaks*. New York: St. Martin's Press.

Rodenburg, P. (2002). *Speaking Shakespeare*. London: Methuen.

Rodenburg, P. (2007). *Presence: How to Use Positive Energy for Success in Every Situation*. London: Penguin.

Scott, A.C. (1982). *Actors Are Madmen*. Madison: University of Wisconsin Press.

Spatz, B. (2015). *What a Body Can Do*. London: Routledge.

Tatinge Nascimento, C. (2009). *Crossing Cultural Borders Through the Actor's Work: Foreign Bodies of Knowledge*. New York: Routledge.

Um, H.K. (1992). *Making P'ansori: Korean Musical Drama*. Unpublished PhD in Ethnomusicology at Queen's University of Belfast.

Um, H.K. (1999). "Food for body and soul: measuring the dialectics of performance," Oideion: Performing Arts Online, July 3. www.iias.nl/oideion/journal/issue03/um/index-a.html. Accessed 18 April 2018.

Um, H.K. (2013). *Korean Musical Drama: P'ansori and the Making of Tradition in Modernity*. Farnham: Ashgate.

Um, H.K. (1997). "Voice Training, Shakespeare, and Feminism." in "NTQ Reports and Announcements," *New Theatre Quarterly*, 50, 183.

Werner, S. (1996). "Performing Shakespeare: Voice Training and the Feminist Actor," *New Theatre Quarterly*, 47, 249–258.

Werner, S. (1997). " Voice Training, Shakespeare, and Feminism." in " NTQ Reports and Announcements." *New Theatre Quarterly,* 50: 183.

Wren, C. (2000). "Far horizons," *American Theatre*, January, 38–39.

Zarrilli, P. (1998). *When the Body Becomes All Eyes: Paradigms, Discourses and Practices of Power in Kalarippayattu, a South Indian Martial Art*. Oxford: Oxford University Press.

Zarrilli, P. (1999). *From Kalarippayattu to Beckett*. Video. Exeter: Arts Archives.

Zarrilli, P., Daboo, J., Loukes, R. (2013). *Acting: Psychophysical Phenomenon and Process: Intercultural and Interdisciplinary Perspectives*. London: Palgrave Macmillan.

Zarrilli, P., McConachie, B., Williams, G.J., Fisher Sorgenfrei, C. (2006). *Theatre Histories: An Introduction*. London: Routledge.

Zarrilli, P., McConachie, B., Williams, G.J., Fisher Sorgenfrei, C. (2009). *The Psychophysical Actor at Work*. London: Routledge.

Zarrilli, P., Sasitharan, T., Kapur, A. (2016). "Special Issue on 'intercultural' acting and actor/performer training," *Theatre, Dance and Performance Training*, 7 (3), 335–339.

1

CONVERSATIONS AND METHODOLOGIES

Embodiment, interculturalism, and practice-as-research

In many of the conversations in "natural/free" voice training texts and interviews, "the human voice" is the "same everywhere" (Rodenburg 1992: 107, 268) and "the voice is the voice" (Berry 2010: 122) regardless of linguistic or cultural context. Anatomy and physiology is key to transferring the exercises between bodies/voices from different cultures and languages. In this way, discourses surrounding embodiment training and interculturalism meet in the voice studio. However, this approach to border-crossing has been heavily criticized for privileging anatomy over cultural influence and has therefore been characterized as an "effacement of cultural and other kinds of difference" that attempts to "transcend cultural conditioning" in favor of "universal" anatomical experience (Knowles 100, emphasis in the original). One aim of this chapter is to examine some of these conversations and offer a more complex discussion of the relationship between culture and voice. Second, I propose that practice-as-research provides a viable methodological approach to investigating this area. A third aim is to offer the reader a basis for understanding the rationale behind the structure of this research within a given historic and artistic context.

Embodiment: The role of vocal anatomy in the "natural/free" voice approach

Rodenburg wrote in her first book, "Whatever their cultural differences the voice of every culture works in the same manner. The biology, mechanics and hydraulics of the human voice are the same everywhere" (1992: 107). This reasoning invests in the body as a stable site for learning. Later in the same book, she also insisted that "The anatomical principles of the voice are the same in each place, the main body of sound the same (1992: 268)." My overseas experience led me to different conclusions.

The anatomy of my voice was different from the anatomy of my KNUA students' voices or the voices of my *p'ansori* teachers. Age, gender, and behaviors, like smoking, influence the physical properties and function of our voices. Our discipline-specific training had also altered our voices. Later, I discuss how the "natural/free" voice training permanently alters the way the body/voice functions by borrowing understandings of body function from the Alexander Technique to produce a "free" voice. In a similar way, *p'ansori* training permanently alters the way the body/voice functions through its practice, producing the *sŏngŭm* [sound/voice] of *p'ansori*.

It was clear to me that the sounds in the Korean language,[1] particularly the placement of the sounds towards the back of the mouth, as well as the "tension-filled" sounds[2] in *p'ansori*, did not comprise a "main body of sound" (Rodenburg 1992: 268) accessible to me when I first arrived in Seoul. The articulation exercises in the training texts I brought with me from the US, particularly those that were influenced by British pedagogy, instructed the placement of sound forward in the mouth, or "trippingly on the tongue"[3] or view the performer's voice as alighting from this forward placement in order to travel a distance when "projecting" the voice in a theatre. These were not placements that were necessarily useful to my Korean-speaking students. Berry wrote:

> In Seoul, South Korea, I found that the sound of the language itself was something I had to deal with: it sounded to me a much more stressed language, more emphatic, and that stress so often came from the throat.
>
> *(Berry 2001: 58)*

Here, I am not referring to "speech principles," which "tend to differ just like musical principles" (Rodenburg 1992: 268). Instead, I am referring to the understanding of sound and sound placement that is felt by the speaker and interpreted by the listener as a cultural act.

Steven Connor suggested that sound has a "phonopolitical" function and specifically reflected on sounds produced in the "back of the mouth," in this instance, the characterization of German as a "guttural language." He wrote that the depiction of German as "guttural" was a "prejudice" that "has roots that reach much further back, having to do with the growing inhospitality of English to sounds produced in the back of the mouth." He argued that "the values of particular sounds and the vocal methods used to employ them often have this phonopolitical force and function" (2014: 11). The *eum-yang* design of "dark" and "bright" vowel sounds in Korean addresses a philosophical and political understanding of sound in language, which encompasses more than the "speech principles" (Rodenburg 1992: 268) to which Rodenburg referred. Later I will discuss the design of the Korean language, its use of pure Korean words and Sino-Korean words,[4] and its "phonopolitical form and function," as well as an understanding of sound in *p'ansori* that differs from an Anglo-American model of "projecting" the voice during performance.

Rodenburg's quotes seemed to focus on the anatomy of the voice as physical properties of the vocal tract. Of course, the vocal tract is not the only site for what is understood as the voice. The voice exists as vibrations that can be felt throughout the vocalist's body as primary and secondary resonance and as vibrations during transmission from vocalist to listener, either through bodily contact or through the air and into the ear. The voice exists within the ear of the listener as a physical property. The voice also exists as electric synapses that carry meaning to the brain. Communication is part of the function of the voice, realized as physical properties, between bodies, not simply within one body (the vocalist).[5] Voicing is both a singular and plural phenomenon. It is "my" voice but does not exist solely in "my" body. This raised for me questions about the relationship between one's own body/voice and the transmission between bodies/voices during voice training, or more simply, issues surrounding "embodiment."

Rodenburg's and Berry's assertions can be understood within the larger key principle of the "natural/free" voice approach that insists the voice is "embodied," literally "in" and "of" *the* body. Anatomy and physiology is understood as the common denominator that links human experience. Berry wrote, "That is why I said that our common ground was the experience of the voice through the movement of muscles" (Berry 1973: 14). The body becomes the site for the voice, the producing mechanism for sounding and voicing, and the kinesthetic awareness of physical acts that influence the training of voice. In short, the body mediates the experience of experiencing voice.

Linklater wrote, "The voice is forged in the body" (Linklater 2016: 59). In the "natural/free" approach, *the* body tends to be one that is conceptualize through a Western, bio-medical model.[6] However, voice and its potential change considerably when the concept of body changes. At KNUA, I often had conversations with my students about the types of voices they admired: "I want a 'thick' voice." Several times I found written in their vocal self-assessments, "I have a metallic sound." Word choice reflected an understanding of voice and vocal function based, in part, on a particular concept of body. In Korean traditional medicine, *o haeng* (lit. *o*/five *haeng*/road or function) is an understanding of certain natural principles and their function within a body. Wood, fire, earth, metal, water were understood as physical properties including firmness, fluidity, body-heat, and mobility. If "metal" is realized as a physical property in the body that can have an effect on sound quality then a "metallic sound" is an aural/oral reality, not simply a descriptive metaphor.[7]

Phillip Zarrilli wrote,

> We organize 'the world' we encounter into significant gestalts, but 'the body' I call mine is not *a* body, or *the* body, but rather a process of embodying the several bodies one encounters in everyday experience as well as highly specialized modes of non-everyday, or 'extra-daily' bodies of practices such as acting or training in psycho-physical disciplines to act.
>
> *(2004: 655)*

Many of my KNUA students viewed their bodies through different mappings of body and this necessarily changed how we talked about the process of "embodying" voice, eventually shaping the developing training exercises.

Conversations surrounding "embodiment" in voice training offer larger issues for voice trainers, not only for those who choose to teach cross-culturally. Many trainers and speech and language therapists work with voices that have changing, multiple relationships to body[ies].[8] If voice is "embodied," literally sited in the body, then whose "body" did Stephen Hawking's voice belong to? Hawking, who suffered from Lou Gehrig's disease [amyotrophic lateral sclerosis] communicated using a DecTalk DTC01 voice synthesizer, an assistive communication device (Greenmeier 2009).[9] He could not communicate with his biological voice and his SGD was not located in his body. Users may choose a voice that comes with their device or can record and add new voices. Voice teachers and speech and language therapists grapple with anatomy and voice when working with cancer patients. Cancer patients who have had a total laryngectomy, or their larynx completely removed, will have undergone surgery to have their windpipe (trachea) separated from their esophagus so that they can no longer force air from their lungs through their mouth to speak. Of the alternative ways of speaking after surgery, patients may be able to use a voice prosthesis (trachea esophageal puncture or TEP), create esophageal speech by swallowing air, or use an electrolarynx, which is a battery-operated machine that produces sound for the patient. Words can be formed when pressing the electrolarynx against the neck and moving the tongue and mouth to form the sound into words (Cancer Research UK 2015).

In these instances, the patient can "voice" using their own biology—in other words their "voice" is sited in their body- but what is traditionally understood as a "voice," sound resulting from vibrations of the vocal folds within the larynx, no longer applies. These examples provoke questions not only about where the voice is sited but also what is voice?

Finally, the writings of voice trainer and transgender actor Rebecca Root[10] exemplify another aspect of the instability of *the* body. When her body transitioned from male to female she wanted to "acquire the sort of voice which would not attract unwanted attention as a TS person, marking me out as a target for ostracism or homophobic behavior." As a TS actor she was often "cast as a 'token' TS person, expected to *look* like one gender but *sound* like another" (2009: 144, emphasis in the original). She asked,

> What makes a person's voice sound male or female and how are those differences reproduced on stage or in life? Is gender identity governed by psychological impulse, overruling the bodily (and vocal) appearance? To paraphrase de Beauvoir, can we *become* men and women?
>
> *(2009: 146, emphasis in the original)*

Her experiences with multiple bodies led her to ask questions of voice training, and importantly for this discussion here, what is the relationship between bodies and voices?

Alexandros Constansis has theorized his sung voice during his experience transitioning and in his article "The Changing Female-to-Male (FTM) Voice," proposed that the FTM voice, "has wider implications . . . to do with the 'biology of culture'; or, to put it another way, with conceptions of 'the natural'" (Constansis 2009). The anatomy of his voice was altered through a drugs protocol (2003–2004) and supported with training techniques Constansis tested first on himself and later taught to his transgender clients. In the field of Voice Studies, "the study of voice quality in transgendered individuals can shed light on how far vocal plasticity can be pushed to overcome the limitations inherent in vocal anatomy" (Kreiman and Sidtis 2011: 144).

Transgender professional vocalists are concerned not only with off-stage uses of voice, or issues of "passing" in order to avoid unwanted attention, but also with on-stage vocal performance. In Root's case, she is interested in character voice construction as a TS actor. She plays "Judy," a transgender character on BBC 2's sitcom *Boy Meets Girl* (BBC Television). In her writing, she cited other artists who also construct character voices for performance, such as actor Ernesto Tomasini's internet project "in which he performed vocally as 'Monica': a sexy Italian housewife. For the men with whom he interacted the lure was her voice: 'the voice became a body, even though there was no body'" (2009: 149). Here, Tomasini's voice "created" a body for and with the listener. How a voice is recognized and how a "body" is assigned to a given voice is a complex process. Kreiman and Sidtis ask, "Can we hear what a speaker looks like?" They wrote,

> Because of the linkage through the speech chain between physical characteristics and perceived voice quality, listeners often treat voice quality as a cue to a speaker's physical characteristics, and make judgments about physical size, sex, age, health, appearance, racial group, or ethnic background, based on the sound of a voice. Such judgments are common on the telephone and are actively exploited in animation and radio advertising, where voices are the only cue available to the speaker's physical attributes.
>
> *(2013: 110)*

Later, in Chapter Six, I introduce studies by Korean phonetician Moon Seung-Jae, which my students and I used in the Namdaemun Market Projects when (re)considering how sound carried cultural meaning in voice and the cues to a speaker's identity. So, the physical attributes of a voice and what a voice can do (anatomically and physiologically) are received by a listener who has certain expectations about what a voice should do, or "social expectation influences listeners' judgements" (2013: 111). Voicing and listening involve production and reception models that cannot be based solely on anatomical function. The "voice of every culture" does not "*work[s]* in the same manner (Rodenburg 1992: 107, emphasis added)."

Within actor training, the construction of character voices raises similar questions about the site of the voice, how voices "work," what a voice is, and whose voice is it. At KNUA, RCSSD and East 15, a standard part of my voice curriculum is the study of "character voices" to ready students for employable skills in voice-overs for commercials, voices for animation, voices for avatars in the gaming industry, voices for storytelling [in which a singular storyteller embodies multiple characters as they do in *p'ansori*], radio dramas, audiobooks, and voices for puppetry, as well as voices in which the student must acquire a particular accent/dialect. Often student-actors will produce a voice reel, which is a series of short recorded texts demonstrating the student's vocal versatility for future employers.

In studying character voices, students have access to online databases of recorded voices to model their vocal character constructions,[11] and can record and collect others' voices, with permission, through field experience. Once recorded, voices are disembodied and can exist as documentation after the body has died. Such voices can be "re-embodied" through performance. When the body of the originator of a famous character's voice dies, such as Mickey Mouse or Kermit the Frog, other performers can step in and reconstruct that character voice. Whose "voice" is this? Is it Mickey Mouse's voice, the voice of the actor, or the voice of the person who originated the character voice? Whose bodies do the voices of Mickey Mouse and Kermit the Frog belong to? Voices can become trademarks and can have copyright. How voices are embodied can raise legal issues.

Discussions surrounding voice tend to create a binary between "embodied" and "disembodied" voices (Cavarero 2005; Connor 2014).[12] Body/voice relationships are much more fluid than these categories suggest. For me, this fluidity offers a creative space. When my students mimetically train to acquire a particular accent or the voice of a famous person, the voice—in this case, the markers that allow an audience to identify the characteristics of a voice as a particular "person" for storytelling meaning—lives in a body that did not originate that voice. The audience, through willing suspension of disbelief, understands that the actor's voice represents another voice from another time/place.

For example, at RSCCD, the Collaborative and Devised theatre strand created a verbatim performance around the events of Hurricane Katrina, which grappled with many of these issues. I taught five British students the vocal markers of President George Bush Jr.'s voice, his accent, nasal resonant placement, hesitations in his speech pattern, and so on. The students then passed his voice between them throughout the performance so that the "Bush" voice issued from different bodies: in one instance, the voice of an older white privileged American male president emerged from the body of a young black British female student. In this way, students used the construction of "character voice" to explore questions of race and power within government responses to the Hurricane Katrina disaster. I had asked the students to consider the literal voice as sonic design of culture. But what are the limits of this technique? Would it ever be appropriate for a white British student to voice one of the African-American characters in this project? Or would that be a kind of vocal blackface? How a voice is embodied can push the boundaries of acceptability and raise ethical questions.

Cavarero insists, "The voice never comes from an object, nor is it addressed to an object . . . It [the voice] does not allow a detached focus on the object because,

properly speaking, it has no object" (2005: 177–178). However, in our performance, through the act of embodying, disembodying, and re-embodying we
passed around the Bush voice, like an object, from performer to performer and
asked the audience to objectify the body/voice relationship for critical analysis.
Separating voice and body can create interesting spaces for artists to explore.

The fluidity between body/voice relationships is also a disciplinary space.
Bodies and voices are not stable sites for learning and this can be useful in studio.
For my purposes, creating an intercultural/interdisciplinary approach, this fluidity
allows me to move between the "natural" voice within the "natural/free" voice
approach and other understandings of voice within Asian modes of training, like
p'ansori. The voice *may* be of a body but it is not *the* body. One cannot assume
universal conditions of body and sound as the means by which voice training
crosses cultures.

Embodiment practices between bodies and voices: Learning *p'ansori* and its adaptations at KNUA

Shortly after arriving at KNUA, I visited several *p'ansori* classes and individual lessons
at the School of Traditional Korean Arts, specifically Ahn Sook-son's lessons with
individual graduate students and Chong Hoi Suk's undergraduate group *p'ansori*
classes. Later, I was graciously welcomed into Choi Yoon-Cho's adapted *p'ansori* for
actor training within the School of Drama and trained as my students did in group
lessons. A month after arriving at KNUA, I searched for one-to-one lessons and was
introduced to *p'ansori* master Han Nongsŏn (1934–2002). I studied with her for two
years. After Mrs. Han's untimely passing in 2002, I transferred to Sŏng Uhyang's
(1935–2014) studio, in part because Han Nongsŏn and Sŏng Uhyang had both
trained under the same master teacher and so I could remain within the same branch
of learning. I was introduced to Sŏng Uhyang by Chan Park who had studied with
her as well as with Han Nongsŏn. Later, I was graciously invited to study with Chan
Park, living with her and her family in their Ohio home, for a ten-day intensive in
2004. Private lessons offered the advantage of training at my own pace but also
meant the lessons were much more intensive. For instance, in Sŏng Uhyang's studio,
I trained two to three hours a day, six days a week, with daily one-to-one lessons
with Sŏng Uhyang. Between lessons, I also practiced with advanced students in her
studio, specifically Bae Il-dong and Seo Suk-Ja, who helped guide my learning,
sometimes under the instruction of Sŏng Uhyang.

For me, learning new skill sets in *p'ansori* lessons was not a kind of "de-education"
process[13] as composer, pianist, and traditional Korean arts practitioner Na Hyo-
Shin describes (Na 2002). Although my *p'ansori* learning experiences were similar
to those described by Na, for me, some of the skills already trained inside my body
provided a necessary foundation for learning new skills. I did not want to "de-
educate" my body of these processes.

Much of my time spent in those first *p'ansori* lessons was devising learning strategies. Often, my *p'ansori* teacher simply could not help me build new learning

strategies because my body and previous training were as foreign to her as her body and *p'ansori* training were foreign to me. With each task, I discovered through trial and error which existing skills were adaptable or not useful. The more aware I became not only of my own body and voice but *her* body and voice, the better my teacher and I were able to communicate. Eventually, we were both looking for and "reading" a particular set of discipline specific signs transmitted from her body/voice to my body/voice.

During this time, I was also devising learning strategies as an American living in Seoul that were similar to the learning strategies I was developing in *p'ansori* lessons. The longer I lived in Seoul, the better I became at "reading"[14] the cultural signs from my students (e.g. why they sometimes lowered their eyes when they talked to me).[15] In *p'ansori*, it seemed to me that the performer and audience were "reading" both discipline and culturally specific signs in the performance. My *p'ansori* training, along with living outside of my own culture, helped me develop a greater awareness of cultural/discipline influenced sound sign-systems that exist both on and off-stage.[16] This growing awareness made me question one of the primary assumptions behind the "natural" or "free" voice approach: the assumption that socio-cultural vocal training fosters "habits" not useful to discipline-specific voice training.[17] What previous training is embedded inside of the bodies of my students through cultural or discipline influence? Does one training need to be "undone" (Linklater 1976: 202) before another training can be learned? Is "de-education" desirable or even possible? Can socio-cultural vocal training benefit voice students during training and/or performance through a kind of vocal/sound sign-system?

I found it necessary to address bodies and voices in cultural context.[18] For my KNUA graduate voice class, I designed lessons and projects that provoked an idea of a "cultural voice." In the Namdaemun Market Projects (Chapter Six), I asked the students to place themselves as experts[19] of their own culture who already had certain skills learned through social vocal training that allowed them to "read" meaning in voices and in sounds within their culture. Through ear-training assignments in-class, verbatim interviews and field recordings, I attempted to help my students become aware of this "off-stage" training that could, through critical examination and devising processes, develop into a sound sign-system in performance.

The process of developing an intercultural/interdisciplinary curriculum at KNUA was, in part, one of rethinking assumptions embedded within the principles and practices of mainstream Anglo-American voice training. This led me to experiment with shifting the principles and practices of the "natural/free" voice approach for the purposes of our classroom. Insights from interculturalism and the debates surrounding "theory" and "practice" helped me to frame my research approach.

Interculturalism: One way of (re)considering voice practice

Bonnie Marranca suggested that interculturalism as a practice, theory, or worldview is as much a "state of mind" as "a way of working" (in Marranca and Dasgupta 1991: 11). The idea that interculturalism establishes a relationship as well as a

particular perspective, or "state of mind," seemed to suggest that intercultural practice was continuously changing. Relationships and perspectives are renegotiated
through their effect/affect on each other. The lack of stability during continuous
renegotiation may be one reason why a *working* definition of "intercultural" was
necessary. For the purposes of my work, a research framework to develop an intercultural voice pedagogy also needed Lo and Gilbert's (2002: 36) "intentional
encounter" in order to create "a more sustained and systematic engagement" with
the key issues of interculturalism.

Building intentional encounters between elements of the "natural/free" approach
and *p'ansori* in my class was necessary for a variety of reasons. First, I arrived at
KNUA so early in its development that the curriculum was still being realized.
Government mandates and rational combining East/West training were clear, but
curriculum structure to build learning strategies bridging *p'ansori* with Western
voice training into their overall acting training was not yet fully implemented.
Second, unintentional encounters such as the random timetabling of *p'ansori* classes
and Western voice classes back-to-back, could provide an opportunity for exchange
but we needed a means to identify any benefits from unintentional encounters and
decide if meaning and purpose lay in the exchange. Otherwise, the students would
become frustrated and question the purpose of the training.

Through timetabling, the School of Drama unwittingly provided what I called
an *environment of transference*; students were transferring knowledge from their
p'ansori class into my voice class in an attempt to "synthesize" the tremendous
amount of training that was required of them. For instance, during class I would
sometimes be asked, "When Linklater talks about 'centre,' does she mean *dahnjeon?*"[20] *Dahnjeon* is a term used during *p'ansori* training. A *dahnjeon* generates *ki*
(energy) and is part of a larger understanding of body through Korean traditional
medicinal praxis. Here the students were referring to the lower *dahnjeon*, which
Sŏng Uhyang described for me as the size of a fist located just below the navel and
inside the body. It would have been easier for me to dismiss these questions or to
ask the students to set aside their *p'ansori* learning and only focus on the set of skills
I was teaching them. Instead, I accepted the context of back-to-back classes and
allowed skills to transfer from one class to another. By doing so, I was inviting my
students to combine, through empirical learning, one understanding of "centering"
from the "natural/free" voice approach with what was commonly called "*dahnjeon*
breathing," adapted from *p'ansori* practice.[21]

In our class, the adaptations of voice training needed to progress alongside the
adapted *p'ansori* learning as an "intentional encounter" over a length of time in
order to create a "sustained and systematic engagement" of the practices both
offered. In this way, the students and I could transfer body-voice knowledge from
one training mode to another. Sometimes this happened strategically and other
times we experimented through trial and error, discovering how different techniques could work together towards a specific learning outcome. This way of working allowed not only the classroom but also our bodies to become *environments of
transference* in which skills encountered each other physically and aurally/orally.

Naming my practice "intercultural" and "interdisciplinary" is a temporary solution as I continue to search for articulations that may more closely reflect what I feel, hear, and see happening in my body/voice and in my students' bodies/voices. Interculturalism as a theory and practice continued to be relevant for me as my practice crossed over from the 20th to the 21st century, even though it continues to carry with it discords and contradictions which make me wary of the difficulties using the term.

According to Knowles, "interculturalism" is an "urgent topic in the 21st century" in part because:

> as cities and nations move beyond monochromatic, as human traffic between nations and cultures (both willing and unwilling) increases, as hybridity and syncretism (the merging of forms) become increasingly characteristic of cultural production everywhere, and as nineteenth-century nationalism gives way to twenty-first century transnationalism, it becomes imperative that the way in which cultural exchange is performed be critically re-examined.
>
> *(2010: 3)*

After my research fellowship (2015–2016) at the International Research Centre, "Interweaving Performance Cultures," Freie Universität, Berlin, Germany, I have been working with the term "interweaving" in my classrooms and investigating if the idea of "interweaving" may offer a fruitful model for embodying voice practices from various cultural contexts. Fischer-Lichte has offered the term "interweaving," as opposed to "interculturalism," to characterize the way certain performance modes "braid" together "new and different kinds of interaction and cooperation in performance" (Bharucha and Fischer-Lichte 2011). However, it would benefit the reader at this point to offer a discussion of "interculturalism" and why this term is problematic.

Conversations from intercultural theatre discourse

The aim of this section is to cherry-pick a few conversations from intercultural theatre discourse that have influenced my developing practice. This helped to create a frame of reference for me when migrating my work from one cultural context to another and grapple with the larger issues of cultural production that emerged from my practice over the years. This section asks:

- What is interculturalism?
- Is interculturalism as a term and/or "way of working" still relevant?
- Is there an identifiable structure, approach or working method that can be employed to inform current practice?
- When developing a structure or working method are binary East/West arguments necessary? Inevitable?

The first issue that has been debated for years has been the creation of a working definition of interculturalism. Definitions of interculturalism continue to be (re) formulated by both scholars and practitioners since it was first used in the 1970s, in part as an attempt to define itself apart from other practices such as multicultural, cross-cultural, transcultural, extracultural, and inter- versus intra-cultural ways of working. The way in which one defines these terms shapes the way one thinks and talks about cultural exchange and influences the way intercultural practice is structured (e.g. Pavis and Lo and Gilbert's model of practice that will be discussed later in this section). Within 20th century theatre practice, cultural exchange has predominantly been mediated by the West. This has raised concerns over socio-cultural, economic, and political power relationships that create the conditions for unfair exchange between artists. One reason for the shifting definitions of these terms over the past 40 years is directly related to a growing understanding of how power relationships affect cultural exchange.

For instance, the term "multicultural" may suggest many or multiple cultures existing side-by-side. In theatre that has been defined as "multicultural practice," the tendency seems to be to create practice that emphasizes similarities between traditions. But by focusing heavily on similarities of the human condition through a philosophy of universalism, multicultural theatre has been criticized for effacing differences and reinforcing dominant Western values. The term "cross-cultural" exchange suggests instances in which two or more cultures meet under certain conditions for an exchange. Like "multicultural," this term has also been heavily criticized when the conditions of the exchange happen within an unfair socio-economic and/or political power relationship. "Cross-cultural" practice like "multicultural" practice are terms that can be found in the earliest writings of cultural exchange in 20th century theatre performance. These terms tend to be used liberally and applied to a broad spectrum of situations. Indeed, Lo and Gilbert have used the term "cross-cultural" as an "umbrella" term to reference the function of other forms of theatre. In their opinion, "multicultural" and "intercultural" are sub-categories of "cross-cultural" exchange (2002: 36).

The term "transcultural" exchange suggests a culture that can transverse or transfer into another culture. Eugenio Barba's work with the Odin Theatre has been called "transcultural" when he brings artists of different cultures together to "barter" or exchange performances and/or performance techniques. Carl Weber criticized such "transculturation" because he felt, "Trans-fer" implies "trans-port," which, consequently, implies "import" as well as "export"—all these being terms of trade and commerce. Quite inevitably, any "'transcultural' experiment will be traded as a device that employs ingredients to make the product more palatable, i.e., marketable" (1991: 27, 29). In Webber's opinion, transcultural performance might be superbly executed, but it is "chop suey," a dish created by Chinese workers in America to resemble Chinese cooking but made from the only ingredients available in their new cultural setting. Weber criticized, "It [transcultural theatre] still won't be a new and different kind of performance where cultural boundaries are transcended" (Weber 1991: 30).

The term "extracultural" suggests an interrogation of culture or the cultural exchange itself from outside the framework of the exchange in order to question power relationships and/or celebrate differences. Lo and Gilbert defined "extracultural" as,

> theatre exchanges that are conducted along a West-East and North-South axis . . . this form of interculturalism goes back to the modernist pioneers who looked to the non-West to rejuvenate Western art. [Richard] Schechner is the best-known contemporary exponent of this practice.
>
> *(2002: 38)*

At the beginning of the 1990s, Bonnie Marranca pointed out that the term "interculturalism" was a "fairly recent addition to theatrical vocabulary" (Marranca and Dasgupta 1991: 11). Patrice Pavis also noted, "The expression 'intercultural theatre' still sounds rather odd to Western ears, even to those critics on the look-out for new trends in contemporary theatre practice" (Pavis 1996: 1). At that time, Erika Fischer-Lichte defined intercultural performance as "constituted by the relationship between the continuation of the own traditions and the productive reception of elements of foreign theatre traditions" (1990: 11).[22] If cultural exchange can be conceptualized as "relationships," this may explain the difficulty mapping a broader pattern of cultural exchange in theatre as a movement or genre. Projects once considered cross-cultural could upon reconsideration be identified as intercultural and later be understood though comparisons with other projects as transcultural. Peter Brook's *Mahabarata* has encountered such various reconsiderations.[23]

Ian Watson's definition of interculturalism as a kind of "creolization" (Watson 2002: 5) of culture seemed to suggest that the parent cultures were somehow "pure," and once these "pure" cultures mixed the result was "disculturisation" (ibid.). Watson's "creolization" argument was similar to Weber's "chop suey" argument when criticizing "transcultural" theatre. Although I acknowledge that intercultural performance practice may lead to "disculturisation" due to power relationships between the participating cultures, I think it is unfair to *assume* "disculturisation" is inevitable as part of the working definition of intercultural practice.

The "creole" or "chop suey" argument relies too heavily on the assumption that culture is a stable, immutable thing or category and only when two cultures mix does culture become unstable or corrupt. If culture is a living thing, always changing, then the introduction of another culture becomes a part of change already in progress. The product of intercultural exchange would not be a mixed product, the crossing or corruption of categories, but a perspective, a "state of mind," a changing relationship. Whether intercultural theatre could offer something brand new and totally different, such as an entirely separate genre, would be as important as offering a new perspective on existing practice. Interculturalism could be understood as a methodology of practice, not a category of practice.

I continue to use the term "intercultural" to characterize my work, in part, because it began at KNUA as an "intentional encounter" (Lo and Gilbert 2002: 36) between Korean traditional arts and Anglo-American voice training as mandated by the curriculum, but also as a practical means by which to try and solve certain curriculum "problems." I take further responsibility for this "intentional encounter" by bringing my KNUA voice curriculum to the UK. Part of what I understand to be "intercultural" practice is the global, migratory patterns of practice (Rebellato 2009: 8, 30–31). These patterns were assisted by the institutions who invited me to work for them, actively cultivating an "international" staff and student body, the work visas I was offered by both the South Korean and British governments, and the support I received within the wider theatre communities that made the work I do possible.

I agree with Bharucha when he asserted, "I would argue that we need the term 'interculturalism' because it is politically necessary for us as artists, as citizens, to find ways of countering the dominance of official state-determined multiculturalism'" (Bharucha and Fischer-Lichte 2011: 4). For Zarrilli, who touched on this conversation in the introduction of the special issue of *Theatre, Dance and Performance Training*, "Whether we label the body-to-body, technique-to-technique, concept-to-concept processes that characterise studio-based exchanges as interweaving or intercultural interaction, it is imperative to be attentive to the dynamics of power operative in each specific context" (Zarrilli, Sasitharan, and Kapur 2016: 335). I find potential in "interweaving" as a verb, a "way of doing" from which a productive model for my work could emerge.

The second key issue concerns mapping or understanding intercultural theatre as a phenomenon in recent theatre practice and discourse. Erika Fischer-Lichte wrote that intercultural theatre as a "pattern of development" has been observed "worldwide" in various cultures in different times "since the 1970s," although she pointed out that "production attitude of one culture's theatre toward the foreign theatre culture is neither wholly new or unique" (1990: 11–12). By 2011, she was suggesting "interweaving" as a new term. In dialogue with Rustom Bharucha, at the International Research Centre, she began the discussion by asking, "Why did we decide not to use the term 'intercultural,' but chose 'interweaving' instead?" For her, the term "intercultural" came "loaded with a certain historical baggage." She was also concerned with collaborations "*within* a culture through its internal diversities" (Bharucha and Fischer-Lichte 2011: 1) This understanding of the term "interweaving" can help to address within Voice Studies the cross-over of categories between "interculturalism" and "intraculturalism." Bharucha responded,

> to what extent are "interweaving" and "intercultural" mutually exclusive categories? . . . the problems associated with "interculturalism" will somehow disappear with the introduction of "interweaving"? . . . Obviously, they don't . . . The question that interests me is somewhat different: Why do we feel the need to reinvent our categories? How and in what circumstances do these new categories manifest themselves?
>
> *(Bharucha and Fischer-Lichte 2011: 3)*

As mentioned earlier, using Brook's *Mahabarata* as an example, projects upon reflection can be reconsidered and renamed by others. But for artist themselves, how and why are names important? For Bharucha, naming a project he was working on in India from "intercultural" to "intracultural" was a result of "the need . . . to create a new category [which] often emerges out of such moments of crisis in one's own research" (ibid.).

Pavis suggested that it "might be more productive to speak of intercultural exchanges within theatre practice rather than of the constitution of a new genre" (Pavis 1996: 1). Can intercultural theatre be mapped as a movement, genre, or phenomenon in theatre or can it only be understood within the particular circumstances of an exchange?

Knowles argued that "theatre has always been intercultural" and that intercultural performance is not new, "though its wide-spread, conscious practice in the western world began only in the twentieth century, and its theorization in the western academy in the 1970s and 1980s" (2010: 6). Fischer-Lichte asked if the specificity of projects and cultural contexts from the latter half of the 20th century emerged independently or do they collectively represent a "phenomenon both fruitful and meaningful?" (Fischer-Lichte 1990: 12). Lo and Gilbert addressed Fischer-Lichte's question by insisting that "intercultural" performance practice could not be understood as an individual "one-off." Lo and Gilbert advocated a "strategic way of rethinking the local and context-specific through the global, and vice versa" in order to develop "a more sustained and systematic engagement with the politics of [intercultural] production" (2002: 48–49). By choosing to discuss a "site-specific study of intercultural projects" instead of engaging with what Lo and Gilbert call the "big picture," interculturalism "privilege[d] content specificity," creating a "false dichotomy between praxis and theory" (2002: 37).

But, does engaging with the "bigger picture," mean trying to find a common denominator for a wide variety of practices that address very different cultures or modes of performance? Does this inevitably mean engaging with "universalism" on some level?

The next key issue in intercultural discourse that impacted my work dealt with the question: How does one structure an approach or working method that can be employed to inform current practice? Fischer-Lichte's proposal of the term "interweaving" or *Verflechtungen* in German is a noun. Bharucha pointed out that in English translation "interweaving" becomes a verb. He responded, "More precisely, 'interweaving performance cultures' comes across to me as an activity, a method, a way of doing things, which is actually quite a beautiful construction" (Bharucha and Fischer-Lichte 2011: 4). The idea that "interweaving" is a verb, an activity, a possible model for ways of knitting together practice, attracts me and in specific instances, I use this term as another "way of working" similar to but more specific than "interculturalism" (a noun) as Marranca and Dasgupta's "way of working" or Spatz's "intercultural theatre" as a kind of "research theatre." As Fischer-Lichte pointed out, "In fact, 'interweaving' doesn't happen by itself; it needs someone who interweaves" (Bharucha and Fischer-Lichte 2011: 5).

At the time I was developing my curriculum at KNUA, I struggled to find a model, or a way of working that I could borrow or adapt. At the turn of the 21st century, several models were available to me, such as Patrice Pavis's hourglass model and Lo and Gilbert's model for interculturalism. However, my frustration with such models were that they seemed to have been designed to articulate how cultural exchange happens, but not necessarily how cultural exchange happened inside the body. Interculturalism and embodiment did not intersect in these models. When trying to apply these models to my classroom, I was trying to make them do something they were not designed to do.

The design of both Pavis's model and Lo and Gilbert's model might be explained through their definition of "interculturalism." Patrice Pavis's later (1998) publication, *Dictionary of the Theatre: Terms, Concepts, and Analysis,* does not have a listing for "interculturalism" or "intercultural theatre," only "cross-cultural theatre." And Lo and Gilbert position intercultural theatre under the "umbrella term" of "cross-cultural theatre" (2002: 32). Both models provided opportunities when source and target cultures might "cross." I needed a model that would represent interaction between multiple sources and multiple targets over time; how interweaving techniques changes and grows within a trainee's body/voice as well as variables such as training resources, space, or teacher/student ratio, among others, that influence that growth.

Using an adapted understanding of "cross-cultural" to structure discussions about intercultural practice leads to the final key issue: binary discussions of "East" and "West" as two opposing forces that meet at the "crossroads" (Pavis 1992). When developing an intercultural discourse structure or working method are binary East/West arguments necessary? Inevitable?

In explaining their use of the term "cross-culture," Lo and Gilbert focus on this East/West dichotomy within intercultural discourse.

> Although one could argue that all theatre is in a sense cross-cultural in that performance work necessitates the negotiation of cultural difference both temporally (across history) and spatially (across geographical and social categories), what dominates critical and institutional interest in cross-cultural experimentations has been the encounters between the West and "the rest."
>
> *(2002: 32)*

Knowles asserted that certain iconic productions, like Brook's *Mahabharata* and Mnouchkine's *Les Shakespeare* (1981–1984), and their "divided reception threw into relief the tendency of intercultural theatre and its scholarship to split the world into a 'west and the rest' binary that was both fundamental and problematic" (2010: 21). What I experienced within the working conditions at KNUA, "the critical and institutional interest in cross-cultural experimentations" (Lo and Gilbert 2002: 32) that have dominated Korean theatre, has not been simply between "the West and 'the rest.'" When postcolonial theatre discourse is integrated into intercultural discourse, the discussion tends to reinforce East versus West binary arguments, predominately focusing on examples of Western colonialization. However, the colonialization of Korea by Japan (1910–1945) has created a very different discourse in Korean theatre. Discussions within *p'ansori* and *ch'anggŭk* discourse (Killick 2010; Park 2003; Um 2013) include arguments over the role of Imperial Japan in the making or breaking of traditional Korean arts. The question of what is "traditional" in the nomination of Korean arts to the level of Intangible Cultural Property is often a question of how much Chinese and Japanese influence remains within an art form before it can claim to be uniquely "Korean." Intercultural performances, such as the 2000 performance of the *Joint Production Chunhyang-ga* by China, Japan and Korea, evidence ways Asian traditional arts interact with each other, in this case, sections of the story of Chunhyang were staged by Zheijiang Xiaobaihua Yue Opera Troupe (China), Shochiku Co., Ltd (a Japanese Kabuki company), and The National Chang-geuk Company.[24] The KNUA directive to foster an artistic "voice" that represents "Koreanness" emerges from this crucible of interaction that includes more than a "West and the rest" perspective.

I chose to apply to my work Marranca's definition of "interculturalism" as a "state of mind" or perspective, as well as "a way of working," or methodology (Marranca and Dasgupta 1991: 11). Added to this I am currently experimenting with "interweaving" as a practical model that guides the ways practices interact within the body/voice of the learner, and between teacher and student during the transmission of voice pedagogy. It seemed that as I taught at KNUA and learned *p'ansori* and KFL, my "state of mind" or perspective on my teaching practice shifted. I thought about voice and voice training differently and this had an effect on my "ways of working." But also, the more I experimented with "ways of working," the more my perspective changed as to what a voice was, what it could/ should do, and how it could/should do it.

My previously learned skills were necessary to acquire new skills in *p'ansori*. I did not "de-educate" or "undo" one set of skills before I was able to acquire a new set of skills. The various skills sets inside my body did not merge into one but remained distinct and intact. As different skill sets encountered each other, they interacted in various ways, and, upon reflection, perhaps I could characterize this as "interweaving." Also, the same skill sets could be "re-woven" to explore how to address different tasks. In this way, one can think of "interweaving" as both an experimental methodology as well as a permanent knitting together of skills that work in symbiosis.

After two years teaching at KNUA, I augmented my task from trying to solve certain curriculum problems to a formalized application of interculturalism as a methodology in a practice-as-research based PhD at the University of Exeter, UK. As definitions for "interculturalism" continue to evolve and previous intercultural projects are (re)considered and (re)named, I agree with Ben Spatz that "It may be that what has been called 'intercultural theatre' is more accurately a kind of 'research theatre' in which interculturalism is the methodology" (Spatz 2015: 62).

Practice as research: Another way to (re)consider voice practice

Shortly after I arrived at KNUA, I decided to train as my students were training, *p'ansori* and Anglo-American voice together, in order to better understand their experience. At the time I did not understand this to be "research through practice" or "practice-based research" or many of the other ways of understanding the relationship between research and practice (Thomaidis 2015: 14–16). I began to understand *p'ansori* initially through practice, but combined this with more traditional print materials research.[25] The research literature helped put the practical training into a broader historical and cultural context that explained how and why particular techniques and methods of training are used to transmit *p'ansori*. Fundamental to my understanding of how the practice of voice training and performance and researching voice could be structured was Chan E. Park's PhD thesis, *P'ansori Performed: From Strawmat to Proscenium and Back* (1995, University of Hawai'i), an auto-ethnographic study of training and performance practices in intercultural and transcultural contexts.[26] I concluded that it would be necessary to develop a structured "dialogue" between the two training traditions that would include both theory and practice to help the students develop skills while also reflecting and critiquing their process within a larger socio-historic context. This "dialogue" also helped me to answer the question, "Why are we doing this?" which would come up periodically during an exercise and help shape the learning objective.

Integrating theory and practice was a part of my training at UW-Madison, in which MFA Acting students were required in their third year to perform two major performance roles and write a Masters of Fine Arts thesis articulating one's practice. While I think Madison offered important intersections between "doing" and "thinking" about ways of doing, on a degree level "doing" and "thinking" were separated. There was no PaR degree option at that time. The terminal degree for practitioners was a Masters of Fine Arts, and the terminal degree for scholars was a PhD. After graduation, in the performance industries in which I worked, there seemed to be a split between "doing" and "thinking" and also in my profession as a voice trainer, realized in an oppositional relationship between "academics" and "practitioners."

Perhaps one of the best examples of this split for the purposes addressed here can be understood thorough the debate that was published in *New Theatre Quarterly* throughout 1996 to 1997, specifically issues 47, 49, 50, and 51, three years before I arrived in Seoul. Sarah Werner's "Performing Shakespeare: Voice Training and the Feminist Actor" (Werner 1996) and the article by Richard Paul Knowles that helped inform her argument (and which was eventually published in 1996 under the title "Shakespeare, Voice and Ideology: Interrogating the Natural Voice" in James C. Bulman's collection of essays, *Shakespeare, Theory, and Performance*) pointed out cultural assumptions embedded within the discursive passages found in the texts of master voice trainers Kristin Linklater, Cicely Berry, and Patsy Rodenburg. However, neither Werner nor Knowles extended her or his interrogation to include the written exercises, which were, according even to Knowles, "the books' central contributions" (1996: 93).

Both scholars pointed out reasons for not including a critical analysis of the companion studio work. Werner cited Knowles (1996), who argued that, although it may "seem unfair" to interrogate only the printed texts of Berry, Rodenburg, and Linkater, their work "*as* texts" have had a major impact separate from that of the studio work (Knowles 1996: 93, emphasis in original). Werner and Knowles focus on the "rhetorical contexts within which those exercises figure and out of which they are developed" (ibid.). Their intention is to interrogate the ways in which those texts "encode and reinforce ideological structures and assumptions that are both deeply embedded in theatrical discourse and too easily overlooked or mystified when their methods are applied in practice" (ibid.).

The intentional limiting of their investigation was problematic for the three voice practitioners whose texts were being discussed. In an unprecedented move, Berry, Rodenburg, and Linklater together wrote a response article to Werner, in which Berry suggested that Werner should "experience . . . their teaching in practice" (Berry, Rodenburg, and Linklater 1997: 49). After Werner responded ("Voice Training, Shakespeare, and Feminism" 1997: 183), Jane Boston published an attempt to mediate the debate (Boston 1997: 248–254), and this seemed to be the last word until Werner revisited the debate in her 2001 book, *Shakespeare and Feminist Performance*. In response to Berry's suggestion, Werner wrote in a footnote that "their response was not to address the historicist and ideological issues I had raised, but to wonder . . . whether I had ever bothered to work on my own voice" (2001: 110). Werner's choice not to investigate practice contrasts with Berry's insistence that "we voice teachers are not talking theories" (1997: 49). Berry wrote in her response to Werner, "It is so dangerous when academic argument/language can have supremacy and weight over actual experience" (ibid.). This exchange is divisive and reinforces the opposition between theory and practice inherent in the way scholars and practitioners have traditionally separated themselves one from the other. Voice teachers do, in fact, talk theories in both implicit and explicit ways. Actual experience is shaped by ongoing theoretical discourse; in turn, theory is shaped by actual experience as it constantly responds to, and attempts to understand, experience. Practice-as-research provides another way of mediating theory and practice.

Investigating the theoretical principles that underpin practice by working through practice is an approach to research currently popular in British higher education institutions. Analyzing the act of embodiment within a teaching/learning process is an alternative model for research, offering other perspectives and helping to interrogate how assumptions within voice training are transmitted. Practice-as-research also provides a certain level of familiarity with the practices, which assists researchers in understanding the writings of practice, particularly the written exercises. The written exercises, like the discursive passages, carry encoded and reinforced ideological structures and assumptions, which are deeply embedded not only within theatrical discourse but also within the training of the actor's body and voice. Embedded, embodied understandings of practice are part of what seems to frustrate Knowles as he looks for resistant readings of Shakespeare. He insists, "I am less interested in how well the methods 'work' than in *what* (ideological) work they *do*" (1996: 93, emphasis in original). Yet Knowles is interested in how well the methods work—he concludes that, within institutional and professional contexts, the methods work too well for resistant readings to take root. As he puts it, "Any attempt to circumvent traditional rehearsal practices is likely to be confronted by the self-protective instincts of actors who believe their training to be ideologically neutral" (1996: 107).

How might such an "instinct" have emerged from the training if, as according to Knowles, actors "tend to skip over" (1996: 93) the discursive passages in a hurry to access the exercises? Deeply embedded responses, which come to feel "natural" or perhaps "instinctive" over long-term practice, come from the repetition of technique during training. In their reading of the discursive passages, Knowles and Werner correctly point out the problem of conflating an actor's experience with human experience. But this interrogation needs to be pushed further back into the voice studio. It is in practice that one can better understand the ways that voice exercises, shaped as they are by anatomical expertise and by suppositions about sociocultural influence, affect how a body/voice essentializes experience. In light of this approach to theorizing voice, the act of transmission becomes part of how "voice training as one of the material conditions for the production of meaning in contemporary performance . . . is routinely overlooked in performance criticism" (Knowles 1996: 93).

In part, the purpose of Werner's book was to insist on the instability of Shakespeare's texts as literary objects. She wrote,

> In establishing the meaning of Shakespeare through the performance of his plays rather than their status as printed objects, performance criticism has also moved along this trajectory, *shifting from a reliance on the text to an examination of the whole creative process.*
>
> *(2001: 17, emphasis mine)*

Yet in examining the work of Berry, Rodenburg, and Linklater, Werner relies on their texts, investing in the "wished for solidity of the text," even after acknowledging that "a number of theatre practitioners have commented to me on the books' occasional distance from their authors' studio methods" (2001: 23). Similarly, one reason why Knowles examines these practices is to "insist that performance criticism of Shakespeare pay attention to the conditions and *practices* that shape the production of meaning in the material theatre" (Knowles 1996: 110–111, emphasis added). In limiting their investigation, Knowles and Werner did not really examine the practices or the whole creative process. They only examined the writings about practice. Moreover, of the writings about practice, they chose to examine only the discursive passages and not the written exercises. In her first book, *Voice and the Actor*, Berry wrote that "the most useful part of this book will certainly be the exercises, for it is the exercises that matter" (1973: 11). If training exercises matter, how and why do they matter? What do they carry in the act of transmission that contributes to "the myriad of other aspects that make up a performance [practice]?" (Werner 2001: 16–17). I will return to this debate in Chapter Two, addressing some of the concepts Knowles and Werner correctly identify as problematic, as a departure point for investigating the structure and learning outcomes of key exercises in the "natural/free" voice approach.

Notes

1 See Chapter Two for Cicely Berry's response to Korean language sounds from her book *Text in Action* (2001).
2 See Chapter Two for Lee Byong-Won's understanding of "tension-filled" sounds in *p'ansori* (Lee 1999).
3 Hamlet's advice to the Players, "Speak the speech, I pray you, as I pronounced it to you, trippingly on the tongue (*The Tragedy of Hamlet* III,ii)," is sometimes used as a reminder, along with tongue twisters, articulation, and sound placement exercises, to place English language forward in the mouth using the tip of the tongue specifically for quick, clear articulation. This suggests a particular location for sound and an aesthetic for speech production that is culturally and historically placed in the Anglo-American actor's body/voice.
4 Words derived from Chinese language.
5 I will return to critically examine different models of communications and a "folk-psychological notion of language use" (Lind et al. 2014), which, I argue, underpins much of US/UK actor training.
6 I will return to this issue in Chapter Three.
7 Refer Berry's descriptor of "metallic quality" to the voice (1973: 12).
8 A few examples of US/UK voice trainers include, but are not limited to: non-medical voice and speech specialists Judy Shahn, retired Senior Lecturer in Voice and Dialects at the University of Washington, School of Drama (USA) and Andrea Caban, Head of Voice and Speech, Theatre Arts, California State University Long Beach (USA), have worked with people recovering from strokes and people living with ALS. Chris Palmer, Head of Voice, and Course Leader MA Practice of Voice and Singing, Guildford School of Acting (UK) has worked with acting students who identify themselves as deaf or hearing impaired and specifically with a student that has Usher syndrome, which causes deaf blindness.
9 According to Greenemeier (2009), assistive communication devices have been used since the 1960s and use of the devices are growing, with an estimated 2.5 million users in the US by 2009.
10 In the interest of full disclosure, Rebecca Root was one of my students on the MA-Voice Studies course at RCSSD and I was her thesis supervisor from which this article was lifted. We have worked together at RCSSD and East 15 Acting School. Root plays "Judy," a 40-year old transgender character in the BBC2 sitcom, *Boy Meets Girl*, the first British sitcom to star a transgender actor and character in the lead role of a romantic comedy.
11 Popular databases for my East 15 students include International Dialects of English Archive (IDEA), BBC Radio Archives, British Library "Sounds Familiar" website, and YouTube clips of famous orators.
12 Cavarero wrote, "The voice belongs to the living; it communicates the presence of an existent in flesh and bone; it signals a throat, a particular body" (2005: 177).
13 Na wrote, "Then the teacher began to sing a melody I recognized, 'Sarangga,' from the *Pansori* repertoire 'Chunhyangga.' I was shocked when she addressed me, asking me to sing it after her. She offered no explanation, and then yelled at me when I couldn't copy her exactly enough. Without giving me time to think or analyze what I needed to do, she told me to sing again. So I kept on singing wrong notes, over and over until,

suddenly, it came out correctly. She said nothing. We continued." www.hyo-shinna.com/Writings/writings.html.

14 In this context, I mean a kind of decoding of embodied socio-cultural signs and behavior.

15 See Chapter Three reference to Korean director, Oh Tae Suk's use of socio-cultural learning, such as lowered eyes, in staging dialogue.

16 In general, I will refer to "on-stage" to mean traditionally recognized performance spaces, such as theatres. I will refer to "off-stage" to mean traditionally recognized spaces not normally considered sites of performance, such as an emergency room, the back of a taxi, or a grocery store. However, later I will challenge my own definitions of "on-stage" and "off-stage," especially in Chapter Six when I detail the use of public space in street performance.

17 See Chapter Two for a larger discussion.

18 I would eventually be influenced by voice trainer Stan Brown's writings (University of Nebraska-Lincoln) in the "cultural voice."

19 Here I am borrowing from Theatre in Education pedagogy, specifically Brian Edmiston's use of Dorothy Heathcote's "Mantle of the Expert" approach that I learned as a teaching assistant under Dr. Edmiston at the University of Wisconsin-Madison 1991 to 1992. See Heathcote and Bolton (1995) to better understand how Heathcote uses this approach as a classroom learning model.

20 For a greater understanding of *dahnjeon* as adapted in my KNUA classrooms, see Chapter Three.

21 I will return to this discussion in Chapter Four.

22 Fischer-Lichte has since changed not only her understanding of "intercultural" theatre but, with the founding of the International Research Centre, "Interweaving Performance Cultures," Freie University-Berlin, has proposed the term "interweaving" instead of "intercultural" to characterize collaboration between performance cultures (refer Bharucha and Fischer-Lichte 2011).

23 Refer to Bharucha (1988) and Rivas (2014).

24 창극 [lit. sung theatre] can also be found spelled in English as "*changeuk*," "*ch'angguk*," and "*chang-geuk*."

25 Because of my level of Korean at that time, it was difficult to access materials in Korean. Most Masters and PhD *p'ansori* theses at Korea's National Library in Seoul have English language abstracts. At that time in Seoul, there were few English language books on *p'ansori*, so I was limited to ordering books over the internet from businesses that would ship internationally. Internet websites provided some access to English language *p'ansori* research, but many conferences do not post full papers on their websites. At that time, KNUA did not invest in memberships to organizations that sent English language academic journals to their library. Eventually, I had a break in my teaching schedule and flew to Hawaii where I had better access to English language *p'ansori* research materials through the University of Hawai'i East-West Center. My experience was similar to the experience of one of my MFA KNUA students, Myun Shin, who had difficulties researching Western voice for her MFA dissertation. Many of the voice books and materials on the internet are only printed in English. During the time she was writing her MFA thesis, there was only one mainstream Western voice text that I knew had been translated into Korean, Chuck Jones' *Make your Voice Heard*.

26 Later she would publish a reworking of her PhD into a monograph titled, *Voice from the Straw Mat: Toward an Ethnography of Korean Story Singing*. Honolulu: University of Hawai'i Press, 2003.

References

BBC Television. *Boy Meets Girl*, www.bbc.co.uk/programmes/b07k4tx0. Accessed 18 July, 2017.

Berry, C. (1973). *Voice and the Actor*. New York: Collier Books.

Berry, C., Rodenburg, P., Linklater, K. (1997). "Shakespeare, Feminism, and Voice: Responses to Sarah Werner," *New Theatre Quarterly*, 49, 48–52.

Berry, C. (2001). *Text in Action*. London: Virgin.

Berry, C. (2010). "The Body in the Voice," *American Theatre Magazine*. New York: Theatre Communications Group, 122.

Bharucha, R. (1988). "Peter Brook's 'Mahabharata': A View from India," *Economic and Political Weekly*, 23 (32), 1642–1647.

Bharucha, R., Fischer-Lichte, E. (2011). "Dialogue: Erika Fischer-Lichte and Rustom Bharucha," *Textures-Platform*, www.textures-platform.com/?p=1667. Accessed 28 March 2017.

Boston, J. (1997). "Voice: the Practitioners, their Practices, and their Critics," *New Theatre Quarterly*, 51, 248–54.

Cancer Research UK (2015). "Speaking after a laryngectomy," www.cancerresearchuk.org/about-cancer/type/larynx-cancer/living/speaking-after-laryngectomy. Accessed 25 November 2015.

Cavarero, A. (2005). *For More Than One Voice: Toward a Philosophy of Vocal Expression*. Stanford: Stanford University Press.

Connor, S. (2014). *Beyond Words: Sobs, Hums, Stutters, and Other Vocalizations*. London: Reaktion Books, Ltd.

Constansis, A. N. (17 May 2009). "The Changing Female-To-Male (FTM) Voice," *Radical Musicology*, 3, 2008, www.radical-musicology.org.uk, 32 pars. Accessed 20 July 2017.

Fischer-Lichte, E. (1990). *The Dramatic Touch of Difference*. Tubingen: Narr.

Greenemeier, L. (2009). "Getting Back the Gift of Gab: Next-Gen Handheld Computers Allow the Mute to Converse," *Scientific American*, August 10, www.scientificamerican.com/article/assistive-communication/. Accessed 25 November 2015.

Heathcote, D., Bolton, G. (1995). *Drama for Learning: Dorothy Heathcote's Mantle of the Expert Approach to Education*. Portsmouth: Heinemann.

Killick, A. (2010). *In Search of Korean Traditional Opera: Discourses of Ch'anggŭk*. Honolulu: University of Hawai'i Press.

Knowles, R. (1996). "Shakespeare, Voice, and Ideology: Interrogating the Natural Voice," in Bulman, J. (ed.). *Shakespeare, Theory and Performance*. London: Routledge, 92–112.

Kreiman, J., Sidtis, D. (2011). *Foundations of Voice Studies: An Interdisciplinary Approach to Voice Production and Perception*. Oxford: Wiley-Blackwell.

Lee, B.W. (1999). "Tension and Release as Physical and Auditory Signs of Affect in Korean Music," paper presented at the Society for Ethnomusicology 44th annual meeting, www.ethnomusicology.org/programs/abstracts_99.html. Accessed 20 April 2018.

Lind, A., Hall, L., Breidegard, B., Balkenius, C., and Johansson, P. (2014). "Auditory feedback of one's own voice is used for high-level semantic monitoring: the "self-comprehension" hypothesis," *Frontiers in Human Neuroscience*, www.frontiersin.org/articles/10.3389/fnhum.2014.00166/full. Accessed 13 June 2018.

Linklater, K. (1976). *Freeing the Natural Voice*. New York: Drama Book Publishers.

Linklater, K. (2016). "The Art and Craft of Voice (and Speech) Training," *Journal of Interdisciplinary Voice Studies*, 1 (1), 57–70.

Lo, J., Gilbert, H. (2002). "Toward a Topography of Cross-Cultural Theatre Praxis," *The Drama Review*, 46(3): 31–53.

Marranca, B., Dasgupta, G. (eds). (1991). *Interculturalism and Performance*. New York: PAJ Publications.

Park, C. (2003). *Voices from the Straw Mat: Toward an Ethnography of Korean Story Singing*. Honolulu: University of Hawai'i Press and Centre for Korean Studies.

Na, H.S. (2002). "A Field of Music" and "Cholla Province," A Composer's Travel Journal. *Korea Times San Francisco*: 18 April 2002–4 June 2002, www.hyo-shinna.com/Writings/writings.html. Accessed 20 April 2018.

Pavis, P. (1996). *The Intercultural Performance Reader*. London: Routledge.

Pavis, P. (1992). *Theatre at the Crossroads of Culture*. London: Routledge.

Rebellato. D. (2009). *Theatre and Globalization*. London: Palgrave Macmillan.

Rivas, T. (2014). "What is Cultural Appropriation: Revisiting Peter Brook's Mahabaharata," originally published on *HowlRound*, http://howlround.com/what-is-cultural-appropriation-revisiting-peter-brook's-mahabharata. Accessed 1 Dec 2017.

Rodenburg, P. (1992). *The Right to Speak*. New York: Routledge.

Root, R. (2009). "There and Back Again? Or, Adventure in Genderland: An Investigation into the Nature of Transsexual Voice, its Presentation in Performance, and the Perception of Gender," *The Voice and Speech Review*, 6 (1), 144–155.

Spatz, B. (2015). *What a Body Can Do: Technique as Knowledge, Practice as Research*. London: Routledge.

Thomaidis, K. (2015). "The Re-Vocalization of Logos? Thinking, doing and Disseminating Voice," in Thomaidis, K. and MacPherson, B. (eds.) *Voice Studies: Critical Approaches to Process, Performance and Experience*. London: Routledge, 10–21.

Um, H. (2013). *Korean Musical Drama: P'ansori and the Making of Tradition in Modernity*. Farnham: Ashgate.

Watson, I. (2002). *Negotiating Cultures: Eugenio Barba and the Intercultural Debate*. Manchester: Manchester University Press.

Weber, C. (1991). "AC/TC Currents of Theatrical Exchange," in Marranca, B. and Dasgupta, G. (eds.) *Interculturalism and Performance*. New York: PAJ Publications, 27–29.

Werner, S. (1996). "Performing Shakespeare: Voice Training and the Feminist Actor," *New Theatre Quarterly*, 47, 249–258.

Werner, S. (1997). "Voice Training, Shakespeare, and Feminism." in "NTQ Reports and Announcements," *New Theatre Quarterly*, 50, 183.

Werner, S. (2001). *Shakespeare and Feminist Performance: Ideology on Stage*. London: Routledge.

Zarrilli, P. (2004). "Towards a Phenomenological Model of the Actor's Embodied Modes of Experience," *Theatre Journal*, 56 (4), 653–666.

Zarrilli, P., Sasitharan, T., Anuradha Kapur (2016). "Special issue on 'intercultural' acting and actor/performer training," in *Theatre, Dance and Performance Training*, 7 (3), 335–339.

2
WHAT IS THE "NATURAL/FREE" VOICE APPROACH?

As offered in the Introduction, the January 2010 special issue of *American Theatre* magazine, "vocal training for the actor" (O'Quinn 2010: 6), set up a way of thinking and talking about contemporary voice practice by listing five master trainers (Berry, Fitzmaurice, Lessac, Linklater, and Rodenburg) as the most influential voice trainers "in the U.S., with a few nods to our British counterparts" (33). However, these trainers represent more than a "nod" to "our British counterparts." Of the five master teachers, only Lessac's work originated within the US, receiving training at "Eastman School of Music and received his BA and MA degrees from New York University" (Lessac Institute 2017). The other four trainers listed are British, receiving their foundational training in London-based conservatoires: Berry, Fitzmaurice, Linklater, and Rodenburg. Of those four, three received their training from the same institution: Berry, Fitzmaurice, and Rodenburg all graduated from the Royal Central School of Speech and Drama (London, England, UK). Kristin Linklater graduated from the London Academy of Dramatic Art (London, England, UK). She returned to teach under her voice mentor Iris Warren, who she cited as an influence in her teaching (Linklater 1976: 2); Berry and Fitzmaurice returned to their alma mater to teach voice: Fitzmaurice cited Barbara Bunch (Berry's earliest teacher) as an influence as well as training under Cicely Berry before teaching voice, verse speaking, and prose reading at RCSSD in 1965 (Fitzmauricevoice.com). Both Berry and Rodenburg cited Gwynneth Thurburn, former Head of Voice at RCSSD, as influential to their work (Berry 2001: 33–34, 2008: 165; Rodenburg 1992: xii–xiii). The "major approaches in voice training" (Gener in *American Theatre* 2010: 33) are heavily influenced by principles and practices emerging from British developments in voice pedagogy, specifically institutional developments from London-based conservatoires.

According to the AT special issue, "Thanks to these voice visionaries, today's actors, singers and performers have a wealth of techniques to chose from" (33).

The implication is that each trainer represents a different approach and so there are many different ways to train an actor's voice. The individuality of each trainer, and by implication that trainer's approach, is reinforced in other prominent publications and discussions surrounding contemporary voice practice. For instance, in the NTQ debates mentioned in Chapter One, Boston insisted that Werner's "declaring that the work of voice practitioners Berry, Linklater and Rodenburg represents a unified body of thought" is "not the case." Boston asserts,

> It is true that they share the common ground of roots in classical systems of actors training, but it is also important to remember that they occupy different positions in the field of voice training and have very different ways of representing their expertise in print and practice.
>
> *(NTQ 51, 1997: 249)*

While there are differences, I argue that these five trainers, and in particular three of the five listed (Berry, Linklater, and Rodenburg) share fundamental principles and practices in their texts and studio practice that can be understood as representing a branch of training emerging from Anglo-American voice pedagogy. I am not asserting that Berry, Linklater, and Rodenburg, nor all five together, "represent a unified body of thought," but the ways in which they think, talk about, and train the voice are compellingly similar.

Perhaps one reason for the similarities in their work is that as trainers of actors' voices all five pedagogues seemed to have been influenced by artistic and intellectual developments in US and UK theatre that shaped their shared areas of interest and approaches to body, voice, breath, and energy. During the 20th century, not only was theatre undergoing great change but also the role of voice in theatre was being reimagined (Kimbrough 2011; Martin 1991). Berry addressed this change, in part, as a "private journey" but believes "the work has changed in the past 50 years, and yet still remains a very central part of the actor's skill. Perhaps most important, it reflects our changing theatre culture" (2001: 29).

Another reason for the similarities may be that as their work grew and developed, the pedagogues interacted. They had knowledge of each other's teachings, sometimes through close professional associations [Rodenburg worked with Berry for nine years at the Royal Shakespeare company (2017; Rodenburg 1992: xiii)] and sometimes through conferences, workshops, and edited publications. For example, one of the most recent interactions between the pedagogues (before Lessac's death in 2011) included the 2009 Voice and Speech Trainers' Association conference in NYC, New York, USA. "Vocal Methodologies from the Source: Lessac, Linklater, Fitzmaurice and Rodenburg" (VASTA 2009). This conference offered practical workshops and conference panels with four of the five master trainers. Although Berry could not attend, I noticed during the conference that her work was referenced repeatedly. The 2009, "Theatre Noise" conference intentionally designed another interaction: Cicely Berry gave a keynote address followed by a public discussion facilitated by me about her work, juxtaposed on the conference timetable of events with a roundtable with Catherine Fitzmaurice about her work, titled "Some Noise Within: Conversations with Catherine Fitzmaurice" (Theatre Noise Conference 2009). At the 2007 *Performance Breath* conference at the Royal Academy of Dramatic Art (London), Fitzmaurice was a keynote speaker (Fitamauricevoice.com). She and Linklater both offered workshops at the conference (British Voice Association 2017; Wayman 2007). Fitzmaurice, Linklater, and Rodenburg participated in the final panel discussion together. Again, although Berry was not in attendance[1], I noticed Berry's work referenced by the pedagogues as well as other important conference participants, such as master voice trainer David Carey. One conference outcome, the publication *Breath in Action* (Boston and Cook 2009) includes a foreword by Berry and a chapter by Linklater.

In collections of writings on practice, their work is often found side-by-side. For instance, in *The Vocal Vision: Views on Voice* (Hampton in Hampton and Acker 1997), chapter one is written by Linklater, chapter two by Lessac, chapter three by Berry, chapter four by Rodenburg, with a later chapter written by Fitzmaurice. The writings of Berry, Linklater, and Rodenburg can also be found in the collection *Well-tuned Women* (Armstrong and Pearson 2000).

Not only has the practice of Berry, Linklater, and Rodenburg engaged with each other's work directly and indirectly through conference participations and book collections, but these platforms also help set up a popular narrative within "the theatre voice profession" (Hampton 1997: viii). Their practices are associated with a "natural" or "free" voice approach that is characterized as "innovative," "visionary," and individual to each trainer. Armstrong and Pearson in *Well-Tuned Women* asserted, "One constant overlap is in the way the different contributions reflect the overall theme . . . how, in being helped to find our *natural* voice, we simultaneously experience a finding of ourselves and our expressivity" (2000: x, emphasis mine). Thus, these master trainers are showcased as specialists working towards a "natural" voice with one aim of the practice being personal development, not only voice training to support overall actor training.

In *The Vocal Vision*, the preface offered, "The prospective Table of Contents contained the names of some of the 'stars' of voice work whom you will see represented in this volume . . . names which have become the equivalent of household words in the theatre voice profession" (vii). Notice the similar characterizations of these master trainers in both *The Vocal Vision* and *American Theatre Magazine*: "'stars' of voice work (1997)" and "pillars of voice work" (Gener 2010: 33). The master trainers are showcased as part of a "vocal vision" (1997) and "visionary innovators in the craft" (Gener 2010: 33). Such characterizations over the course of a decade created a popular conception of modern voice training centered around a handful of top master trainers and emphasized the individuality and inventiveness of their approaches; this discourse has continued into the millennium. By focusing on their inventiveness, conversations usually do not examine borrowed and adapted practices from the past, linking their teaching to a larger tradition of British training.[2]

However, outside of the "theatre voice profession," the narrative surrounding these three master trainers is a bit different. Several actor training sources deemphasize

Berry, Linklater, and Rodenburg's "individual" approaches, grouping them and attributing their "innovations" to ongoing developments in actor-training. This tends to uncouple their work from larger, older traditions of voice training and instead suggests that their work emerged out of much later developments in mid-20th century actor training, specifically as "post-Brook school of voice texts" (Knowles 1996 in Bulman, 95; Looser 2005: 36) or suggests their work as having emerged from a Brook/Grotowski approach to training. Robert Gordon wrote,

> Possibly Grotowski's praxis has had an influence that permeated the mainstream theater through cross-pollination with the tradition inaugurated by Michel Saint-Denis. The earliest information about Grotowski's praxis in Britain was through his impact on Peter Brook.[3] Whether their work was actually informed by a knowledge of Grotowski's practices, whether they absorbed such ideas through coming into contact with Peter Brook, or whether the parallel in teaching practices can be attributed to zeitgeist, there is little doubt that the approaches of the three most influential British voice teachers of the last fifty years—Cicely Berry, Kristin Linklater, and their younger contemporary Patsy Rodenburg—are in some respects strikingly similar to that of Grotowski.
>
> *(2006: 299)*

While such conversations do parallel Berry's reflection that modern voice training was influenced by a "changing theatre culture" (Berry 2001: 29), it does not balance the "innovative" developments in modern voice training with its foundational pedagogical traditions.

It is not the intention nor would it be possible within a chapter to exhaustively examine or map the complex territory of modern voice training. Instead, one aim of this chapter is to understand the "natural/free" voice approach within the context of these popular narratives. I hope to raise certain questions about what is a "natural" or "free" voice and, by using select examples, to antagonize these narratives. I argue that while Brook and Grotowski may have influenced voice training [Brook wrote the foreword to Berry's first book (1973) and Linklater quotes Grotowski in her first book (1976: 24)], the practical exercises that lay the foundation for the training emerged from earlier developments. If Brook and/or Grotowski, well known for their cross-cultural practices, particularly their interest in Asian practice, had been significant influences on Berry, Linklater, and Rodenburg, why was I finding it so difficult to create other cross-cultural interactions between voice and Asian practices in my voice classrooms?

In our class texts, Berry wrote that the exercises "appearing in this book are foolproof" (1973: 17) and Linklater wrote, "The framework of the exercises is impeccably designed and has an enduring potency" (1976: 2). I was having difficulty, not simply *adjusting* the exercises to my Korean speaking students but applying core voice principles and practices—even before attempting to interface Anglo-American voice pedagogy with Korean *p'ansori*. The investigations in this chapter reflect my attempt to understand why this might be. The conclusions I drew, at that time, fed the choices I made when shifting certain principles and practices as necessary preparation for interweaving the two main training traditions I work with into an intercultural/interdisciplinary voice approach.

In this chapter, I first focus on the practices and writings of practice of Cicely Berry, Kristin Linklater, and Patsy Rodenburg, because I used their work specifically at KNUA. They comprise what I am calling the "natural/free" voice approach. Here, I use this term in a limited, specific way to describe my understandings of their key principles and practices based primarily on their first books, as foundational practices from which their work developed: Berry's first book *Voice and the Actor* (1973), Linklater's first book *Freeing the Natural Voice* (1976), and Rodenburg's first book *The Right to Speak* (1992). Readers may also refer to recordings of their practices that demonstrate certain aspects of their training in studio. Added to this is my embodied knowledge of their practices from workshops taken with the three master trainers. In short, I argue:

- All three began their writings on practice by examining physical as well as social and environmental habits as the source of vocal inhibitions (Berry 1973: 7–8; Linklater 1976: 11–12; Rodenburg 1992: 8). They all understood negative socio-cultural and environmental influences as establishing bad "habits" in the body/voice.
- These bad "habits" were physically realized as excessive muscular contraction or unnecessary "tension," inhibiting the process of vocalization (Berry 1973: 10; Linklater 1976: 1; Rodenburg 1992: 19–20).
- In order to increase the student's physical awareness of this unnecessary "tension," all three practitioners touch the student's body in a way similar to F. M. Alexander's use of touch in the Alexander Technique as a part of "directing awareness" (Alexander 1910: 129; Berry 1973: 63–64, 79–80, as well as the video *Shakespeare Out Loud*; Linklater 2003: video *Teaching Voice*; Rodenburg 1994 video *A Voice of Your Own*).
- Once the students became aware of this "tension," the three trainers used their voice exercises to "release" the muscular contraction (Berry 1973: 24, 27; Linklater 1976: 19; Rodenburg 1992: 173).
- One way the body/voice released this "tension" was through a more efficient skeletal/muscular relationship (Berry 1973: 23–30; Linklater 1976: 19–24; Rodenburg 1992: 131–133, 183), which I argue are adaptations of earlier techniques such as Alexander-based spinal alignment practices (Alexander 1910: 120–129).
- The three trainers also designed voice exercises to help "recondition" (Linklater 1976: 2) the student's body/voice, relearning how to function in efficient ways, another similarity to Alexander's "reeducation" process (Alexander 1910: 107–119).
- All three turned away from the 1950s 'voice beautiful' school of training that relied on mimetic training practices towards a more "individual" approach (Berry 1973: 16; Linklater 1976: 185; Rodenburg 1992: 118).

- All three organize the overall framework of their practical voice training in a similar way, beginning with spinal alignment or "posture," leading to a focus on breath, then sounding, and finally speech. This development is similar to older approaches to training, like that of Thurburn's training progression as outlined in her 1939 publication *Voice and Speech* (127).

Next, I place their writings and practice in socio-historical context; the radical politics and changing theatre culture in the US and UK during the 1960s and 1970s is often cited as the crucible from which Berry, Linklater, and Rodenburg's practices emerged, specifically linking the work of Berry with Peter Brook (Berry 1973: foreword by Brook; Boston 1997 in NTQ 51: 250; Kingsley in Carson 2013: 46; Knowles 1996 in Bulman, 93) and Berry, Linklater, and Rodenburg to the work of Jerzy Grotowski and Stanislavski (Blair 2008: 27; Gordon 2006: 299–300; Linklater 1976: 24). I examine two practices that evidence a significant shift in voice pedagogy, away from the "voice beautiful" approach popular in the 1950s, towards the "natural/free" approach: rejecting the use of rib reserve breathing in favour of "natural" breath and repositioning the use of or discarding the use of an articulation teaching tool called "bone prop."

However, I argue that although this period may have significantly shifted certain practices, other core practices and ideas from earlier traditions remained. Thus, within this discussion I introduce earlier understandings of "natural" and "free" in voice training, the influence of W. A. Aiken on Berry, Linklater, and Rodenburg in training actors' voices using a Western biomedical model, and relationships to body and voice through adaptations of the Alexander Technique in voice training. I argue that notions of "natural" and "free" already underpinned voice training as early as the turn of the 20th century and position the body/voice relationship in practice in a particular way that is fundamental to Anglo-American voice training but makes it difficult to integrate other mappings of the body/voice found in Asian practices.

One aim in this section is to investigate how techniques trained into an actor's body/voice carry with them particular socio-cultural and historical contexts and in this way can be understood as embodiments and reenactments of cultural values and ideas of what a voice can/should be and what a voice can/should do. Through critical analysis of the "natural/free" voice approach, this chapter asks, "what is voice?" specifically, what is a "natural" or "free" voice? What can/should it do and how can/should it do "it?" From that analysis, the following chapters then ask what shifting principles and practices of this tradition are needed to interact with adaptations of *p'ansori*, as the necessary preparatory work to embody, literally put into the body, an intercultural/interdisciplinary voice training approach?

In the final section of this chapter, I list and explain which principles and practices of the "natural/free" voice approach I adapt for integration into my intercultural/interdisciplinary approach to training actors' voices. Later chapters will detail how those selected exercises and the ideas underpinning those exercises are negotiated in the studio.

What is a "natural" or "free" voice?

Kristin Linklater was born in Scotland in 1936. She trained as an actress at the London Academy of Music and Dramatic Art (LAMDA) and subsequently returned there to teach voice production as Iris Warren's assistant. In 1963, she moved to the US and set up a studio in New York. She has worked with the Royal Shakespeare Company; Tyrone Guthrie theatre; the Festival Theatre, Stratford, Ontario; the Lincoln Center Repertory Company; the Negro Ensemble Company; the Open Theatre; and Shakespeare and Company. She co-founded Company of Women in 1977, presenting all-female, multiracial productions of Shakespeare's plays. From 1965 to 1977, she held the post of Master Teacher of Voice at New York University Theatre Program. She has received major grants from the Ford Foundation, the Rockefeller Foundation, the Mellon Foundation and the National Endowment for the Arts. In 1981, she became a Guggenheim Fellow. She is Professor Emeritus at Columbia University in New York City, NY, USA (Columbia. edu). She teaches workshops internationally and currently runs a teacher's certificate training program for her method through the institute she founded, The Linklater Centre for Voice and Language and has also recently opened The Linklater Voice Centre, Orkney, Scotland (Linklater Voice Centre 2017). She has articulated her voice training methodology in three books: *Freeing the Natural Voice* (1976), *Freeing Shakespeare's Voice* (1992), and *Freeing the Natural Voice: Revised and Expanded* (2006).

Although I have experienced Linklater's teaching first hand through several workshops, for the purposes of this chapter, I will mainly discuss her training approach as articulated in her writing with occasional reference to her practical teaching from video evidenced in a 2001 voice training workshop at The Center for Performance Research in Wales, as documented by Arts Archives. The aim is to introduce two major concepts of her work:

- The "natural voice" focuses on the "person."
- The process of "freeing" the voice differentiates between what is "natural" or appropriate physical usage and what is an "habitual" pattern of physical usage, often mistaken as "natural" because of its physical familiarity.

Linklater wrote, "The natural voice is transparent-revealing, not describing, inner impulses of emotion and thought, directly and spontaneously. The person is heard, not the person's voice" (1976: 2). Introducing her understanding of the "freeing" process, Linklater cautions that the "natural" voice should not be mistaken for that which feels "familiar." She wrote, "I must underline at the outset that in our perception of our own voice there is a vital difference to be observed between what is 'natural' and what is 'familiar'" (ibid.). This concept is borrowed from the work of F. Matthias Alexander, who Linklater acknowledged as an important influence in her American work. "Also it was in America that I was introduced to the Alexander technique, which helped clarify the psychophysical nature of the voice work" (1976: 4). She wrote,

He [Alexander] showed that habitual patterns of physical usage impose a dictatorship on the body which can only be broken with careful psycho-physical re-conditioning on the deepest level. His influence is clear in much of the voice work that has developed since then.

(1976:2)

Patsy Rodenburg (OBE) was born in 1953 and trained at the Central School of Speech and Drama. She is currently Head of Voice at Guildhall School of Music and Drama, London, England for over 30 years and course leader on the MA in Training Actors (Voice) program (GSMD 2017). She is also Director of Voice at the Michael Howard Studios in New York City and with them has recently established The Patsy Rodenburg Centre for Voice and Speech offering The Rodenburg Master Teacher Certification Program. She worked at The Royal Shakespeare Company (RSC) alongside Cicely Berry (nine years) and was appointed a Board Member at the RSC in 2013. She was also Head of Voice at England's Royal National Theatre for 16 years (PatsyRodenburg.com 2017). She has written five books articulating her voice training methodology: *Presence* (2007) also titled *Second Circle* in the US; *Speaking Shakespeare* (2002); *The Actor Speaks* (2000); *The Need for Words* (1993); and *The Right to Speak* (1992). She has also produced an instructional video entitled, *A Voice of Your Own* (1994) and newly released eight DVD series titled *Shakespeare in the Present* (2016).

Although I have experienced Rodenburg's teaching first hand through workshops, here I am referencing her practical exercises not only through her writing but also through her instructional video *A Voice of Your Own* (1994), in part because there is a close relationship between this video and her first book (1992): Rodenburg opened her video with an image of a baby crying to introduce her understanding of a "natural voice." Rodenburg's voice-over narration on the video was read from her own writings of practice, the beginning pages of *The Right to Speak*.

> The *natural voice* and its potential are what we came into the world with at birth. It is our basic vocal equipment that matures and flourishes (barring sickness) as we age. Our first experience of natural voice was in that initial gasping primal scream, that first chance we were given to "catch our breath." Life and our subsequent experiences should ideally enrich and broaden the natural voice, transforming it into a powerful instrument of self-expression.
>
> *(Rodenburg 1992: 19)*

If the video and book are understood together, they introduce two major concepts of her work and, I suggest, founding principles of the "natural/free" voice approach:

- the "natural voice" is an instrument of individual "self" expression; and
- this off-stage "self" is the fundamental influence of the "natural voice."

Like Linklater, who contrasts the "natural" with the "familiar," Rodenburg contrasts the "natural" with the "habitual":

> Throughout my work I refer a great deal to the "natural" as opposed to the "habitual" . . . life batters and restricts us in such ways that most of us settle into what I term an *habitual voice*: a voice encrusted with restrictive tendencies that only awareness and exercise can undo and counteract. The natural voice (or what others term "free" or "centred" voice) is quite simply an unblocked voice that is unhampered by debilitating habits.
>
> *(1992: 19)*

Contrasting the "natural" with "habitual" may perhaps be an adaptation of Alexander's work on habitual tensions. Rodenburg wrote, "Alexander technique teachers are valuable allies for a good voice teacher. Voice work includes working with the whole physical apparatus" (Rodenburg 1992: 63). In her foreword to Kelly McEvenue's book, *The Actor and the Alexander Technique* (2001), Rodenburg wrote, "Kelly and I first met at the Stratford Festival Theatre, Ontario, Canada, in 1984. This began a creative working partnership that has grown over the years and constantly enhances my teaching" (ix). Although not as explicitly stated as in Linklater's writing, Rodenburg's writing seems to evidence in an indirect way the impact the Alexander Technique has had on Rodenburg's work.

Cicely Berry (OBE 1985; CBE 2009) was born in 1926 and trained at the Central School of Speech and Drama (CSSD) in London, returning there to teach after graduation as well as later in her career (Berry 1987: 288). She joined the RSC in 1969 at the invitation of Trevor Nunn and was Director of Voice from 1969 to 2014. Currently, she remains as Advisory Director of the RSC and is Associate Director at Theatre For A New Audience, in New York, USA, and has an ongoing relationship with a Brazilian youth theatre company Nos de Morro (RSC.org). She has repeatedly taught workshops in Brazil and South Korea, and has taught workshops in Columbia, China, Zimbabwe, India, and across Europe. She has articulated her teaching methods in five books: *Voice and the Actor* (1973), *Your Voice and How to Use It Successfully* (1975), *The Actor and the Text* (1987, 1992), *Text in Action* (2001), and *From Word to Play* (2008). She also has a video called *Shakespeare Out Loud* (2002, 2010) and a DVD series *Working Shakespeare* (2003).

I reference Berry's teaching through workshops I have taken with her, specifically a five-day intensive voice workshop in Seoul, South Korea (2000), her writings of her practice, and occasionally recordings of her practical voice exercises. Berry's video *Shakespeare Out Loud* (2010) mostly relates to her later work, particularly her 2008 publication *From Word to Play*. However, many of the exercises sampled in this short video are adapted from her earlier work and can be found in the written exercises of her earlier training texts.

From her earliest writings Berry chose to use the term "free" voice, but the underlying principle is similar to Linklater's and Rodenburg's understandings.

To begin with, I prefer the word "free" to the word "relaxed", as the latter gives the impression of being floppy and heavy, and therefore perhaps dull, whereas "free" implies being relaxed but ready for action, alert but not tense. You constantly have to differentiate between the tension you need and the tension you do not need. To make any movement certain muscles have to have tension- what you do not want, however is unnecessary tension, because all unnecessary tension is wasted energy- it is energy being kept in and not made available for communication.

(Berry 1973: 22)

Here, Berry introduced two major concepts of her work as well as founding principles of the "natural/free" voice approach:

- A "free" voice is one that is "alert but not tense."
- "Free" also denotes a process by which one must distinguish between good tension, "tension you need," and bad tension, "tension you do not need."

Rodenburg also made this distinction between good and bad tension, but used the terms "healthy" and "useless" tension in physical usage (1992: 120). For Rodenburg, "tension" is useful in survival or daily structural maintenance, but in performance, "so much of the tension that blocks our voice is used unnecessarily" (1992: 120). Much of the focus of the "natural/free" voice approach deals with the negative effects of "tension." I will return to this discussion later when I introduce *p'ansori* training, which places excess amounts of muscular contraction in the body in order to produce a particular aesthetic.[4]

Just as Berry and Rodenburg differentiated between good and bad tension, for Linklater, good tension is, "relaxing in order to do something" in contrast with "relaxing for the sake of relaxation." Bad tension is "unnecessary tensions." Linklater wrote,

The ability to relax must be cultivated slowly and with specific intent, otherwise it degenerates into the state of general collapse that Jerzy Grotowski rightly disparaged: "One cannot be completely relaxed as is taught in many theatre schools, for he who is totally relaxed is nothing more than a wet rag." There is, however, a vital difference between relaxing for the sake of relaxation, which inevitably includes mental collapse, and relaxing in order to do something. The aim is to remove unnecessary tensions so that the muscles are free to respond to impulse, without the short-circuiting created by habit.

(1976: 24)

The similarities between the three methodologies set the founding principles of the "natural/free voice" approach.

- All three methodologies set their goal as the "natural" or "free" voice.
- The "natural" or "free" voice is linked to the "life experience" of the off-stage "person's" individual "self" expression.

- The "natural" or "free" voice develops from a body that is relaxed and "alert," not "collapsed" or "floppy."
- The "natural" or "free" voice is defined by its opposite, the voice blocked by "habits" and "tension."
- "Tension," as muscular contraction, can be both good and bad, but for the most part, the "natural/free voice" approach focuses its training on exercises to release this bad "useless" tension or excessive muscular contraction.

The "blocked" voice

The "blocked" voice is often characterized as one in which habitual tension disrupts the "natural" anatomical and physiological functioning of a voice. This places a great deal of attention, especially in the beginning of the training, on understanding voice as part of a physical body. In Berry's first book, she used simple anatomical drawings and studio photos to communicate her understanding of breath and sound production physically. Throughout her book, she continually returned to anatomy as one of the fundamentals of her work.

> The more you do the exercises the more you will realize that it is the satisfactory use of the muscles that you must rely on, for when the muscles themselves are working right the sounds will be properly defined. You are only doing what an athlete does, and that is preparing the muscles you need to do a particular job.
>
> *(1973: 44)*

For Berry, the strength of the book lies in the nature of the exercises, which increase one's understanding of the voice through "physical awareness" (1973: 11).

This link between the voice and body through a Western biomedical model is a core practice in contemporary voice training, often credited to W.A. Aiken who worked with both RCSSD founder Elsie Fogerty and her successor Gwynneth Thurburn (Fogerty 1930: Acknowledgements, vi; Thurburn 1939: vi). Boston wrote, "Most of the main tenets of 20th-century voice theory can be traced back to Dr. W. Aiken. Elsie Forgerty, founder of the Central School of Speech and Drama in London, first recruited him to the profession in 1912" (in Turner 2007: xiii). Linklater also cited Aiken as influential to her work. She wrote, "Any systemized work that I do on vowels is based on the vowel scale drawn up by W.D. Aiken and expounded in his book *The Voice*" (Linklater 1976: 163; refer Aiken 1900, 1910). A diagram of the resonator scale by Dr. W. A. Aiken is published in Elsie Fogerty's *Speech Craft* (1930: 38–39).

However, a quick perusal of elocution handbooks published in London before 1912 evidences that voice and speech training for performers was already founded on understandings of anatomy and physiology before Fogerty and Aiken worked together. *Bell's Standard Elocutionist: Principles and Exercises* (1878, 1887) includes an anatomical description of breath production and "the organs of articulation" (14; archives.org). In *Voice, Speech and Gesture: Practical Handbook to the Elocutionary Art*

(1897, 1908) the first chapter, "The Voice," is written by Hugh Campbell, MD, author of "The Throat and Lungs in Health and Disease, etc" (1), and includes: detailed anatomical drawings, a section on "different methods of breathing" (35–42) and a section on the "hygiene of the vocal organs" (43–53) that focuses on vocal health. This suggests that a British tradition of voice training is grounded in a scientific biomedical model that survived throughout the 20th century: through a changing theatrical culture (Berry 2001: 29) in which certain practices of the "voice beautiful" approach were rejected, through a reimagining of the role of voice in 20th century dramatic theories (Kimbrough 2011; Martin 1991), survived through the politically turbulent 1960s and 1970s, and the influence of Brook and/or Grotowski (Gordon 2006; Knowles 1996 in Bulman). This understanding of the body/voice relationship that underpins modern voice training sets up a way of thinking and talking about what a voice is and what a voice should do, especially in terms of vocal health. What a voice is begins with a discussion of its anatomic materials (object-body), an understanding of the whole through the sum of its parts. This would become a central point of focus in my developing pedagogy at KNUA as I tried to interweave a voice tradition that understood "embodiment" through a biomedical mapping of the body with other mappings of the body that my KNUA students were bringing into my classroom, specifically understandings of *ki* and *dahnjeon*. This also led to a (re)consideration of what is vocal "health" in light of a traditional *p'ansori* training practice, called *sankongbu*. I will return to these issues in Chapters Three and Four.

Like Berry, Linklater also used anatomy to understand vocal function as well as increase physical awareness. In Linklater's first chapter, "How the Voice Works," she provides a "simple physiological outline of the mechanics of the voice," although freely admits,

> from this point on I shall not be using exact scientific terminology. I have chosen to describe the voice metaphorically, analogically and by its perceivable features. While this simplification may make the voice scientist quail it has proven the best approach for the voice user.
>
> *(1976: 6–7)*

Almost 80 years earlier, Campbell wrote similarly in *Voice, Speech and Gesture,*

> It will not be needful to give more than a very general account of the organs of speech, for, in the first place, it is impossible without making careful dissections to obtain a full knowledge of them, and if anyone has a mind for this, he can find all the necessary information on anatomical works; and, in the second place, a brief description will be sufficient to enable the reader to understand the general principles of voice-production.
>
> *(1897: 114)*

The drawings in Linklater's book are not anatomical but sketched cartoons, drawn by Douglas Florian, that give the impression of the exercises' objectives. However, this is not to suggest that Linklater pays little attention to anatomy and physiology as foundational to voice training. Later, in the revised *Freeing the Natural Voice* (2006), Linklater offered as Appendix an excerpt from *Anatomy and Physiology of the Voice and Choral Pedagogy* by Robert Stataloff, MD, DMA (2006: 375–380), and most recently wrote in *The Journal of Interdisciplinary Voice Studies*, "The craft of voice training depends on a detailed understanding of how the voice works anatomically" (2016: 59).

Like Linklater, Rodenburg also rejected overly medical approaches to voice and her first book did not contain any anatomical drawings.

> Some books on voice also seem to me to be terribly clinical and strain too hard to be like medical texts. These are useful for practitioners and teachers but harder for the general reader. When my own students use them I always notice how they invariably get lost or lose interest.
>
> *(1992: ix)*

Thus, in her 1992 training text, explicit use of anatomy and physiology does not appear but in her later writing, *The Actor Speaks* (2000), she offers early in the book an anatomical description of how the voice functions as a "vocal process" (6–8). She wrote,

> On the first day I explain to my students how their voices work. Most have no idea about how the voice functions and usually confuse voice work with speech work . . . I begin by going through the anatomy of the voice, identifying the chain of physical relationships which help us produce sound.
>
> *(2000: 5)*

Rodenburg's rationale is similar to RCSSD's Head of Voice Gwynneth Thurburn who wrote in 1939,

> There are a few physical laws which need consideration, and some knowledge of anatomy and physiology should be attained, but a detailed study is necessary only to the specialist. Indeed, a detailed study, unless it goes far enough, is more likely to hinder than to help as a general rule, but it must be borne in mind that without a foundation upon physiological and physical laws the sounds made are apt to be governed either by habit or individual preference.
>
> *(1939: 22)*

Here, Thurburn also introduces another important idea fundamental to the "natural/ free" voice approach: misuse of vocal anatomy may be due to "habit."

The "blocked" voice and "habits"

Part of the process of becoming physically aware through work is developing the ability to identify excess tension and release that tension through exercises. The roots of this tension may be physical, but it may also be caused by social and environmental factors.

For Linklater, the "natural" voice is blocked and/or distorted by physical tension as well as emotional, intellectual, aural, and spiritual blocks (1973: 1). Linklater wrote that these "blocks" were "psycho-physical" in nature and designed the exercises in her book to remove these "blocks." She wrote, "This book contains a detailed series of exercises, combining imagery and imagination with technical knowledge, that can lead to enough understanding of the psycho-physiology of the voice to recondition your *habitual* way of communicating" (1973: 2, emphasis mine). Whereas a simple understanding of the anatomy and physiology of the voice is introduced in chapter one, "How the voice works," the "blocked" voice, introduced in chapter two, "Why the voice doesn't work," describes how this anatomical structure is disrupted (1973: 12). She specifically detailed how the "effects of emotion on breathing," and "postural *habits*" interrupt the "free play of the vocal folds" and how "*tension* in the larynx and throat *blocks* the voice" (15, emphasis mine).

A "blocked" voice is one that can no longer respond with spontaneity because "that spontaneity depends on reflex action and most people have lost the ability, and perhaps the desire, to behave reflexively" (1973: 11). According to Linklater, reflex action is "short-circuited by secondary impulses" that are "formed unconsciously and by people other than oneself, in childhood" and a habit is formed (11–12). The beginning of the "freeing" process starts by identifying habits that create unnecessary tension in the body, prohibiting the "free" play of the vocal mechanism. "The first step toward freeing the natural voice is to develop an ability to perceive habits and register new experiences" (19).

Rodenburg, like Linklater, understands the "habitual" voice as affected by the tensions acquired through daily living.

> Habits physically manifest themselves as holds or barriers to the sounds we make . . . Any useless tension, anywhere in the body, can constrict the freedom of the voice. The way we stand or sit, for instance, the ways our heads, necks or spines are correctly or incorrectly aligned, the carriage of our shoulders, upper chest and torso, the habitual set of our mouth and jaw- all of these influence the balance and functioning of our voice. Any one of these can be the land-mine sitting in the path of the voice's free passage.
>
> *(1992: 19–20)*

The physical, anatomical relationship between muscular constriction and inefficient voice usage is influenced by social and environmental factors, inhibiting vocal usage.

> I want to look at how the voice gets blocked, the different kinds of strain and tensions we make our voices suffer and how the voice can be released from all this anxiety and extended in range and colour. Mostly, I want you to see

for yourself how the conspiracy against your right to speak evolves. How background, gender, injury or illness can taint the sound we make.

(1992: 8)

For Rodenburg, social and environmental factors create "habitual" tensions that change the "natural" voice into a "habitual" voice.

For Berry, "the condition of life conditions the speech" (1973: 8). She details ways in which "environment" as one of four factors that "continually affect the individual's voice" (7–8). I will return to a discussion of how contemporary voice training talks about the influence of socio-cultural factors and "tension" later in Chapter Five.

This understanding of how a voice is "blocked" can be found in earlier writings, such as Thurburn's 1939 publication *Voice and Speech*. She wrote,

> A good voice is one in which the organs are properly used and which will improve the quality of the voice. A bad sound is one in which there is *tension* or constriction in some of the muscles involved, and will in time inevitably impair the satisfactory functioning of the voice.

(12, emphasis mine)

Like Berry, Linklater, and Rodenburg, Thurburn understands the anatomy and physiology of the voice as inhibited by "tension." She sometimes explained the term "tension" as "contraction in those [muscles] which are not required" (43). She wrote, "Undue tension in any part of the body will interfere with the easy functioning of the vocal organs . . . bodily tension of any kind . . . inhibits a free response" (41). Thurburn's use of the term "free" is linked to muscular efficiency, similar to the way Berry, Linklater, and Rodenburg sometimes use "free" to also discuss efficient body/voice relationships. In addition, like the three pedagogues, for Thurburn, vocal function depends on "building up a new set of habits" (14). She wrote, "the aim should be to train the organs so that they habitually function well" (ibid.).

In "unblocking" the voice, Berry, Linklater, and Rodenburg all begin not only with understanding the body/voice relationship through anatomy and physiology, but also a body/voice relationship between the skeletal and muscular framework that is conditioned by habits. All three address posture and/or spinal alignment: Berry offers pictures of "incorrect posture" and "correct posture" (1973: 6, 62–63), Linklater's chapter three, "The Spine," (19–24) asserts, "the efficiency of the vocal apparatus depends on the alignment of the body and the economy with which it functions" (20); and Rodenburg wrote,

> [The spine] is one of my main target areas as a voice teacher. When someone enters the room for an initial voice class with a collapsed, slumped or stiff spine I know that the whole vocal system has to be opened and realigned.

(131)

In the "elocution era," posture was also a concern in relation to efficient vocal function. Campbell wrote, "The attitude of the speaker is a matter of some moment. He should stand upright, keeping the chin somewhat raised so as to give *free play* to the larynx and to *allow* of the voice being directed upwards" (45–46, emphasis mine). Here, Campbell (1897) used key teaching words repeated 80 years later by Berry, Linklater, and Rodenburg: "free" and "allow." In this instance, "free" is understood as the unencumbered movement of vocal anatomy and physiology. "To allow" is the result of action taken by the speaker to create a hospitable environment from which sound can issue. I will return to these key words later in this chapter when addressing Knowles critique of "freedom" (96, 99, 102, 104, 105) and "allow" (96, 102) in the texts of Berry, Linklater, and Rodenburg.

Whether directly or indirectly influenced by the Alexander Technique, Berry's first exercise in her first book reads surprisingly like an adaptation of Alexander's "orders." Alexander used the "orders" to re-condition the actor's spinal alignment in order to better support breath and sound production. I will refer back to this Berry exercise when I detail a comparison between Berry and Alexander later in this chapter. Berry wrote,

> Take the time to feel these sensations of lengthening and widening and freedom in the different sets of muscles. Actually say to yourself: Back spread, Shoulders spread and free, Lengthen down to the bottom of the spine, and feel the wholeness of the back, Wrists free, Elbows free, Neck free, and lengthening out of the back.
>
> *(1973: 23–28)*

Berry's later work, *The Actor and the Text* (1987, 1992), seemed to support the use of the Alexander Technique. She wrote, "many actors find great benefit from work in the Alexander Technique which teaches a conscious awareness of bodily alignment, and through this a freeing of physical tension in both movement and stillness" (25).[5]

If all three master trainers were influenced by older training practices, specifically certain practices found in Thurburn's and Alexander's work, which they cite as influences, this may explain the similar way they understand the body and the similarities in training the body/voice relationship.

- All three introduce spinal alignment, or "posture," as a means by which to increase breath and sound support.
- All three examine physical as well as social and environmental habits as the source of vocal inhibitions.
- All three understand the role of tension/release as a linear process: negative excessive muscular control acquired from "daily" life is released through training. And this trained release is meant to be a permanent change in the way the anatomy of the body/voice functions. The learner is not meant to return to their habitual patterns but embody new, more efficient habits.

The "natural/free" voice and rib reserve

Berry, Linklater, and Rodenburg all mention "rib reserve" in their first books (Berry 1973: 26–27; Linklater 1976: 122, 142; Rodenburg 1992: xii) and I suggest that a reading of their "natural/free" voice approach to breath capacity, and how they define one understanding of "free," should be read in relation to their experiences with rib reserve.[6] Rib reserve training was possibly borrowed from singing training and/or elocution training and was very popular from the 1930s through to the1950s, in part because of fashionable ideas of vocal delivery in performance.[7] By rejecting this performance style in favor of a more "naturalistic" style of acting, voice trainers also rejected the training techniques, like rib reserve, that helped produce this performance style.

Berry mentioned rib reserve breathing early in her first book (1973: 26–27), as part of a larger breath capacity exercise. The first part of the exercise (24–25) is intended to "open up the ribs" (25). The next part of the exercise is intended to "exercise the diaphragm" (ibid.). She wrote,

> Here you have separated the diaphragm breath from the rib breath, but only for the purpose of being aware of each set of muscles. In fact they both work together, and *freedom* of the lower ribs helps the movement of the diaphragm . . . To make good sound it is essential that both sets of muscles are working at their best, but interrelated and *free*.
>
> *(26, emphasis mine)*

She differentiated her understanding of "freedom" and "free" by contrasting it with rib reserve breathing, which she characterized as "unreal" (27). She wrote,

> I should like to make it quite clear that I do not believe that you should work keeping the two movements separate—that is, *holding* the ribs out firmly and only using the breath from the diaphragm, what has been known as rib-reserve breathing. To me this is *unreal* and makes for a great deal of *tension*.
>
> *(26–27)*

Three key teaching words, "holding," "unreal," and "tension" are repeated by all three master trainers. In this way, "free" is understood in part as a musculature that is not "held" or "locked" in place but moves without "tension." The sound produced is one that is "real," or "natural."

Later in her writing, Berry offered a personal oral history of her experience with rib reserve in the foreword to *Breath in Action*. She wrote,

> Training at the Central School of Speech and Drama between 1943 and 1946 under the direction of the wonderful Gwynneth Thurburn, I was reared on "rib reserve". This involved opening out the ribs, separating the

rib movement from that of the diaphragm, so that the chest was enlarged both by widening and by deepening the movement of the lungs. This gave the voice a strong chest resonance, while we spoke on the diaphragm breath. It was all physically demanding and I often found it to be over-technical and difficult. However, it was the method taught then, in 1948, I went back to teach there full-time on the actor training programme.

(2009: 11)

Berry reconsidered the role of rib reserve for actors' voices when in 1970 she joined the RSC and "began consciously to think about breath in a different way" (11). According to Berry, she joined the RSC at a time when "styles of acting began to change . . . We no longer wanted to hear that well-rounded, 'poetic' sound for it was no longer relevant" (12). Audiences, influenced by television "wanted to hear *real* people speaking" and "to hear the actor's own personal truth" (12, emphasis mine). I read Berry's description as aligning the aesthetic principles of naturalism with what is often considered a "natural" sounding voice—a voice that is "real" is one that could be heard in off-stage environments but adapted for the stage. She continued,

And it was at this point that I found the whole concept of rib reserve no longer useful. It was too much aligned to the technical constraints of singing, of fulfilling a time frame or phrase, of finding music within the phraseology. It was clearly not about finding and discovering the thought itself.

(2009: 12)

In her first book (1992), Rodenburg provided a personal account of her experience of being trained in rib reserve.

I learnt "rib-reserve breathing" in order to extend my child's breath capacity to ridiculous lengths. This is the breathing you get from holding your ribcage up for *unnaturally* long periods of time. It can be physically deforming. All I remember was aching from my centre through to my shoulders and up to my ears as I strained to keep the ribcage hoisted.

(1992: xii, emphasis mine)

I read this personal account much in the same way I read Berry's accounts, as oral histories that are not incidental to understanding their practice and should not be discarded. Rodenburg's account frames her pedagogical approach historically through personal experience. Her practice of "rib reserve" technique had a direct influence on her current practice teaching with what she considers a more "natural" approach to voice.

Rodenburg set up a way to think about a "natural" breath by contrasting it with the "unnatural technique" (Rodenburg 2000: 65) of rib reserve. In her later text, *The Actor Speaks*, she wrote a description of the practice,

> Before I went to the Central School of Speech and Drama I was taught rib reserve. Your breath in and went "on support", which meant you *held* or you *locked* your ribcage up and worked from the abdominal area of muscles with the ribs staying up. We use to go "on support" at the beginning of the class and let our ribs down only at the end of the lesson. A bit of string was tied around our rib-cage. If the string loosened the teacher could see our ribs slipped . . . This high rib position is obviously *unnatural*.
>
> *(2000: 64–65, emphasis mine)*

Part of the reason this technique is understood as "unnatural" is because "locking of the rib-cage for long periods of time creates shoulder *tension*, abdominal *tension* and back *tension*" (65, emphasis mine). As mentioned earlier in this chapter, the "natural/free" voice approach avoids "tension" and trains to release excessive muscular contraction. Logically, the "natural/free" voice would avoid training techniques that do not embrace its values, fostering what is believed to create unnecessary "tension."

Rodenburg only teaches rib-reserve technique "in rare circumstances" (65) and a description of how to train rib reserve can be found on page 66, the advantage being that "rib reserve turns the voice into a power tool" (66). However, she noted, "I think it is fair to say that this *unnatural* technique might be needed when the art form itself requires the *unnatural*. An aesthetic in art is not always *natural*" (65). Here "natural" is defined by its opposite, "unnatural." Also, "natural" is understood as a sound aesthetic that carries with it assumptions about how sound represents emotion within the actor's performance. Rodenburg continued,

> I think that this technique helped to create all those clear, intellectual British actors who sounded to American ears rigid and passionless. Great voices, but missing real souls [because] the *locking* of the rib-cage tightens all the abdominal muscles and consequently cuts the actor off from his or her *emotional centre*. The tight abdomen makes accessing feeling almost impossible.
>
> *(2000: 66)*

In this way, "tension" is characterized as blocking not only the "natural" physiological function of the breathing mechanism (the "blocked" voice) but also inhibiting the performer from accessing emotion. The idea of an "emotional centre" is also found in Linklater's writing. In this way, the training is shaped by a value system embedded within a particular style, or aesthetic.

Like Berry and Rodenburg, Linklater positioned a conversation about rib reserve in light of changing styles or aesthetics. Linklater wrote,

> I would like at this point to bury an old ghost who says that it is necessary in performing Shakespeare to be able to speak twelve lines on one breath. This is not so. Sometimes it may be necessary to have the emotional stamina to maintain an unbroken line of emotional drive for twelve, sixteen, or thirty

lines, but within those there are a myriad of changing thoughts, and breath must serve them by changing also . . . It is not an impossible physical feat but the results belong to a style popular forty years ago and are meaningless to modern ears.

(1976: 142)

As a result of this changing aesthetic in performance, Linklater rejected rib reserve that would have made 12 lines on one breath possible and developed techniques that would instead foster a "natural capacity" for the breath.

Any attempt to sustain breath by *holding* it back or preserving it sets up *tensions* that defeat the objective. This is why the old-fashioned exercises in "rib reserve" are so counter-productive. The effort involved in *holding* the ribs open for as long as possible, in order to maintain a reserve tank of air, inevitably creates *tension* that contracts the *natural* capacity.

(1976: 122, emphasis mine)

Like Berry and Rodenburg, Linklater's dislike of rib reserve is partly because of the "tension" it creates in the body through "holding" the ribs in place. This "tension" inhibits the performer from accessing the necessary emotion that "drives" the thought. Linklater wrote,

In an emotionally driving, demanding speech the breathing musculature must be very fit in order to supply fast, subtle changes to keep the thought content alive and to intensify as the emotions intensify, but the overall line is maintained intellectually.

(1976: 142)

From this, the next paragraph introduces the idea of an emotion "center" (143), similar to Rodenburg's understanding that tension created by rib-reserve "cuts the actor off from his or her emotional centre" (2000: 66). Linklater wrote, "The experience of an inner center for sound may help to bring the voice into more satisfying contact with the feeling" (1976: 143).

In this way, Berry, Linklater, and Rodenburg all associate rib reserve breathing with a technique that trains the voice towards an out-of-fashion aesthetic, with the implication that it is no longer in use. However, in *Breath in Action* (2009), David Carey (who lists Berry, Linklater, and Rodenburg as influences on his teaching)[8] offered in his chapter an exercise to train modern actors a "paired rib-reserve" exercise (194). He wrote, "this exercise is based on J. Clifford Turner's approach to rib-reserve training in *Voice and Speech in the Theatre*" (Ibid.), which is a training text printed during the Voice Beautiful era, 1950, but has since been re-issued five times: the sixth edition (2007) was edited by Jane Boston, current course leader for the MA/MFA Voice Studies program, RCSSD, which trains future voice teachers. In Turner's book, Turner attributed his understanding of "rib-reserve" breathing to his early training with W. A. Aiken. Turner wrote, "For the use of the term 'rib-reserve,' and for many of the views expressed in the following pages, I am indebted to the late W. A. Aiken, M.D., whose pupil I was at one time privileged to be" (1950, 2007: 18). Aiken's influence can be directly and indirectly linked to some of the top voice trainers in Britain. This situates the body/voice relationship not only within a biomedical model but a way that is based on Aiken's approach to integrating anatomy and physiology within voice pedagogy. Let me reiterate that I am not attempting to map a history of voice, nor tie voice trainers down to one influence, insisting that they "represent[s] a unified body of thought" (Boston in NTQ 51, 1997: 249). Instead, I am attempting to understand where the similarities in their work come from and how those similarities reinforce a particular way of thinking about, talking about, and training the voice within an Anglo-American voice tradition.

Rib-reserve, a "natural" breath and Grotowski

The "natural/free" voice is defined, in part, through the comparison of those earlier techniques from the Voice Beautiful era that were deemed "unnatural," or "unreal." Key teaching terms as "natural," and "free" are often associated in the popular narrative as having emerged from the radical politics of the 1960s and 1970s, along with practices of Brook and Grotowski. Like Berry, Linklater, and Rodenburg, Grotowski characterized his voice training approach as "natural" and compared them with earlier approaches that he felt were "unnatural." Like the "natural/free" voice approach, Grotowski also referred to "good habits." He wrote, "Voice training in most countries and at nearly all schools is wrongly conceived and practiced. The *natural* voice process is hampered and destroyed. *Unnatural* techniques are learnt and these spoil the original *good habits*" (Grotowski 1968: 153, emphasis mine). Grotowski's use of language (e.g. "good habits" and "natural voice") as well as his "organic" approach to training actor's voices is cited as having influenced the "natural voice" approach, although only Linklater quotes Grotowski directly in her first book (1976: 24). The similarity in language is one reason why Berry, Linklater, and Rodenburg's training texts have been characterized as "post-Brook school of voice texts" (Knowles 1996: 95). While a certain amount of influence may have occurred, I argue that a comparative examination of rib reserve and "natural" or "free" breathe training did not necessarily emerge from the influence of Brook/Grotowski.

One of the very first exercises in Berry's first book is an exercise my KNUA students and I did with Berry when she taught a voice workshop in Seoul, South Korea, 2000. Berry asked the students to place the backs of their hands against their ribcage where it bulges the most to feel the greatest movement and to breathe out slowly to ten counts. Here she used a kinesthetic approach to the work; in this instance, Berry asked the student to both feel the movement from within the body as well as feel the movement more objectively outside of the ribcage through the placement of the student's own hands on their body, monitoring the movement. Berry wrote,

Breathe in for three counts, hold a moment and check shoulders and neck. Open your mouth and breathe out for ten counts. Wait until you feel the ribs needing to move and breathe in again, and so on. Remain conscious of the muscles between the ribs controlling the outgoing air, because it is those muscles you want to stimulate, and always wait for the feeling of those muscles wanting to spring out before you take in air again. When you are ready increase the count to fifteen.

(1973: 28–29)

Notice the similarities between Berry's breath capacity exercise and Jerzy Grotowski's breath capacity exercise adopted from Hatha Yoga:

The three phases succeed one another in the following rhythm:
Inspiration: 4 seconds
Hold the breath: 12 seconds
Expiration: 8 seconds

(Grotowski 1968: 117)

Although Berry's exercise does not hold the breath for 12 seconds, suspending the ribcage as one might do in rib reserve breathing, Berry and Grotowski share a similarity in approaching inhalation on a three or four count, holding the breathe, then exhaling the breathe on an eight or ten count.

However, Berry's exercise above is also quite similar to Thurburn's exercise from 1939. She wrote, "With the backs of the hands lightly touching the sides of the chest, wrists dropped, shoulders relaxed" (54). Thurburn took the student through a breath exercise, breathing in then out "counting 1, 2, 3 aloud." Eventually, as the exercise progressed, she asked the student to "breath in, count six, relax and repeat several times" (56). Was Berry's exercise influenced by Grotowski via Brook in the 1970s or earlier, from Thurburn, whom she trained under, during the 1940s?

Grotowski's next exercise, which he wrote is "taken from the classical Chinese theatre" seems quite similar to the method of rib reserve breathing.

While standing, place the hands on the two lowest ribs. Inspiration must give an impression of beginning in the very spot where the hands are placed (therefore pushing them outwards) and, continuing through the thorax, produce a sensation that the air column reaches right up to the head. (This means that, when breathing in, the abdomen and lower ribs dilate first, followed, in smooth succession, by the chest). *The abdominal wall is then contracted while the ribs remain expanded,* thus forming a base for the air stored up and preventing it from escaping with the first words uttered. *The abdominal wall (contracting inwards) pulls in the opposite direction to the muscles which expand the lower ribs (contracting outwards), keeping them thus for as long as possible during expiration.*

(1968: 117–118, emphasis mine)

Grotowski concluded,

> An exercise such as this is not intended to teach respiration for respiration's sake, but prepares for a respiration that will 'carry' the voice. It also teaches how to establish a base (the abdominal wall) which, by contracting, allows the easy and vigorous emission of the air and thus the voice.
>
> *(1968: 118)*

He insisted twice in the concluding paragraphs that these techniques were intended to foster "organic respiration" and "breathing is an organic and spontaneous process" (118–119). Certainly, Berry, Linklater, and Rodenburg's understanding of a similar exercise they called "rib reserve" was understood as "unnatural," not the "organic" breathing process Grotowski suggested his exercise promoted.

In Rodenburg's video, she demonstrated a similar sustained breath exercise over a 15 count that is remarkably similar to Berry's counting exercise. No such counting exercise seems to exist in Linklater's first book. Instead, Linklater insisted,

> No purpose whatsoever is served by learning to sustain a breath over a longer and longer span of time; all that happens is that the natural elasticity of the breathing muscles is impaired, and capacity is reduced because the effort involved creates tension and tension contracts.
>
> *(1976: 45)*

Linklater, the only pedagogue of the three who referred to Grotowski directly in her first book (1976) during a time when Grotowski's work was popular, rejected training the breath using counting exercises, which Grotowski advocated in his 1968 publication.

The "natural/free" voice and bone prop

Like rib reserve breathing, another practice used by elocution teachers was a tool called "bone prop," a small wooden dowel held between the teeth to keep the jaw placed during articulation exercises. One aim of using a bone prop was to help isolate muscles, increase awareness, and promote muscular efficiency during articulation. Both Thurburn and Fogerty mention bone prop in their training texts (Fogerty 1930: 39; Thurburn 1939: 69), and, with this, both use Dr. W. A. Aiken's "diagram of the resonator scale" (Fogerty 1930: 38; Thurburn 1939: 73).

In 1939, Thurburn suggested students could purchase a bone prop from "Messrs. John Bell & Croyden, 50 Wigmore Street . . . It is called Aiken's Bone Prop for Vowel Position, and is made in various sizes" (69). In 1973, Berry wrote similarly, "They [bone props] are available from John Bell and Croyden of Wigmore Street, London" (49). Her vowel list (48) resembles the "Diagram of the Resonator Scale" found in both Fogerty and Thurburn's texts (Fogerty 1930: 38; Thurburn 1939: 73). Berry's "tongue-tip" exercise in which the student is instructed to "insert the bone-prop" (1973: 53–54) is very similar to Thurburn's "Tongue" exercises (1939: 69). Berry explained the advantages of working with a bone prop,

> As you can see, the movements involved in making vowels and consonants are comparatively small and take place within a small area. (It is interesting to notice how little actual movement you can make while keeping the speech intelligible). Therefore, the smallest variation of placing and movement can make a relatively big difference to the speech. Because it is difficult to isolate the awareness of these muscles, you have to exercise each muscle separately in order to recognize what happens. To do this you need the jaw open to a comfortable degree and you need to keep it open. Unless you can keep it open and steady two things are likely to go wrong with the exercises: you will not be able to separate the *awareness* of the precise movements of the muscles of the lips and tongue from the movement of the jaw; and if the jaw is not open to a certain degree you will not be able to exercise the lips and tongue fully, so the exercises will not be properly effective. This is why it is valuable at the beginning to use a bone-prop or something similar to prop the jaw open while doing the exercises.
>
> *(1973: 49, emphasis mine).*

For Berry, part of the benefit of using bone prop is to increase physical "awareness," one of the aims of the "natural/free" voice approach. However, "propping" the jaw open during the exercise could lead to "holding" and "tension," which must be avoided in the "natural/free" approach. So, Berry cautioned,

> Great care should be taken to find the right size as, obviously, too wide a one will create tension in the jaw, something which must be avoided . . . If you can use one without setting up over-much tension in the jaw then so do, because it increases the effectiveness of the exercises enormously and the benefit is felt more quickly.
>
> *(1973: 50)*

Berry's difficulty is clear. The bone prop was a tool from her training and part of the tradition of training the voice when she began teaching during the 1940s and throughout the 1950s. But when instructing students by way of her book, published in the 1970s, a different value system was being embraced. Fogerty and Thurburn do not caution the student about "tension" when using bone prop in their texts.

My KNUA postgraduate students and I worked with Berry using a bone prop when we took her voice workshop in Seoul (2000). I found the prop to be very useful, but the "awareness" it helped me discover was not what I would describe as a "natural" or "free" awareness of my voice. Instead, the work increased my understanding of how my articulators work together to produce vowels, consonants, and vowel/consonant combinations, and where those combinations resonate inside of my mouth as a result of decreased or increased spatial relationships between the upper and lower teeth. In short, it provided the opportunity to establish efficient relationships between my articulators. Efficiency is one of the goals of a "free" voice. I concluded that "free" in this context addressed the sense of easiness after rebuilding more efficient relationships. This exercise helped me understand that a "free" voice, in this context, is a constructed, trained voice by way of technique. A "free/natural" voice is crafted.

In Linklater's first book, she seemed to agree in principle that in training the articulators, "The isolation of the lips and tongue from the jaw is important for clear speaking" but she rejected the use of a bone prop as a tool for achieving those ends. She wrote, "But take the principle to an extreme and you arrive at one of the most pernicious props of the elocution brigade: the bone-prop" (162). Linklater's description of a bone prop is peppered with descriptors that make the practice sound as disagreeable as possible to the values of "free" or "natural" voice use. She wrote,

> This is a small instrument about an inch high that the student is asked to place between the teeth and bite in order to keep the mouth rather wide open and the jaw *immobilized* while the lips and tongue perform *diction* exercises. A cork is sometimes used, lengthwise, to provide an even greater *obstacle* to overcome. I have heard a speech from Shakespeare be subjected to the indignity of this test, and I am sure the actor who trains his diction thus on the text of a play will never effectively perform the play. The only way in which the lips and tongue can function in such conditions is with huge exaggeration and the diligent student will program *gross mouthings* in the place of articulation, *killing* any hope of *natural* music in speaking. Also programmed by this method is jaw *tension* which leads to throat *tension* and breathing *tension*.
>
> *(1976: 162, emphasis mine)*

A bone prop "kills" "natural" speech not only through the "tension" it creates when the jaw is "immobilized" but also because the student performs "diction exercises," which is an approach to word, language, and text that is in opposition to the "individual" student finding their "own" interpretation to text, not "program[ed]" from an external source. Linklater wrote,

> Interpretation of the text must not be imposed from the outside, it must be released from within . . . Because a spoken text is revealed through an individual who is unique, it makes no sense for another individual (for instance, a teacher) to say how any given text should be spoken.
>
> *(1976: 185)*

However, there is some evidence to suggest that the "elocution brigade" embraced similar values, such as "individualism," "free," and "natural," but through the explicit use of the *technique* of training. For instance, Thurburn, as one example of a proponent of bone prop, believed this tool "will permit *free* movement" by "having established an open mouth as a first principle" in order to "develop activity and sensation in the muscles concerned in the process of articulation" (1939: 66, emphasis mine). Thurburn wrote, "Most teachers of Voice Production are very well aware of the criticism leveled against teaching this subject. It is said that it develops consciousness of delivery, and that many good speakers listen to the sound of their own voice" (67). But she insisted,

> all *technical* work is conscious in its early stages, and the aim is to make it automatic so that it should never obtrude . . . the speaker who has studied fully and *forgotten his technique* will never give the impression of enjoying the sound of his own voice.
>
> *(1939: 67, emphasis mine)*

Thurburn is concerned with a student sounding "natural" and as an "individual"— the same values Linklater embraces. Thurburn wrote, "It is the business of the teacher to see that his pupils' voices are in such condition physically that they are able to respond *naturally* and unconsciously *to the minds of their owners*" (81, emphasis mine).

Rodenburg, who developed her training techniques 20 years later when certain fundamentals of the "natural/free" voice approach had been established, would not necessarily need to adapt and/or reject an older practice, like bone prop, in the way Berry and Linklater did. Rodenburg mentioned her experience with bone prop to explain why she chose not to use it. Rodenburg wrote,

> As a child my voice and speech training was traditional. Bone props stretched my mouth open and I lived in continual fear of swallowing these instruments of torture (there was even a string attached to the prop so it could be yanked out if it inadvertently slipped back into the throat). I recently experimented with one presented to me by a student. As I placed it in my mouth fear instantly gagged me, I traveled back twenty-eight years and broke out into a cold sweat. I instantly spat it out. I have never taught with a bone prop though there are some people who find them very useful aids to clear speech.
>
> *(1992: xiii)*

During the seven years I taught at RCSSD, bone prop was taught in both the undergraduate acting conservatoire and on the MA Voice Studies teacher training course. At that time, mostly Annie Morrison's adapted design was preferred (refer Morrison 2017a). Morrison demonstrates the use of her bone prop in videos that can be downloaded from Vimeo. In the introduction to her articulation drills she said,

> These vowels are used in drama schools to produce a wide range of resonant colour and tone in the voice. They exist in an idealized form of RP [received pronunciation]. These drills are designed to help you speak clearly in your own accent.
>
> *(Morrison 2017b)*

Morrison noted that this tool was to help speech clarity "in your own accent," perhaps because traditionally bone prop was coupled with vowel charts, like Aiken's "diagram of the resonator scale," which used RP vowels as a standard for speech. The use of bone prop and the speech standard it continues to be linked with, the class/race defining received pronunciation, is still hotly debated in the field of voice training (Dal Vera 2000; Knight 2012).

The role of "technique" in the "natural/free" voice approach

In moving away from certain techniques, like rib-reserve and bone prop, in order to develop a more "natural" or "free" approach, the "natural/free" voice gave the impression that it rejected technique and/or repositioned it as secondary to vocal expression, sometimes characterized as "inner feeling" (Berry 1992: 228) or "inner self" (Linklater 1976: 4).

For instance, in the beginning of Linklater's *Freeing the Natural Voice*, she made a point of telling the reader that the aim of the training was not to develop a "technique." She wrote, "The approach is designed to liberate the natural voice rather than to develop a vocal technique" (1976: 1). I suggest that rejecting "technique" was part of the "changing theatre culture" Berry referred to in her oral history (2001: 29). Voice Beautiful techniques like rib reserve were understood as "unnatural" and in this way helped define what was considered "natural." However, in rejecting "technique" the "natural/free" voice did not always acknowledge the techniques that did remain within the exercises.

Berry described changes in voice pedagogy through two significant markers: the emergence of the American "Method" acting approach in Great Britain and the development of a "new style of [theatrical] writing" for the stage (1992: 288). She wrote,

> When I started to teach in the late 40's, my work was geared to "voice production" in a quite conventional way: this meant the training of the voice to be clear and interesting, to release tension, and make sure the speech was articulated "correctly" – i.e. acceptable to class standards. But two things had a great bearing on the work I did: one was an interest in language and how it could be communicated and the other was the effect of Method work on the approach to acting and how that was interpreted here [England].
>
> *(1992: 288)*

Berry noted that her husband, Harry Moore, "an American actor and teacher who had trained in the Method studio in New York" (ibid.) influenced her. This personal experience paralleled developments in which

> a new approach to acting took root—the Method, influenced by Stanislavsky; and this radically changed the actors' perception of language and how it should be presented ... its influence on this side of the Atlantic was

considerable—it made us want something different. The result was that the actor's position regarding text shifted: because motive and *inner feeling* did not always coincide with structure and rhetoric, no longer was the way to speak classical text a clear-cut process.

(1992: 288, emphasis mine)

Berry noted the contrast between "inner feeling" with "structure and rhetoric." The tension between "expression" and "technique" in training an actor's voice is attributed to the different values that "Method" acting introduced. She wrote,

> Not only did the actor have to make choices regarding the presentation of language, those who went to listen also had to make choices: the audience was divided in that some people went to the theatre wanting to hear the play the way it used to be/sound—others began to want to hear something new.
>
> *(1992: 288)*

Linklater also marked this moment as an important shift not only in actor training but also voice pedagogy. In her first book she wrote, "By the fifties the influence of an emotionally vital American theatre had begun to inspire the British to fill out their technique with more gut content" (1973: 3). She characterized British theatre and American theatre in the 1950s and 1960s as "an imbalance between the creative use of *inner self* and communicative skill" (1973: 4, emphasis mine). The colloquial term she and Berry used, "inner," to characterize actor training in the US is an understanding of "Method" acting as emotionally and psychologically motivated. She characterized British actor training during that same timeframe as an "outside inwards" approach, or an approach in which the body is trained first in "technical skill" (1973: 3), which would then ideally become an internalized response. She wrote,

> Meanwhile, in London, working from outside inwards ways of developing the actor's being into a sensitive, integrated, creative instrument had grown-originated by Jacques Copeau, developed by Michel St. Denis and Litz Pisk and nurtured at the Old Vic Theatre School.
>
> *(1976: 3)*

In the US, "in the thirties, forties and fifties, Stanislavsky's books, the Group Theatre and the Actor's Studio moved American actors forward in psychological and emotional exploration to the point where they virtually abandoned the study of 'external skills'" (Ibid.). As a result, "the search for an equilibrium between technique and emotional *freedom* has occupied actor-training for half a century, and in the history of actor development, America and Britain have been consistently out of step with one another" (1973: 3, emphasis mine). Here "technique" is contrasted with "freedom," a value of the "natural/free" voice approach.

Berry and Linklater's marking of the "Method" at a particular moment in US and UK history points to certain disciplinary shifts as well as specific cultural interactions between the UK and US in Anglo-American voice pedagogy. However, Linklater noted that as early as the 1930s her mentor, Iris Warren,

> moved the science of voice production from British actors into a new phase by adding psychological understanding to physiological knowledge . . . The voice exercises remained, but were gradually altered by the shift from external, physical controls to internal, psychological ones. The criterion for assessing progress lay in the answer to the question "how does it feel?" rather than "how does it sound?" The ultimate aim was, and is, to *free* yourself through your voice.
>
> *(1973: 3, emphasis mine)*

From Linklater's account, the idea behind the term "free" and the exercises that "were gradually altered by the shift" already existed in British voice pedagogy before the rise of the "Method" in the 1950s and 1960s, with its emphasis on psychological motivation in character construction. The suggestion is that physical understandings of "free" were augmented through the added psychological dimension that Iris Warren offered. As a result, Linklater asserted, "The voice work that I brought with me had evolved over the years to the point where it married well with the American methods of acting" (1973: 3). The term "free" can also be found in the writings of Thurburn (1939: 41), as well as a description of the relationship between "expression" and "technique" (1939: 43). Perhaps the introduction of the Method in the UK in the 1950s refreshed ongoing conversations in voice practice from the 1930s about the place of "technique" and "expression" in the development of a "free" voice?

Rodenburg's understanding of the development of the "natural/free" voice approach is similar to Linklater's account. Rodenburg also referred to "outside/inside" and "inside/outside" approaches (1992: 113). However, unlike Linklater, Rodenburg feels that America and Britain have not been "out of step with one another" but that American "inside/outside" approaches have dominated contemporary voice training, the result being, "the word 'technique' became a dirty one and many useful approaches became suspect" (1992: 114). She wrote, "Over the past twenty-five years most vocal training (and most books on the subject) has stressed quite the opposite approach: working from the inside out" (1992: 113–114).

Rodenburg suggested that previous

> rigid restrictions had made speaking a dull and deadly activity learned by rote[9] . . . so the pendulum during the late 1950's and throughout the 1960's and 1970's had to swing naturally away from outside technical training of the voice to intense inner work that stressed *changing the self before we could change our voice and our speech.*
>
> *(1992: 114, emphasis mine)*

Although Rodenburg advocates working "from the outside in," the first half of her book focuses on the "self" and "self-expression," how the "self" is influenced by "life experience," and how the individual must assert one's "right to speak." In short, she seems to first explore an "inside/out" approach in the first half of her book before she addresses the "outside/in" or "technique" in the second half of her book.

This division between "outside" and "inside" can be found in the writings of all three practitioners and tends to set up a way of talking about embodiment training in oppositional relationships of "technique" and "expression."[10] The term "technique" during this time was traditionally understood (perhaps misunderstood?) as an "outside" approach to training the body through muscular skill development. This placed voice training in a difficult position. The socio-political principles of training were moving away from "technique" in other areas of theatre, but 20th century voice training was based on "technique." So how does a voice trainer in the 1970s adapt their training and previous teaching experience to the new demands of a "changing theatre culture?" Perhaps by emphasizing teaching language such as "free" and "natural" that already existed in the practice and which dovetailed with language used by leading theatre makers, like Brook and Grotowski, while downplaying the "technique" embedded within the exercises?

The Alexander Technique and the "natural/free" voice

Rejection of "technique" in favor of a "natural" approach is not singularly found in the "natural/free" voice approach and did not only emerge during the 1960s and 1970s when rejecting Voice Beautiful techniques, like bone prop and rib reserve breathing. Similar language can be found in earlier training approaches, like the Alexander Technique, when practitioners want to distinguish themselves and their approaches from earlier trainings or when practice is undergoing some form of reconsideration. Here I would like to look at the influence of the Alexander Technique as "technique" within the "natural/free" voice approach as one example of the way an earlier "technique" was modified by voice pedagogy to address a changing theatre culture. Linklater explicitly cited the Alexander Technique as an influence (1976: 4), and, most probably, as argued earlier in this chapter, has indirectly influenced Berry and Rodenburg's work.

According to the Society of Teachers of the Alexander Technique (STAT; 2017), a UK based organization, Australian-born Frederick Matthias Alexander (1869–1955) was a young actor who was plagued by recurring vocal problems (alexandertechnique.co.uk).[11] After consulting with medical professionals who were unable to provide a cure, Alexander began years of experimental voice and body research that would eventually be understood as The Alexander Technique. By 1894, Alexander was successfully practicing his technique in his studio in Melbourne, Australia, which later moved to Sydney and finally, in 1904, to London. It was in London where Alexander established the "Little School," a children's school with curriculum influences from Italian educator, Maria Montessori. Also, "Alexander spent some time in the USA, where he met and gave lessons to philosopher John Dewey, the "father of the American education system" (alexandertechnique.co.uk). Alexander remained in London until his death in 1955. During his life, the Alexander Technique was hugely popular in Australia, Britain, and the US, and according to STAT, "people came to the United Kingdom from around the world to train as teachers of the Technique. Today there are 18 professional affiliated societies world-wide" (alexandertechnique.co.uk).

As mentioned earlier, Linklater suggested, "His [Alexander] influence is clear in much of the voice work that has developed since then" (1976: 2). Many practi-tioners would be able to recognize Alexander's influence in British actor training, particularly through the curriculum development at major UK conservatoires. For instance, Linklater's alma mater, the London Academy of Music and Drama (LAMDA), has been teaching the "Alexander Technique" in its three-year acting course (LAMDA prospectus 2004). Berry and Rodenburg's alma mater, the Central School of Speech and Drama (CSSD), has taught Alexander Technique "as part of the voice programme on BA Acting and has been for many years now" (Colman, e-mail interview, 5 February 2004). Guildhall School of Music and Drama, where Rodenburg teaches voice, included the "Alexander Technique" as part of its three-year acting program (GSMD prospectus 2004). In 2004, the Royal Academy of Dramatic Art (RADA) listed in their prospectus four Alexander Technique teachers on staff. These teachers were not listed under the sub-headings of either "Movement," "Voice, Speech and Dialect," or "Acting and Text," but as separate staff under the heading "Alexander Technique" within the larger head-ing "Acting Teaching" (RADA prospectus 2004). Other mainstream, institutional acting programs list the Alexander Technique either as a separate discipline within the larger acting program or as part of the movement training within the acting program. But by having the Alexander Technique as part of the acting program at all, institutions provide an environment of transference in which the acting student has the opportunity to transfer her knowledge of the Alexander Technique princi-ples to her understanding of voice principles. In my own MFA Acting program in the US, I had the privilege of three years private training in the Alexander Technique alongside my acting training.

During the NTQ debates, mentioned in the Introduction, Knowles pointed to the confusing way Berry, Rodenburg, and Linklater used the term "free" and "freedom" (1996: 97, 99, 104). He wrote, "'Freedom' is among the most slippery of these concepts, and I have suggested it lies at the heart of each of these texts" (96). Knowles noted how "free[ing]" methods are used to "allow" a process to happen "naturally." Knowles wrote,

> [Berry] presents her exercises, that is, as methods by which to "allow"—a word most often used, ironically, in the imperative mood—"the text," or "Shakespeare," to speak through the body "naturally," unencumbered by the actor's conscious or conditioned shaping—what Brook has already introduced as "the conditioning . . . of a warped society" (Foreword 3). The actor/reader

is repeatedly urged to "allow the words to do their own work" (108), to "take their own value" and "lead you" (124), to "allow the rhythm to take you" (124), confident that, if "you" do, "the meaning will be clear" (108). Freedom, then is constructed in *Voice and the Actor* as a kind of surrender; instinctive and involuntary (11, 24, 116, 132) rather than conscious (15, 22, 31, 101).

(1996: 96)

Knowles linked Berry's use of the terms, "free," "natural," and "allow" with Berry's relationship to Peter Brook. Knowles asserted that Brook's production of *Midsummer* is evidence of the developing ideology found in Berry's 1973 book, in which Brook wrote the foreword. Knowles wrote,

> But first, some history. As I suggested above, and as is the case for so much of the mythologized contemporary tradition of Shakespearean production in English, it all began with Peter Brook. In the beginning was the *Dream*, and the *Dream* was the word; it is not incidental that the first *words* in the first of this tradition of voice texts are delivered by Brook, as the author of the Foreword to *Voice and the Actor*. Berry pays tribute to Brook as a kind of "onlie begetter"'citing the experience of working on his Dream as having given her confidence in her work, and drawing on that experience to lend Brook's authority to her method (Parker 32–3).
>
> *(Knowles 1996: 93–94)*

Knowles attributed the "ideological underpinnings" of Linklater, Berry, and Rodenburg's work to the, "psycho-physical work of Peter Brook and others" (107). But he did not suggest to whom the "others" referred, and did not position Brook as a collaborator. By parodying the New Testament, "In the beginning was the Word, and the Word was with God" (John 1:1), Knowles reinforced the myth he parodied by focusing his writing only on Brook, as the "Father" of a tradition instead of one contributor to a history of influences in voice training. He did not ask how Berry's work may have influenced Brook. Does collaboration only flow from director to voice coach in a top-down hierarchy? Could terms such as "free" and "allow" have influenced Brook, through Berry, from an already established British training tradition? Knowles noticed that Brook's language is similar to Berry's in that "natural" is contrasted with "habits" created through "the conditioning . . . of a warped society" (1973: foreword: 3). This language is surprisingly similar to language used by Alexander 70 years earlier.

As early as 1902, Alexander set his psycho-physical training in opposition with older traditions by defining his approach as "freer." I am providing the reader with a large section of Alexander's writing to introduce to the reader his understanding of his practice through the structure and vocabulary of his writing of practice. I will return later to compare the structure of his writing and use of language with similar usage in the writings of the "natural/free" voice approach.

Over twenty-two years ago in Australia, I was teaching what I still believe to be the true meaning of *free expression*. My pupils in this case came to me for lessons in vocal and dramatic expression. Now by the old methods these pupils would have been taught to imitate their master very accurately in vocal and facial expression, in gesture, in the manner of voice production; and it would have been at once apparent to any one acquainted with the manner and methods of the teachers, where each pupil had received his training. Furthermore, pupils educated by those methods were taught to interpret each poem, scene, or passage on the exact lines that were considered correct by their respective teachers.

My own method, which at that time was regarded as very *radical* and *subversive*, was to give my pupils certain lessons in re-education and co-ordination on a basis of conscious guidance and control, and in this way I gave the reciter, actor, or potential artist the means of employing to the best advantage his powers of vocal, facial, and dramatic expression, gesture, etc. He could then safely be permitted to develop his *own characteristics*. A few suggestions might be necessary as to interpretation, but the *individual manner was his own*. No pupil of mine could be pointed to as representing some narrow school of expression, although most of them could be recognized by the confidence and *freedom* of their performances.

(1969: 105)

Alexander contrasts his "freer" training approach with what appears to be mimetic training traditions. Notice his use of the word "freer" to describe the difference between methodologies. His approach was "radical" and "subversive." Berry, Linklater, and Rodenburg work would also be characterized as "radical" in that it was "innovative" and "visionary." The descriptions of their practice in their first books implied that they were offering alternative, or "radical," approaches in contrast to the Voice Beautiful approach that came before them. For instance, Rodenburg explicitly positioned herself as an advocated for the learner in subverting the "conspiracy" against one's "right to speak" (1992). Notions of "freedom" are framed by Alexander's use of the term "freer" by which to cultivate an "individual manner." Individualism is contrasted with mimetic training traditions: Alexander's "freer" techniques develop an "individual manner" and "confidence" that produced a "freedom" in performance, but mimetic training traditions are positioned as a "narrow school of expression."

Berry, Rodenburg, and Linklater cultivate a similar understanding of "freedom" by associating it with the "individual," one's own "natural" voice. Berry wrote, "For the actor, on the other hand, the voice is an extension of himself" (1973: 16). Linklater, like Alexander, contrasted individual expression with what appeared to be one understanding of mimetic training. She wrote,

Interpretation of the text must not be imposed from the outside it must be released from within. When the block and limitation of conditioned thinking are removed, depth of understanding are uncovered beyond the scope of acquired knowledge. The task is to allow the text access to those depths and let it play on you . . . It is only laziness on the part of a teacher or a director to take the short cut of telling an actor how to say a line rather than sharing the understanding of the line. Such teaching or direction demeans the actor's intelligence, saps confidence and diminishes *individual* creativity.

(1976: 185, emphasis mine)

However, either by vocal modeling or a more conscious effort by the learner to fulfill teacher expectations, a certain amount of mimetic training is likely to occur. Even Alexander admitted that "a few suggestions might be necessary as to interpretation." Through positive and negative reinforcement, the teacher is reconditioning the student's vocal behavior. Alexander's explicit use of the term "re-education" points to behavior modification in a way that the term "freeing" and "individualism" in the "natural/free" approach do not. However, in Alexander's writing and the writings of Berry, Linklater, and Rodenburg, there is little in-depth investigation of how cultural and discipline-specific expectations shape the final "individual" performance. Knowles commented,

Linklater's movement away from the accidental of cultural conditioning that constrain the voice, towards freeing the "individual emotional and imaginative capacity" in the service of "the human truth it expresses" (45) is ultimately an individualistic and generalized one. In attempting to transcend cultural condition en route to "the atmosphere of universal experience" (186) she allows for the *effacement* [emphasis his] of cultural and other kinds of difference.

(1996: 100)

Also, by setting "individualism" in opposition with mimetic training, "individual" approaches to acting seem to exist outside of an acknowledged training lineage. Mimetic training typically points to its training traditions through observable lineage trademarks and can act as a backdrop to any noticeable "individual" choices the performer makes.

My own experiences with mimetic training have been positive. I began playing violin at the age of four through the Japanese Suzuki Method, which is a mimetic training approach. At that young age, I had not yet learned the skills needed to synthesize music through intellectual processes of reading music and understanding music theory, which would begin later at age seven through the state school system. Unaware of the principles behind Western time and key signatures, I simply repeated what I saw and heard, developing a direct connection to physical, muscular response and muscle memory recall. Music was literally embodied, put inside my body, through the training of my muscles and the muscular reaction to my developing ear-training. My first state school music teacher did not support my Suzuki lessons, which I took concurrently, and called me a "trained monkey" because of the mimetic training I received in order to play the violin without reading music. However, during violin lessons with this teacher, he would often play a passage and ask me to follow his example, very similar to the mimetic training techniques I followed in my private Suzuki lessons. At the time, the only difference I understood between the two lessons was that the state school teacher played from written music and the Suzuki trained teacher played from memory, but both were asking me to follow, model or mimic their example.

Behavior modification in training continued beyond the scope of the studio. When studying music at university one of my violin teachers encouraged me to attend as many concerts as possible in order to "absorb" the performances of master violinists. In each of the acting conservatoires in which I have taught, students are required to attend live theatre productions; master performers are role models to developing artists-in-training. They model behavior that students are often asked to emulate.

When Linklater lamented "the banishment of words from the body" (1976: 172) in modern Western education, she did not mention that the eras of oral/aural rhetoric training she praised practiced mimetic training techniques to embody language. Like my early experiences in violin, aural/oral voice traditions, such as rhetoric, do suggest an "interpretation of the text" that is "imposed from the outside." Simply because the form is not present visually, either through music composition or printed text, does not mean that the student is "freer" during the training process.

It was only when I returned to mimetic training later in life through *p'ansori* that I was reminded of the advantages of ear-training and sight analysis and considered ways of bringing this approach to training actors' voices in my classroom. I will return to this fundamental problem later when I discuss this issue in relation to integrating *p'ansori* and the "natural/free" voice approach. Specifically in Chapter Six, I explore how to combine one discipline based on mimetic training principles (*p'ansori*) with another discipline that seemingly rejects those principles (the "natural/free" voice approach) in constructing verbatim performance pieces and character voices in the Namdaemun Market Projects.

Alexander pointed to the "freedom" in his technique. Rather than call it a "natural" process, he described it as a process of "re-education." Although "free" may suggest a lack of form or structure, in the "natural/free" voice approach, the training exercises are very structured and sequenced. They lead the body in a linear process that first assumes negative tension within the student's musculature, and through the exercises, trains the body to release that negative tension.

In the "natural/free" voice approach, "natural" and "organic" processes are taught in a similar way that "technique" is taught, through sequenced exercises repeated "doggedly" over a length of time. Linklater wrote,

> I strongly recommend that you develop a sequence of exercises that takes you from conscientious physical relaxation through all the steps taken from Chapter 3 to 13 and in that progression. Do not alter the sequence or make arbitrary jumps within it until you are quite sure of what you are doing. In the

beginning it may seem *unorganic* [emphasis mine]. Your body and your voice may seem to tell you that you don't need such-and-such an exercise whereas this other one is essential. Unfortunately your "instinct" may be some ingrained, crafty habit fighting to maintain your vocal status quo; if you doggedly persist in doing the most unpopular exercises along with the others you will be covering every aspect of the whole regularly.

(1976: 118)

For my students at KNUA, imagine how confusing Linklater's advice must seem: She is asking the students not to trust their "instinct" because that which feels "natural" or instinctual may simply be "habitual." Instead, an "unorganic" feeling will create a "natural voice." "Organic," "natural," "free" are terms that may confuse instead of explain the idea of "re-education" and do not point to a process of behavior modification in classroom learning.

Through demonstration, Linklater, Berry, and Rodenburg, role model how to release "tension" and cultivate a "freer" voice. The word "free" is understood through physical/aural demonstration. In the practice itself, I find more instances of mimetic training than are acknowledged in the writings of practice through the use of the terms "freedom" and "individualism."

Alexander dismissed notions of freedom without structure by contrasting his work with the work of the "Free Expressionist" movement in schools. He wrote,

> The method of the "Free Expressionist" is to associate music with the first of these arts. Now music and dancing are, as everyone knows, excitements which make a stronger emotional appeal to the primitive than to the more highly evolved races . . . But in the schools where I have witnessed children's performances, I have seen the first beginnings of that madness which is the savage's ecstasy. Music in this connection is an artificial stimulus and a very potent one. And though artificial stimuli may be permissible in certain forms of pleasure sought by the reasoning, trained adult, they are uncommonly dangerous incitements to use in the education of a child of six.
>
> *(1910: 73–75)*

Through this comparison, Alexander's writing does not simply frame his practice, but sets up a way to talk about practice. He sets in opposition the "primitive" versus "the more highly evolved races." He also points to the "emotional appeal" of music within the Free Expressionist's classroom structure as "savage's ecstasy" in contrast with the "pleasure sought by the reasoning, trained adult." Now compare Alexander's writing with Linklater's understanding of how the voice becomes blocked. Linklater wrote,

> The animal instinct level of emotional response to stimulus, deep in the unconscious mind, is largely conditioned out of us as we grow up. There should be a balance of conscious control and instinctual response in mature

behavior, but so much human behavior is unconsciously controlled by habits conditioned in childhood by arbitrary influences such as parents (or lack of them), teachers, peers or fellow gang members, movie stars, pop stars, that if we come to a point in our lives where we want access to the primitive sources of laughter sorrow, anger, joy (as an actor must), they may seem to have been civilized or brutalized out of us.

(1976: 11–12)

Where Alexander wrote of the difference between "savage" and "reason," Linklater contrasted the "animal" with "civilized." Now compare Alexander and Linklater's writing with Rodenburg's writing. Rodenburg wrote,

In the West we live in such vocally orally suppressed societies that the sudden experience of vocal freedom can severely shock anyone trying it out for the first time . . . Our society simply does not encourage us to be vocally free or expressive. You have to go to other areas of the world like the Mediterranean, Africa, the Orient or the Caribbean to experience genuine vocal freedom in action. Such a riot of sounds will often jostle most Westerners . . . Too often we only like to hear the voice of so-called "first class citizens", well-bred and well-toned. Ironically, it is usually the "other" classes of citizens whose voices still retain the habits of natural release.

(1992: 27)

For Rodenburg, the "well-bred" Western voice (class/race distinction) is "suppressed" while large sections of the world are collapsed together as the "other" in a generalized understanding of "genuine vocal freedom." Rodenburg did not situate this cultural comparison within her own experience, unlike other sections of her writing that clearly link her personal experiences with her pedagogical approach. As a result, her statements could easily be misread as reinforcing the racial divisions she attempts to dispel. For instance, based on my work with Korean young men at KNUA, before and after their required military service, I disagree with Rodenburg's statement that the "manufactured 'male sound'" produced by "push[ing] down" the lower register "is most prevalent in the West and not such an issue in the East. Male Oriental speakers tend to be much freer than Occidental ones" (1992: 47).[12] Here Rodenburg set up a vocal comparison between entire races of people, just as Alexander compared races of people, without contextualizing the information.

There is a difference between Alexander rejecting the "savage," Linklater embracing the "primitive," and Rodenburg championing the "other." But the oppositional relationships within the discourses remain. I worry that Alexander's racist comments, disappointingly representative of his Victorian time, have been replaced with contemporary generalizations of the "other" that are just as harmful. The "natural/free" voice approach is still discussing the voice in categories borrowed from Victorian England. Can this approach to understanding the voice continue to be useful in a global teaching environment?

The "natural/free" voice and "re-education"

"Re-education" is a fundamental of Alexander's work. In his first book, *Man's Supreme Inheritance*, he uses a quote from writer and Alexander Technique admirer, Aldous Huxley, to explain his own use of education and "re-education." Alexander begins "Part II" of his book:

EDUCATION

It is because the body is a machine that education is possible. Education is the formation of habits, a superinducing of an artificial organization upon the natural organization of the body; so that acts, which at first require a conscious effort, eventually become unconscious and mechanical.

Huxley

RE-EDUCATION

It is because the body is a machine that (Re)-education is possible. (Re)-education is the formation of (New and Correct) habits, a (Re-Instating of the Correct) artificial organization upon the natural organization of the body; so that acts, which at first require conscious effort, eventually become unconscious and mechanical.

(1910: 107)

One outcome in the Alexander Technique is that an act "eventually becomes unconscious and mechanical." Similarly, in 1939, Thurburn insisted, as mentioned earlier in this chapter, that "all technical work is conscious in its early stages, and the aim is to make it automatic so that it should never obtrude" (67). In 2008, master trainers Carey and Clark Carey (2008: 7) as well as Houseman (2008: 311) were advocating a similar approach through a "learning cycle." Carey and Clark Carey wrote,

[t]he learning cycle begins when we move from unconscious incompetence (habitually using muscles in a way that is inefficient without realising it), to conscious incompetence (gaining an awareness of the inefficient pattern). From there we can work our way to conscious competence (introducing a new use of the muscles through exercise and focused attention), and finally to unconscious competence (using the muscles in a more efficient way without having to think about it).

(2008: 7)[13]

There is a deeply rooted tradition in Anglo-American voice training in which techniques are used to consciously "re-educate" the body and then, at some point during the training, to "forget" the technique so that it appears "unconscious and mechanical," which could be characterized as performing in ways that could appear "natural." In this way, new habits are formed that appear responsive without marking the skill as learned behavior. I argue that the "natural" voice is not "natural" but a "re-educated" voice that appears "natural" by developing habits that eventually become "unconscious" response. I also suggest that this "natural" or "free" voice, when compared with the "blocked" voice, is positioned as a "correct" way to speak, in the same way that Alexander insists his "re-education" process creates "new and correct" habits. One's "own," "individual" voice is measured during training through an aesthetic, in which the result is characterized as "correct."

Like the assertions found in Berry, Rodenburg, and Linklater's work, Alexander claimed that bad, inefficient habits are learned through social training.

> My first claim is that psycho-physical guidance by conscious control, when applied as a universal principle to "living," constitutes an unfailing preventive for diseases mental or physical, malformations, and loss of general efficiency. It is commonly considered that these conditions are brought about by such evils of civilization as the limitation of energy, and by that loss of so-called "natural conditions" which civilization entails.
>
> *(109)*

Alexander's notion of the "evils of civilization," revisited in Rodenburg's work as a "conspiracy" (1992: 19–20) and Linklater's work in which the "natural voice" is blocked "through living in the world" (1976: 1) are problematic for several reasons. The "evils of civilization," a society's "conspiracy" against one's "right to speak," and "living in the world" are not geographically, historically, or culturally specific sites. The suggestion is that all civilizations, all societies, everywhere in the world do harm to the vocal user and would not be beneficial to discipline-specific vocal training or performance. I will return to address this further in Chapter Five.

"Allowing" as technique

If the term "to allow" were to be understood through Alexander's practice combined with the trainer's use of "directing awareness" through touch, the term "to allow" can be understood as an adaptation of a particular pedagogical approach to encouraging muscular release. Edward Maisel, editor of Alexander's collected writings, attempted to clarify Alexander's use of the term "free" as a method that "directs" a process of "re-education."

First, Maisel rewrote one version of Alexander's "orders" in order to clarify what he understood the word "free" to mean.

(1) Let the neck be free (which means merely to see that you do not increase the muscle tension of the neck in any act).
(2) Let the head go forward and up (which means merely to see that you do not tense the neck muscles by pulling the head back or down in any act).
(3) Let the torso lengthen and widen out (which means merely to see that you do not shorten and narrow the back by arching the spine).

(1969: Introduction, xxvi)

Maisel's clarification may or may not be successful for the reader, but one can see that Maisel acknowledges a terminology problem and strives to remedy the situation. In the end, Maisel concluded,

> But these are instructions which are no instructions at all. They cannot even be carried out literally. Taken together, they point to one unified sensation, a single felt experience that seems to permit or expedite the desirable elongation of the spine which constitutes "the true and primary movement in each and every act." Or as Alexander enigmatically summarized these three directions: "All together one after another."
>
> *(1969: Introduction, xxvi)*

According to Maisel, Alexander himself struggled with defining the terminology he used in his work. His difficulty with articulating a practice technique using language can be recognized in Berry, Linklater, and Rodenburg's work as well. How does one articulate kinesthetic experience? Linklater wrote,

> How do you teach relaxation? By touching the pupil's body and feeling whether the muscles are responding to the messages being sent to them. How do you induce a new use of the voice? By taking hold of the body and moving it in new directions which break conditioned, habitual movements.
>
> *(1976: 4)*

Verbal instruction, at times during training, is simply inadequate. Maisel wrote,

> Beyond this normal resistance to verbal instruction, however, Alexander had to contend with another, more basic problem, which was inherent in what he was attempting. His task was like sending a kiss by messenger. The experience he sought to impart was one which by its very nature eludes utterance. As is usually pointed out you cannot describe 'blue' to a man who has never seen the colour blue. How then do you convey a new feeling, a new pattern of physical sensation, to a man who has never known it?
>
> *(1969: Introduction, xxvi)*

Maisel wrote that eventually Alexander understood the limitations of language as an educational tool within the practical work and turned to the training itself to convey his ideas.

> Initially, Alexander had attempted- in words, futile words- to teach the new feeling by *telling* [emphasis his] his pupil how to attain it . . . But instead of relying upon words in situations where of one cannot speak, might there not be some other form of communication? Might it not be possible to impart one's message in some other way? In meeting and solving this problem,

Alexander developed a means for conveying kinesthetic experience—which is perhaps the most valuable part of his work.

(1969: Introduction, xxix)

Part of the pedagogy of Alexander, and I assert its adaptation into the "natural/free" voice approach, is the hands-on learning; the practitioner literally lays her hands on the student, directing awareness to the area that the student needs to focus on.[14] Through touch, not only the practitioner but also the student increases the kinesthetic experience of the work. Kinesthetic experience is sending and receiving messages between the student and the instructor without the need for, or in addition to, language.[15] In my experience with Alexander training, the term "to allow" references a key practice and, when used with touch, encourages the student to muscularly respond to a new pattern of behavior. The term "to allow," *as I have used it in the Alexander Technique,* is a conscious action, not as Knowles described it, "surrender; instinctive and involuntary" in his analysis of Berry's use of the term in her writing.

The problems Maisel described with Alexander's work and the frustrations of language are compounded when teaching voice internationally in other languages. In my experience, the shifting meaning of the words "free," "freedom," "allow," or "natural" usually meant stopping during the exercise to explain how this same word should be retranslated into a new Korean word. The multiple meanings of "free" in English as used by these authors are separate ideas that need separate Korean translations. Using these key words, "free," "freedom," "allow," and "natural," which lay at the heart of the "natural/free" voice approach, in an international classroom and translated into another language made it clear to me how confusing and impractical the language could be.

While critics of the "natural/free" voice approach, like Knowles and Werner, argue the ideological problems behind the language, I am arguing that the language simply is not practical in certain contexts for delivering the educational objectives.

Each explanation I give in English must then be given equal time to translate into Korean. This means that teaching instructions during exercises leave the students literally "holding" a position, waiting for the next bit of instruction. Within the "natural/free" voice approach, this "holding" creates "tension" and is unacceptable.

In order to solve my own practitioner's problem with the language of the "natural/free" voice approach, I returned to Maisel's observation, "these are instructions which are no instructions at all." As the voice exercise instructions in my Korean classroom "could not be carried out literally" they became counterproductive to the work. I discarded as much language as I could, using only key words, demonstrating the position for the students (a mimetic training device), and directed awareness through touch to increase kinesthetic awareness.

Taking this experience with me into my British classrooms, I noticed that language still remained a problem even without in-class translation difficulties.[16] For instance, Alexander Technique teacher, Eleanor Rosenthal, insisted that the

language of the instructions must distinguish between "doing" and "directing."
She wrote,

> In recent years some Alexander teachers seem to be blurring the distinction
> between doing and directing, and a recent mass market paperbound book
> omits the concept of directing entirely. However, learning to direct is an
> integral and useful part of the Alexander Technique, and anyone who is
> taught what purports to be the Technique without being taught how to
> direct is, I think, being serious [*sic*] shortchanged. As Alexander says, in the
> passage quoted above, doing triggers ones' old, habitual, muscular responses;
> directing permits one to change them.
>
> *(1981: 19)*

Notice that in distinguishing between the two terms, "directing" "permits" one to
change. This word choice is similar to "allow" that Knowles points to in Berry,
Rodenburg, and Linklater's work. For Rosenthal, the difference between "doing"
(triggering muscular response) and "directing" ("permitting" change) is fundamental to Alexander's work. When teaching, I am just as careful with terminology as
I was working in translation at KNUA. Issues of "language" are always present in
multilingual classrooms. This awareness helped me reconsider the terminology
practitioners use to write and talk about practice.

Adapting the "natural/free" approach

By examining Berry, Rodenburg, and Linklater's work within not only a historical
perspective but also in relationship with other embodied practices, I suggest that
the "natural/free" voice approach is another way in which to transmit techniques
even as Linklater asserts that it is not a "technique" (1976: 1). I suggest that the
"natural/free" voice does propose a form of voice that fulfills a particular function,
an aesthetic that appears "natural" and "individual."

Reading their writings only as prose pieces and attributing their ideology to
Brook and/or Grotowski mistakenly suggests that the "natural/free" voice approach
developed only as late as the 1960s. A rereading of Berry, Rodenburg, and Linklater's
practice through Thurburn and Alexander's work suggests that fundamental philosophies of body/voice and foundational techniques of the "natural/free" voice
approach most possibly existed as early as the 1900s.

In the beginning of this chapter I asked the research question, what shifting
principles and practices of voice training are needed to embody, literally put into
the body, an intercultural/interdisciplinary vocal training approach? There are several major shifts I feel are needed in order to adapt certain principles and practices
of the "natural/free" voice to an intercultural/interdisciplinary approach.

The first fundamental shift must be the way trainers talk and think about the
voice and training. All three practices talk about developing a "free" or "natural"
voice achieved through a process of "freeing" the body. Terms such as "natural"

or "freeing" or "organic" are not practical in an intercultural context because these terms are culturally influenced perceptions, not fixed definitions. The terms can also be misleading because vocal training creates a rehearsed response that appears "natural," as opposed to *being* natural (i.e. "untrained"), like the baby crying at the beginning of Rodenburg's video. "Natural" and "free" are descriptive metaphors that do not help explain the complex processes they represent.

The "freeing" process is a term that hides the fact that training itself develops a discipline-specific performance aesthetic, an aesthetic that must be learned and agreed upon during performance by both performer and audience. Instead of using these terms, I have stripped away language that I feel is impractical in my classrooms while continuing to construct a training vocabulary better suited to explain complex processes in a practical way. I also use the word "technique," not as a descriptive negative, but as a historical/cultural practice passed from teacher to student. I also shift voice training away from discussing the voice in oppositional relationships such as East versus West or "inside/out" and "outside/in" approaches to training and performance. I believe such categories limit the way one thinks about the potential of the voice.

A second shift must be the way the body is understood as a home for the voice and its contributions to vocal function. All three master teachers use anatomy as a universal, stable site for teaching/learning that invests in similarities. I would like to shift this principle towards addressing the body in its cultural context. First, all three master teachers examine physical as well as social and environmental influences as the sources of habits that "block" vocal function. My approach detailed in Chapter Six reconsiders the way socio-cultural vocal training can be used in professional voice training as an asset by developing a student based, culturally understood sound sign-system that depends on culture to create meaning with the audience during performance.

Also, all three master teachers primarily address the negative role of tension, or muscular contraction, during vocal function. I would like to shift this focus to reconsider a more balanced approach to both muscular contraction and release, without such a heavy focus on release exercises. I demonstrate this shift in focus in Chapter Four when I (re)consider the role of breath in training actors' voices by integrating Korean understandings of *eum-yang* from *p'ansori* into a complementary muscular contract/release cycle.

There are three particular practices I adapt to my intercultural/interdisciplinary approach to training actor's voices. First, I continue to use the "natural/free" voice approach adaptation of Alexander's "directing" through touch. I believe this practice helps focus the student's attention on particular parts of the body, increasing body awareness. I do this with permission of the student after a discussion about appropriate touch. I combine this with *p'ansori* mimetic training principles that model the form visually and orally. In this way, the student has two different external gauges, touch and modeling, to help him/her reeducate muscular relationships.

Second, I adapt the "natural/free" voice approach to teaching spinal alignment, originally borrowed from Alexander practice. I believe this not only creates muscular efficiency but will allow the spine to act as a transportation system for the vibrations of sound to travel through the body. I combine this practice with my understanding of *ki* energy.

Finally, I adapt my understanding of the "natural/free" voice approach as a psycho-physical process by critically analyzing the difference between psycho-physical and bodymind. Chapter Four will further detail my understanding of the bodymind relationship through contemporary discourses of embodiment.

In the next chapter, Chapter Three, I continue exploring this research question through a comparative study of the "natural/free" voice approach with *p'ansori* as well as prepare the reader for adapting certain principles and practices of *p'ansori* for integration into an intercultural/interdisciplinary approach to training actors' voices.

Notes

1 According to Jane Boston, who co-curated the conference with Rena Cook, Berry had been invited but could not attend due to illness (2016; personal e-mail correspondence, 27 May 2016).

2 Conversations on VASTAVOX, a yahoo-based listserv created by VASTA (Voice and Speech Trainers Association) to mediate conversations between VASTA members but is also open to the public, such as posts between 9 and 15 August 2016 "Biographies" and 24 June to 19 September 2016 beginning with Linklater's post "What's it all for?", evidence voice trainers arguing over their understandings of voice pedagogical history, and biographies of master voice trainers and the place of understanding theatre and voice history within acting training. Other than the often quoted *Voice in Modern Theatre* (1991), there are few texts known in mainstream practice for documenting the progress of voice training for actors.

3 According to Gordon, "Brook had invited [Grotowski] to London in 1966 to conduct some laboratory work in preparation for the RSC's production of US, as acting on their own instincts for change" (2006: 299).

4 See Chapter Three.

5 Also refer Martin (1991: 174).

6 The actor would keep the ribcage lifted throughout the performance, using the additional room in the ribcage to increase the amount of air the actor could take. Rodenburg, Linklater, and Berry each provide a definition of "rib reserve" in their writing.

7 For one example of a rib reserve breathing exercise, refer Elsie Fogerty's *Speech Craft* (1930: 31–32), although she does not name this exercise "rib reserve," instead "the special breath control needed for voice" (31).

8 Carey worked with Cicely Berry at the RSC for four years, 1982 to 1986, course leader for the prestigious MA in Voice Studies at RCSSD, Senior Voice Tutor and Acting Head of Voice at RADA, and currently is Voice and Text Director at the Oregon Shakespeare Festival (USA). In the biography at the end of *The Shakespeare Workbook* it reads, "David's pedagogy is an *eclectic* one which draws on the work of leading voice teachers of today, such as Cicely Berry, Kristin Linklater and Patsy Rodenburg" (258, emphasis mine). Refer *The Shakespeare Workbook and Video: A Practical Course for Actors* by David Carey and Rebecca Clark Carey (2015: 256–258).

9 A euphemism for mimetic training.

10 I return to this discussion in Chapter Three when I compare Western Voice dualistic understandings of "technique" and "expression" with Asian, specifically Zeami's, understandings of the relationship between "technique" and "expression," or "the mind of the flower."

11 Also refer to Alexander's own account of the origin of his practice in *The Use of the Self* (1932, 2001: 23–36).
12 Refer to McAllister-Viel, T. (2007: 216–223).
13 I will return to this "learning cycle" in Chapter Four when addressing the different ways in which Anglo-American voice training and Asian vocal arts, like *p'ansori*, position the role of "self" and consciousness in training.
14 See photos in Berry's *Voice and the Actor* demonstrating Berry's use of touch in teaching her voice work (1973: 63, 79–80).
15 This is not to suggest that this pedagogical approach is not without its own ideological influence. While teaching at the University of Wisconsin-Madison, USA, my university employers, sensitive to sexual harassment issues, asked that I frame my "hands-on" approach within a larger discussion about appropriate, non-sexual touching and trust issues. In Korea, my position as a female touching certain conservative or self-identified religious male students told me they were uncomfortable being touched by a woman. If the class was made up of an odd number of students resulting in a male/female partnership, sometimes one or both students would choose to sit out of the exercise instead of touch each other. Several of my male Korean students returning from required military service were happy to show off their well-developed muscles and would tighten their stomachs when touched to impress certain female classmates or me, reducing the effectiveness of the teaching approach. At the University of Exeter, England, UK, one female student asked me not to touch her "fat" when referring to her stomach region. I am aware that touch could mean something different to students other than a pedagogical approach to learning.
16 My classrooms at RCCSD and East 15 serve[d] students who speak primary languages other than English, students usually understand English as a foreign language or English as a second language. Therefore, I am able to teach in English without the use of in-class translation. However, at times, there still remain translation difficulties for an English as a foreign/second language student and I work with these students individually.

References

Aiken, W.A. (1900, 1910). *The Voice: An Introduction to Practical Phonology*. London: Longmans, Green & Co.
Alexander, F.M. (1910, 1918). *Man's Supreme Inheritance*. London: Chaterson.
Alexander, F.M. (1932, 2001). *The Use of the Self*. London: Methuen.
Archives.org. https://archive.org/details/bellsstandardelo00bellrich. Accessed 30 March 2017.
Armstrong, F., Pearson, J. (ed). (2000). *Well-tuned Women: Growing Strong Through Voicework*. London: The Women's Press Ltd.
Bell, D. C., Bell, A. M. (1878, 1887). *Bell's Standard Elocutionist: Principles and Exercises*. https://archive.org/details/bellsstandardelo00bellrich Accessed 30 March 2017.
Berry, C. (1973). *Voice and the Actor*. New York: Wiley Publishing.
Berry, C. (1987, 1992). *The Actor and the Text*. New York: Applause Books.
Berry, C. (2001). *Text in Action*. London: Virgin.
Berry, C. (2002). *Shakespeare Out Loud*. [video] Sydney: ABC TV arts.
Berry, C. (2003). *Working Shakespeare*. [5 DVD series]. New York: Applause Theatre and Cinema Books/Hal Leonard Corp.
Berry, C. (2008). *From Word to Play*. London: Oberon Books.
Blair, R. (2008). *The Actor, Image, and Action: Acting and Cognitive Neuroscience*. London: Routledge.
Boston, J. (1997). "Voice, the Practitioners, Their Practices, and Their Critics," *New Theatre Quarterly*, 51, 248–254.

Boston, J., Cook, R. (2009). *Breath in Action: The Art of Breath in Vocal and Holistic Practice*. London: Jessica Kingsley Publishers.

Boston, J., Cook, R. (2016). Personal e-mail correspondence 27 May 2016.

British Voice Association. (2017). www.britishvoiceassociation.org.uk/archive/performance-breath-2007.htm. Accessed 30 March 2017.

Campbell, H., Brewer, R.F., Neville, H., Harrison, C., Corder, F., Hawley, S. (1897). *Voice, Speech, and Gesture: A Practical Handbook to the Elocutionary Art*. London: Charles William Deacon & Co.

Carey, D., Clark Carey, R. (2008). *The Vocal Arts Workbook and DVD: A Practical Course for Developing the Expressive Range of Your Voice*. London: Methuen Drama.

Carey, D., Clark Carey, R. (2015). *The Shakespeare Workbook and Video: A Practical Course for Actors*. London: Bloomsbury Drama.

Columbia.edu. (2017). http://arts.columbia.edu/theatre-arts-professor-kristin-linklater-wins-2011-lilly-award. Accessed 30 March 2017.

Dal Vera, R. (ed.). (2000). *Standard Speech: Essays on Voice and Speech*. New York: Applause Books.

Fitzmaurice, C. (2009). "Some Noise Within: Conversations with Catherine Fitzmaurice," at *Theatre Noise Conference*, Royal Central School of Speech and Drama, London, England, UK. http://crco.cssd.ac.uk/418/1/Theatre_Noise_website_as_pdf.pdf. Accessed 30 March 2017.

Fitzmaurice Voicework. (2017). www.fitzmauricevoice.com/about.htm. Accessed 30 March 2017.

Fogerty, E. (1930). *Speech Craft: A Manual of Practice in English Speech*. London: J.M. Dent & Sons Ltd.

Gener, R. (2010). "'Pillars of Voice Work,' in Special Section: Approaches to Theatre Training," *American Theatre*, 27 (1), 33.

Gordon, R. (2006). *The Purpose of Playing: Modern Acting theories in Perspective*. Ann Arbor: University of Michigan Press.

Grotowski, J. (1968). *Towards a Poor Theatre*. London: Methuen Drama.

GSMD (2017). www.gsmd.ac.uk/acting/staff/staff_biographies/department/16-department-of-acting/669-patsy-rodenburg/. Accessed 30 March 2017.

Hampton, M., Acker, B. (1997). *The Vocal Vision: Views on Voice by 24 Leading Teachers, Coaches and Directors*. New York: Applause.

Houseman, B. (2008). *Tackling Text: A Step-By-Step Guide for Actors*. London: Nick Hern.

Kimbrough, A. (2011). *Dramatic Theories of Voice in the Twentieth Century*. Amherst: Cambria Press.

Kingsley, B. (2013). "The Architecture of Ideas," in Carson, S. (ed.). *Living With Shakespeare: Essays by Writers, Actors, and Directors*. London: Vintage, 45–55.

Knight, D. (2012). *Speaking with Skill: An Introduction to Knight-Thompson Speech Work*. London: Bloomsbury.

Knowles, R. (1996). "Shakespeare, Voice, and Ideology," in Bulman, J. (ed.). *Shakespeare, Theory, and Performance*. London: Routledge, 92–112.

Lessac Institute. (2017). http://lessacinstitute.org/about/arthur-lessac/. Accessed 30 March 2017.

Linklater, K. (1976). *Freeing the Natural Voice*. New York: Drama Book.

Linklater, K. (1992). *Freeing Shakespeare's Voice*. New York: Theatre Communications Group.

Linklater, K. (2003). *Teaching Voice*. [video] Exeter, England, UK: Arts Archives. info@arts-archives.org.

Linklater, K. (2006). *Freeing the Natural Voice: Imagery and Art in the Practice of Voice and Language*. London: Nick Hern.

Linklater, K. (2016). "The Art and Craft of Voice (and Speech) Training," *Journal of Interdisciplinary Voice Studies*, 1 (1), 57–70.

Linklater Voice Centre. (2017). www.linklatervoice.com/kristin-linklater-voice-centre. Accessed 30 March 2017.

Looser, D. (2005). *Freeing the Natural Voice? Performance, Gender, Society*. Unpublished PhD thesis, Master of Arts in Theatre and Film Studies, University of Canterbury, Christchurch.

Maisel, E. (ed). (1969). *The Alexander Technique: The essential writings of F. Matthias Alexander*. London: Thames and Hudson.

Martin, J. (1991). *Voice in Modern Theatre*. London: Routledge.

McAllister-Viel, T. (2007). *Casting Perceptions: The Performance of the Gendered Voice as Career Strategy*. New York: Applause Books.

McEvenue, K. (2001). *The Actor and the Alexander Technique*. London: Methuen.

Performance Breath Conference. (2007). At the Royal Academy of Dramatic Art, London, England, UK.

Morrison, A. (2017a). www.themorrisonboneprop.com/about.html. Accessed 30 March 2017.

Morrison, A. (2017b). https://vimeo.com/30619101. Accessed 30 March 2017.

O'Quinn, J. (2010). "Editor's Note," *American Theatre Magazine*, 27 (1), 6.

Parker, K. (1985). "Goodbye, Voice Beautiful," *Plays and Players* 382 (July 1985), 32–33.

PatsyRodenburg.com. (2017). www.patsyrodenburg.com/PatsyRodenburg.com/Biography.html. Accessed 30 March 2017.

Royal Shakespeare Company. (2017). www.rsc.org.uk/news/happy-birthday-to-cicely-berry. Accessed 30 March 2017.

Rodenburg, P. (1992). *The Right to Speak*. New York: Routledge.

Rodenburg, P. (1993). *The Need for Words*. London: Methuen.

Rodenburg, P. (1994). *A Voice of Your Own*. [video] New York: Applause Books.

Rodenburg, P. (2000). *The Actor Speaks*. New York: St. Martin's Press.

Rodenburg, P. (2002). *Speaking Shakespeare*. London: Methuen.

Rodenburg, P. (2007). *Presence: How to Use Positive Energy for Success in Every Situation*. London: Michael Joseph, Penguin Group.

Rodenburg, P. (2016). Shakespeare in the Present. [video]. www.shakespeareinthepresent.com/index.php. Accessed 17 April 2018.

Rosenthal, E. (1981). "Alexander Technique: Notes on a Teaching Method," *Contact Quarterly*, Fall (1981), 19.

Society of Teachers of the Alexander Technique (STAT). (2017). http://alexandertechnique.co.uk. Accessed 29 March 2017.

Theatre Noise Conference. (2009). At the Royal Central School of Speech and Drama, London, England, UK. http://crco.cssd.ac.uk/418/1/Theatre_Noise_website_as_pdf.pdf. Accessed 30 March 2017.

Thurburn, G. (1939). *Voice and Speech: An Introduction*. Digswell Place: James Nisbet and Co. Ltd.

Turner, J. C. (2007). *Voice and Speech in the Theatre*. 6th ed. Boston, J. (ed). London: Methuen Drama.

VASTA. (2009). Voice and Speech Trainers' Association conference in NYC, New York. USA. "Vocal Methodologies from the Source: Lessac, Linklater, Fitzmaurice and Rodenburg," www.vasta.org/history-of-conferences. Accessed 30 March 2017.

Wayman, L. (2007). "Performance Breath–An Essential Exploration of Body, Voice and Word" in *British Voice Association Newsletter*, www.britishvoiceassociation.org.uk/archive/performance-breath-2007.htm. Accessed 29 March 2017.

3

WHAT IS *SŎNGŬM* [성음] IN *P'ANSORI* [판소리]?

Chapter Two introduced the reader to one understanding of a "natural/free" voice as a branch of Anglo-American voice training. Chapter Three introduces to the reader one understanding of the *sŏngŭm*, or "sound/voice" (Um 2013: 221) or "vocalization" (Park 2003: 309) within *p'ansori*, as I have learned it from Human Cultural Treasures Han Nongsŏn and Sŏng Uhyang over the course of four years, and briefly with Dr. Chan Park. In this chapter, as in the previous chapter, I investigate certain principles and practices in preparation for integrating adaptations of the two source traditions that comprise the foundation of my approach. It is beyond the scope of this chapter to offer but a summary of *p'ansori* as context for discussing the *sŏngŭm* as embodied practice, which I do through interviews with professional *p'ansori* performers and master teachers, my own experiences training in *p'ansori*, and through comparative study with "natural/free" voice training.

In this chapter, I first offer the reader a brief overview of *p'ansori*. Next, I introduce my understanding of *p'ansori* vocal performance dynamics and means of embodying role. I specifically examine the relationship between (what I am calling) text and vocal text, how character voices are built using this text/vocal text relationship, and the relationship between sung and spoken voice as vocal forms that frame the meaning of the text/vocal text. These are the *p'ansori* aural/oral performance structures that will later inform the intercultural/interdisciplinary training and inform devised original in-class projects, which will be detailed later.

Then, I examine the *p'ansori* training practices that create the unique sound of *p'ansori sŏngŭm*. The first section focuses, in a limited way, on training within studio practice: video sample one is a cutting from one of my lessons with Sŏng Uhyang with analysis of my process learning *p'ansori* as a foreigner. Video sample two is a cutting of Bae Il Dong demonstrating one kind of vocal ornamentation in *p'ansori*, part of the vocal techniques and the expected aesthetics of *sŏngŭm* that will be referenced in later chapters. The second section focuses on an aspect of *p'ansori* training outside of the studio, specifically *sankongbu* 산공부 [mountain study], and how this shapes *sŏngŭm*. *Sankongbu* assists in the development of *sŏngŭm* and underpins a cultural understanding of how one should learn *p'ansori* through "laborious vocal training," which is "essential in attaining the status of a professional *p'ansori* artist" (Um 2013: 159–160). Finally, I compare *p'ansori* training with the "natural/ free" voice training practice and how "natural" is understood through both practices. Through this comparative study, I provide an opportunity for voice practitioners and trainers to (re)consider fundamental assumptions made about the materials of training (voice, sound, breath, resonance) as universally understood concepts and as "natural," "human," behaviors. Instead, this comparison sets up an understanding of voice training as a socio-cultural and discipline specific construct, with "technique" positioned as the possible bridge between these two traditions. In this way, I address the research question: what shifting principles and practices of voice training are needed to embody, literally put into the body, an intercultural/ interdisciplinary vocal training approach?

A brief overview of *p'ansori:* Definitions

P'ansori is a beautiful and complex vocal art form that tells a story using alternating forms of *ch'ang* 창 [sung] passages and *aniri* 아니리 [spoken] passages with *pallim* 발림 [gestures]. The single *p'ansori* performer is accompanied by a drummer playing a *puk* 북 or double-barreled drum. The performer stands in the center of a playing mat, or *p'an* 판 [performance area], with the accompanist sitting to the performer's left, also on the playing mat. A full-length *p'ansori* performance, *wanch'ang* 완창 [complete singing], may take up to eight hours to perform, which requires a great deal of strength and stamina from both the performer and accompanist. During the telling, the performer vocally embodies multiple characters and interacts directly with the accompanist and audience. The accompanist and audience interact with the performer during the telling by shouting out *ch'uimsae* 추임새 [specific calls of encouragement], such as *olsiggu!* [no direct translation] or *chotta!* [good!].

P'ansori performer and scholar Dr. Chan Park described *p'ansori* as a "story-singing tradition" (2003: Preface) but investigated a much more complex understanding of the term based on its etymology: *p'an* can be understood as both the playing area, or straw mat, as well as "wholehearted participation" (1). *Sori* can be understood as "singing" but "*sori* goes beyond just 'singing' to become narrative expressiveness, a musical metalanguage . . . that is acquired through method and process" (1). *Sori* references the particular sound of *p'ansori* as well as the *p'ansori* voice that created this unique sound. In this way, "*p'ansori* is the performance of an oral or vocal narrative, that is, *sori* within a given context, *p'an*" (1). Or, more simply, *p'ansori* can be understood as a playing area [*p'an*] for its voice\sound [*sori*].

Yi Pohyong suggested that the origin of *p'ansori* began with songs from outdoor entertainers as *p'annorum* 판노름 (Yi in Um 2013: 34). Eventually these songs became separated from this context and while the prefix *p'an* was maintained, referring to a place where people gather together, the suffix –*norum* [play or entertainment] was replaced with *–sori* [song] (Um 2013: 34). This connects *p'ansori* with oral folk traditions of the lower classes and illiterate, traveling performers before it was written down and later embraced by the upper classes and Korean royalty. The origins of *p'ansori* are also connected with Korean shamanism (Pihl 1994: 8; also refer Chong Nosik 1940 in Phil (trans.) 1994: 38; Jang 2014: 10; Um 2013: 33–34; Yi 1982). According to Um, "*Muga* 무가(shamanist ritual music) from Cholla Province and *p'annorum* 판노름 (folk entertainment) have been accepted as the main origins of *p'ansori*" (2013: 55). However, it is important to note that mapping the history of an art form, like *p'ansori*, is not a linear process. As *p'ansori* developed, it continued to interact with other art forms, sometimes returning to renew relationships with the forms that first helped develop it. "For example, shamanist chant influenced *p'ansori* at an early stage, after which *p'ansori* fed back to shamanist chant at a later period by introducing elements of upper class culture" (Um 2013: 55).

Jang notes the difficulties in mapping oral forms like *p'ansori*, in part, because oral traditions tend to be passed down from one generation to the next through direct oral/aural transmission. Also, the social status of *p'ansori* meant that "the literati who left us documents before the mid-eighteenth century did not pay much attention to folk music since they considered it to be unworthy" (Jang 2014: 6).

P'ansori and border-crossing

In addition to these various definitions and etymological origins, *p'ansori* as an art form has been introduced to non-Korean, English-speaking audiences based on comparisons with Western vocal art forms. *P'ansori* is sometimes described as "Korean opera." Marshall Pihl wrote,

> Some writers have used the expression "one-man opera" to explain the term. The oddity of the expression aside, it does succeed in conveying the four essential characteristics of *p'ansori*: it is a solo oral technique, it is dramatic, it is musical, and it is in verse.
>
> *(1994: 3; also refer Howard 2006a: xii; Killick 2010: xvii)*

Former Dean of the School of Drama at The Korean National University of Arts, described *p'ansori* as "an indigenous theatre of Korea" (1980: Introduction). The difference between the characterisation of *p'ansori* as "opera" versus "theatre," for me, suggests a switch in emphasis from a primarily sung voice form to a primarily spoken voice form. This difference also reflects the way *p'ansori* has been defined, characterized, and promoted in different ways through the (re)writing of its history and the lens of specialization.

Um notes that defining what *p'ansori* is has "become a key issue across several academic disciplines . . . This debate, which began in 1966, also signified both a changing academic paradigm as well as the emergence of *p'ansori* as a state-sanctioned bona fide tradition" (Um 2013: 5). Thus, during the 20th century defining *p'ansori* for the purposes of nominating it as an Intangible Cultural Property was one part of positioning this art form as "a national cultural symbol" (Um 2013: 1). This opens larger questions about "the preservation movement" as "interventionist . . . involving elements of presentation and restructuring" (Howard 2006a: xiii). Because definitions are not neutral descriptions, shifting definitions perhaps say more about those defining *p'ansori*, and the socio-cultural context from which those definitions emerge, than the art form itself.

For instance, during my first five years in Seoul, *p'ansori* shifted from being called "Korean opera" to "Korean blues," perhaps because of similar associations between *p'ansori* and American blues as folk art traditions with messages of struggle, as well as certain voice/sound characteristics. Like the "blues" sound that is linked to particular types of emotions, the *sori* or *sŏngŭm* of *p'ansori* is well suited for the performance representation of *han* (sometimes translated as "grief"); I have also heard *p'ansori* characterized as "the voice of Korea," which exemplifies what Um pointed to as "the development of a cultural nationalism" that has been "supported and promoted by academics and non-academics alike, creating an 'authorized heritage discourse' on *p'ansori*" (Um 2013: 4–5). This approach has been seen as sometimes necessary in creating an image of *p'ansori*, as one cultural symbol of South Korea that can be promoted overseas.

Um noted, "One particular feature of *p'ansori* writings in the 1990s and later demonstrates the impact of globalization and the interpretation or adaptation of *p'ansori* in modern Korea" (Um 2013: 5). Indeed, my monograph focuses, in part, on the adaptation of *p'ansori* to actor training within The Korean National University of Arts, School of Drama, and later to UK acting conservatoires, as part of the impact of globalization on training pedagogies. This will, necessarily, change the way I define, characterize, and position *p'ansori* here.

Brief history

In studying *p'ansori*, most scholars begin with an attempt to map out an origin story and from that detail other significant developments. The earliest recorded evidence for the existence of *p'ansori* is a version of *Ch'unghyang-ga* in Chinese verse published by Yu Chinhan in 1754 (Taehan Min'guk Yesurwŏn 1973: 213). The assumption is that most oral art forms, like *p'ansori*, existed before its first written record, and so *p'ansori* most probably existed well before 1754 (Jang 2014: 3; Um 2013: 35).

The origins and history of *p'ansori* are mostly associated with the Choson Dynasty—AD 1392 to 1910.[1] Um compared the way Kim (1978), Kim (1978), Im (1981), Yi (1984), Yu (1990), Yi (1982), and Chŏng (1998) usually divided the history of *p'ansori* into three or four periods or stages, but *p'ansori* history could also be divided into as many as seven periods, according to the way in which scholars understand *p'ansori*: linking *p'ansori* developments with historical events, socio-cultural developments (e.g. shifting patronage from lower to upper class), or following performance styles and the roles of particular singers (Um 2013: 37–38).

One important period for most *p'ansori* scholars is around the turn of the 19th century, which is sometimes referred to as the "golden age" of *p'ansori*. Um wrote that "the notion of tradition and the artistic identity of *p'ansori* are firmly anchored in nineteenth-century Korea as well as in the pre-modern and pre-colonial" (Um 2013: 33–39). In general, the first half of the 19th century is referred to as the "age of the eight great singers" or *p'al myongch'ang* 팔명창, in which eight male singers greatly influenced the structure and performance of *p'ansori* through their own personal styles. During the latter half of the 19th century, "age of the later eight great singers," or *hugi p'al myongch'ang* 후기팔명창, vocal technique underwent further development.

In the 20th century, the "age of the five great singers," or *o myongch'ang* 오명창 (including the period of Japanese occupation, 1910 to 1945) the *p'ansori* canon was reduced from 12 to five major stories, which is still generally considered the traditional *p'ansori* repertory. Each of the five *p'ansori* are linked with one of the five cardinal Confucian relationships: *Sugung-ga* (Song of the Underwater Palace) is linked to the relationship between subject and king; *Chunhyang-ga* (Song of Chunhyang) is linked to the relationship between husband and wife; *Hungbo-ga* (Song of Hungbo) is linked to the relationship between brothers; *Simchong-ga* (Song of Chong Sim) is linked to filial piety; and *Chokpyok-ga* (Song of the Red Cliff) is linked to the relationship between friends.

During this stage, the introduction of *sin'guk* 신극 or "new theatre/drama" was a form of Western style theatre brought to Korea by Japan at the turn of the 20th century. This influenced the development of "*p'ansori*-based ensemble" performance, called *ch'anggŭk* 창극. According to Pihl,

> Before 1903 "one singer, one drummer" was the traditional performance approach in which a solo *kwangdae* [traditional name for a *p'ansori* performer] performed both as narrator and as the individual characters of his story. From 1903–1935, came the period of *p'ansori*-based ensemble *ch'angguk*, in which a "lead singer" took over the function of narrator while male and female singers played the characters, but no new material was added to the libretto. Finally, after 1935, rewritten, dialogue-based *ch'angguk* was introduced and newly created, historical works emerged.
>
> *(1994: 51; also refer Killick 2010)*

The next stage of *p'ansori* is usually determined by post Japanese occupation (roughly 1945 to the mid-20th century) in which the Korean peninsula underwent a Period of Trusteeship (USA and USSR,1945–1948) with the eventual split of the peninsula at the 38th parallel (1948) resulting in The Republic of Korea (South Korea) and The Democratic People's Republic of Korea (North Korea). Most scholarship on *p'ansori*, as well as the focus here in this book, is on South Korea.

After the Korean War (1950–1953), South Korea implemented a series of government initiatives that greatly influenced the development of *p'ansori*. According to Hahn Man-Young,

> As it entered the 1960's [*sic*], the Korean government endeavoured to establish a growing industrial economy. This was particularly true as the incoming

regime of Pak Chung-hee introduced a series of five-year development plans. Western culture became dominant as one result of this policy and indigenous traditions continued to fade. In folk and music circles, students who were willing to undergo the long apprenticeship which Korean music traditionally required disappeared. Naturally, too, young people did not want to learn skills which could never provide sufficient income for life in a rapidly developing country . . . Further, many of those who had trained as musicians switched to more economically viable occupations, and the old age of many who still had musical skills threatened the demise of our indigenous heritage.

(Hahn 1990: 36)

In 1963, the Korean government reacted and implemented the Intangible Cultural Property scheme, or *Muhyong munhwajae* 무형 문화재, in which *p'ansori* was designated Intangible Cultural Asset No. 5. Hahn wrote,

Talented holders of traditional forms, *poyuja* 보유자, were awarded Human Cultural Asset [*In'gan munhwajae* 인간문화재] status. They were given monthly stipends in exchange for which they were required to teach and perform, the latter generally once annually. Students, [*chonsusaeng* 전수자], received a small monthly payment and were assessed for their progress in learning annually. Students who reached a prescribed standard were awarded a certificate and appointed Master Students [*isusaeng* 이수생]. Master students might later be chosen to succeed.

(Human Assets; Hahn 1990: 36)

In 1959, the Department of Traditional Music within the College of Music at Seoul National University was established. In 1960, the *Kugak yesul hakkyo*, 국악 여술학교 or Traditional Music Arts School, was formed. After the Korean government's support system became actively involved, traditional music courses were introduced to other universities and by the mid-1980s, the number of courses had moved into double figures. Eventually, Korean traditional music was given 50% of music class time in Korean primary and secondary schools and according to Hahn Man-Young, "The subject is now firmly established as part of the school curriculum" (Hahn 1990: 37–38). Today, students can attain undergraduate and post-graduate (MA and PhD) degrees in traditional Korean arts.

Alongside government schemes that sought to preserve *p'ansori* as a traditional Korean art form, other artistic interactions were happening in the 1960s and 1970s. For instance, Korean avant-garde theatre director, Oh T'ae Sok (1940 to present) explored ways in which *p'ansori* could be incorporated into Western theatre forms (Kim and Graves 1999). By 2000, his experimentations integrating elements of *p'ansori* with adaptations of Shakespearian plays would tour worldwide. When his version of *Romeo and Juliet* (Mokwha Repertory Company) toured at the Barbican (London, UK) in 2006,[2] My program noted the following:

Oh Tae-suk emerged as an avant-garde theatre artist in the 1960s, opposing the then dominant *shinguk*, a generic term referring to modern Korean theatre modeled after realistic European and American drama. While "Western" in its framework, Oh's theatre is decidedly Korean in sentiment and spirit and the result of forty years of relentless experimentation in search of a new theatre aesthetic that merges Western dramaturgy with Korean traditions. Oh's original plays and his unique directing methods have made his name virtually synonymous with post-*shinguk* in Korea.

http://londonkoreanlinks.net/2006/12/04/oh-tae-suk-romeo/

Oh Tae-suk would be one of the Korean theatre artists my students at KNUA would study as part of their actor training while training in voice with me and, later, I would incorporate Oh's approach to investigating "Koreanness" into the Namdaemum Market projects. I will return to this in Chapter Six.

After the first democratically elected government of South Korea was established (1987–1988), the "final" stage of *p'ansori* history to the "present," is addressed (Um 2013; Yi 1982). In the 21st century, *p'ansori* can be found in a variety of different forms. Several scholars have written on new developments in *p'ansori* (Creutzenberg 2011; Howard 2006b, vol. 2; Um 2008: 24–57, 2013: 181–205; Willoughby 2006) such as newly written *p'ansori* by a young generation of *p'ansori* performers and fusion experiments with Western jazz, such as Bae Il Dong's collaboration with trumpeter, Scott Tinkler, and drummer, Simon Barker, on their album *Chiri*, 2010. International conferences and symposiums, such as "Pansori in Europe: Between Mediation and Appropriation" (14–15 July, Berlin, Germany) aim to explore *p'ansori* "beyond the borders of Korea" and "cross-border artistic collaborations" (Creutzenberg 2011). In music composition, Dongjin Kim (1913–2009) is another example of interactions between *p'ansori* and Western music.

> Although traditional *p'ansori* operas are sung with a gritty and husky voice that lacks any sense of resonance, Kim adapted this harsh style for Western singers by introducing what he called "shin-ch'ang-ak" (New Singing Music). The purpose of shin- ch'ang-ak was to allow singers to retain their normal vocal technique while preserving key elements of traditional *p'ansori*.
>
> *(Kim 2012; abstract; also 10, 12–14)*

In this way, modern *p'ansori*, like early *p'ansori*, interacted with other forms and cultures and this has been essential to its development. While it is important to understand *p'ansori* as an indigenous Korean vocal art form, integral to the cultural identity of South Korea, it is also important to recognize how other cultural and disciplinary interactions have historically helped develop *p'ansori* and will, I suspect, continue to develop *p'ansori* in the future.

At this point, it would benefit the reader to see/hear a sample of *p'ansori* so the reader has a visual and aural understanding of this art form. There are several samples available through public access, such as YouTube, or subscribing though the National Gugak Center website. Just as scholarly definitions of *p'ansori* demonstrate explicitly or implicitly the position of the scholar within a certain context, video also offers one perspective that can alter certain material conditions that affect interpretation, such as the position of the camera and place of video editing as part of the context that shapes one understanding of *p'ansori* practice. I understand the difficulties of using video to represent a live art form in framing an understanding of that art form. The inadequacies of video as a medium for live art is a perpetual problem for those wanting to discuss performance. Although video samples do not demonstrate a performer/audience relationship in real time, it does allow the video viewer the opportunity to understand *p'ansori* as a performing art that exists at the moment when performers and viewer/audience together create meaning.

Many of the video samples found on YouTube offer close-up shots of the vocalist and rarely the drummer. Long-shots usually situate the vocalist in the center of the frame, and when subtitles are used, usually only the vocalist's words are subtitled, not the drummer's *ch'uimsae*. This perhaps gives the video audience the impression that a *p'ansori* performance is primarily about the vocalist. But in *p'ansori* there is a saying 일 구수, 이 명장 [first the drummer, second the singer] that suggests that the drummer is of primary importance. Because appreciative audience members and *p'ansori* connoisseurs, called 귀명장 *kwimyeongjang* [lit. "ear-renowned singers"] have slowly depleted over the years, scholar Yeonok Jang wrote that the saying has now been updated, "first the audience, second the drummer, and third the singer" to "call attention to the significance of the audience in *p'ansori* performances" (Jang 2002: 137).

Some samples offer subtitles in Korean (refer An Suk Son's televised performances of *Sugungga*; www.youtube.com/watch?v=RRSPlKFJbWk). Subtitles can be useful for novice Korean audience members because *p'ansori* often contains phrases no longer in contemporary usage, references to unfamiliar battles and historical figures, and can help some Korean viewers understand the pronunciation of certain outdated Sino-Korean words or the Cholla province dialect that is often used in *p'ansori* performances. Reading the *p'ansori* language while simultaneously listening to the performance provides an opportunity to "read" or understand the entire performance as a kind of performed text. Thus, the printed text on screen becomes an important part of the over-all video "performance text."[3]

Embodying role

The singular *p'ansori* performer inhabits multiple characters during the telling: characters found within the story, the Narrator, and the role of Performer when bantering with the audience or drummer.[4] During performances I have attended, the *p'ansori* storyteller as Performer has commented on the telling, like asides, addressed to the drummer or audience, such as "This part is very sad." Sometimes, Performer has commented on the performance itself, complimenting the audiences' participation or the expertise of the drummer. At times, Performer can incorporate a moment between the role as Performer with the role of Narrator. For instance, after singing a lament, Performer improvised a line suggesting that the character after such singing would need a drink of water to soothe her throat. Performer turned her need for water into part of the telling through narration. Performer then can take a sip of water from a glass that has been left on stage at the start of the performance by a stagehand, or in other performances I have seen, the vocalist simply asked at the wings of the proscenium stage for a glass of water and one was brought to her by a stage hand. She then asked the audience for their patience while she sipped from a glass of water before continuing with the telling. Slipping in and out of the role of Performer was not incidental to the performance, nor was the performer "breaking" character by stepping out of role. Switching roles between the world of the tale and the real-time world of the telling is a convention accepted by the audience within this performance form. To me, it seemed this was one way the performer created a sense of community with the audience. Performer not only acknowledged the audiences' presence but invited the audience to cooperate and participate as co-creators. This participation seemed just as involved and explicit as moments when the audience offered *chimsae*. Using these perform-ance conventions to participate, the audience seemed to also play a role—the role of Audience.

One way the audience understands how and when the *p'ansori* performer is in role and when she switches from one role to another is through the use of character voices. Kim Woo Ok matched three types of *aniri* [spoken] voice with character development: descriptive delivery for the reading of classics, colloquial for use in conversation between characters, and recitative for use in 계면조 *kyemyeonjo* [sorrowful mode: think of the sound of a Western minor triad] for describing sad moments (Kim 1980: 96–97). He also noted how *ch'ang* [sung] modes are used in developing character voices: *kyemyeonjo* for sad, sentimental voice, 우조 *ujo* [grand mode: think of the sound of a Western major triad] for description [what I under-stand as "narrator's voice"] and masculine character voices, 평조 *pyeongjo*, [Kim trans. "peaceful mode"] for use in cheerful scenes, 솔령재 *sollongje* for soldiers or warrior-like characters, and 경조 *kyongcho* from Kyonggi Province, to represent characters from Seoul (Kim 1980: 103–104).

Although Kim carefully delineated the differences of each role, in performance character voices are not always delivered separately; like other storytelling forms in which one performer must inhabit multiple roles, the performer sometimes embodies two characters at once through the use of, what I am calling, text and vocal text. For instance, in Lee Chu Eun's version of 수궁가 *Sugung-ga* [trans.="The Story of the Underwater Palace"] (Lee 2000)[5] the scene in which Tortoise calls Tiger down from the mountain, Lee Chu Eun performed the text "Tiger comes down" as "Tiger comes dooooooown!" with a vocal glide descending in pitch and a vocal gesture that sounded like a stylized "growl" on the word "down."[6] The text is Narrator's but the vocal text, the way in which the words are spoken, intro-duces the character voice of Tiger. In this way, the storyteller inhabits two roles, Narrator and Tiger, at once. In order for the audience to understand this moment, they must locate their listening in several places; They are listening to the narrative information, in other words the "who, what where" of the story in order to follow the story structure, but also the audience is listening to the vocal gestures to glean additional information about the story, such as character description.

The vocal text "Tiger comes dooooown" suggests Tiger is physically strong and powerful. This introduction of Tiger as an intimidating figure through vocal gesture sets audience expectation about what Tiger must look like and how he might behave through how Tiger, as any tiger, should sound. This is contrasted later in the story when Tiger's voice changes according to his changing circumstances; after meeting Tortoise, Tiger attempts to eat Tortoise. While trying to defend himself, Tortoise bites Tiger's penis. Tiger's voice changes and becomes high pitched and breathy in Lee Chu Eun's version. As Tiger begs Tortoise to let go, his voice breaks and he laments, in recitative *aniri* in *kyemyeoncho*, that Tiger has yet to fulfil the responsibility of a dutiful son and have children. Tiger laments that he should have had children earlier. Through the contrast of Tiger's initial character voice and this situational voice, audience expectation about how a fierce tiger should sound is thwarted, and this leads to the comedy of the scene.

The interplay between the text and the vocal text allows for more complex storytelling. The vocal text does not always have to support the text. Tiger begs for Tortoise to let go in recitative *aniri* in *kyemyeoncho*. *Kyemyeongcho* is translated into English as a "sorrowful mode." However, this does not necessarily reflect the spirit of the scene. When *kyemyeoncho* is used by Tiger in this scene it does not function to elicit sadness from the audience. Instead, *kyemyeongcho* used here functions as comedy. The sorrowful mode is not a serious lament over a real death but a comic twist on the "death" of a family lineage should Tiger's penis be bitten off by Tortoise. The comedy depends on the audience understanding the sound signifier of a lamentation, in other words, the "vocal text," contrasted with the text of the comic situation.

Form and function of the voice within the telling

Part of the mimetic training, as I experienced it, in *p'ansori* sets up when and where to use 아니리 *aniri* [spoken passages] and 창 *ch'ang* [sung passages]. I interpret sung voice, spoken voice, recitative chant [*ch'angcho* 창조], and lamentation as forms for the voice that frame the information delivered to the audience. The form of the performer's voice fits the performative function of the telling. When I discuss form and function here of the sung and spoken voices in role I am *not* referring to traditional understandings of the *aniri* and *ch'ang* modes, like *cho* 조 [Park trans. "melodic modes"] or *che* 제 [Um trans. "style"], for developing character voices. For detailed investigations of *cho* and *che* see Park (2003: 178–189) and Um (2013: 78–100, 101–122).

For instance, in Lee Chu Eun's version, the scene in which Tortoise bites Tiger's penis begins in sung voice, a form which best serves to mimic howls using vocal pitch glides, elongated vowels, and vocal ornamentation. The open throated gestures that accentuate the pitch break suggest a kind of violence of action through the sound representation of that violence via the pitch break. If the painful cries were performed using spoken voice, the sounds would carry a more realistic vocal quality that might encourage listener empathy. In my opinion, the function of the sung voice form in this instance supports the comedy of the scene by distancing the listener from more realistic sounding painful cries, so that the listener can laugh and enjoy the comedy.

Immediately after Narrator describes the biting action using sung voice, Lee Chu Eun switched to spoken voice in role as Performer to joke with the drummer about the action in the scene. Performer would need to make this quick comment using spoken voice, like an "aside," because the sung voice form would draw too much attention to it and away from the main action of the story. The spoken voice form that follows the sung narration of the bite places Lee Chu Eun in several positions to tell the story: Narrator through sung voice remains in the narrative of the story while Performer through spoken aside comments on the action. This quick switch in form, from sung to spoken voice, aurally signals to the audience Lee Chu Eun's character switch from Narrator to Performer. The form of the voice signals the function of role so that the audience will not be confused. Once these vocal forms are established as storytelling conventions, the performer can more easily switch role without losing the audience.

What is *sŏngŭm*?

In order to better understand *p'ansori* vocal dynamics and embodiment of role, it would help the reader to understand how *p'ansori* voice is trained to perform in this manner. The unique sound of the *p'ansori* voice is developed, in large part, during training, then refined throughout a performer's career in front of various audiences.

For Park, acquiring the *sori* is "the culmination of [many] things: inherent vocal and tonal presence, stylistic 'authenticity,' musical deftness, strength, and aesthetic sensibility . . . a trained *p'ansori* voice is typically husky, resonating with *ki* (strength) and subtle expressiveness simultaneously" (2003: 157). This section will not be able to look at all aspects of this acquisition, as several issues would deserve their own chapters.

In defining *sŏngŭm* and its role in *p'ansori*, Park begins with "the ancient Confucian Book of Rites (Yegi, Liji)" as the origin for music itself.

> Music rises as the mind is moved. First, the mind moves as it is touched by things external. The mind, touched, moves and it creates sound. Sound is distinguished in clear and turbid, slow and fast, high and low, and these qualities interact with one another, creating changes. The changes create melody, called "um."
>
> *(Park 2003: 189)*

Thus, the *um* of *sŏngŭm* is linked to melody, sound and "mind." I will return to a discussion of "mind" and to this particular quote in Chapter Four. "Sound," which is described through contrasts, "slow and fast, high and low," is one way in which "the dialectical principle of the *yin* and the *yang*" explain "the vocal structure of *p'ansori* (Park 2003: 190 citing *Sinyok yegi*, trans. Kwon Odon: 374)."[7] For Park, again quoting *Sinyok yegi* (399) "voice is the acoustic reflection of the mind. Where the mind is the agent of music, virtue is invisible except in music, and in music one cannot shelter a deceitful heart" (Park 2003: 189). In this way, training the voice towards *sŏngŭm* is not simply training the voice towards particular skill sets through technique, or as Park put it "Singing is not just vocal but mental and ethical, not merely acquisition of oral tradition but transformation of self" (Park 2003: 202).

Park wrote, "In vocal music, the vocal cords (song) are the instrument for realizing 'um', and thus the term *sŏngŭm*, 'vocal music' or the 'music of the voice'" (189). However, it is also clear from Park's use of *Sinyok yegi* that *sŏngŭm* is much more than its definition as "vocal music." For her *sŏngŭm* can be equated to the "life" of *p'ansori*. She wrote,

> Throughout the history of *p'ansori*, singers have zealously pursued the ultimate "life" of *p'ansori*, the *sŏngŭm*. The centrality of its musical existence has inspired multiple definitions and applications of the term . . . in the context of *p'ansori* singing, *sŏngŭm* signifies the following: 1) a natal property: favorable or unfavorable quality of the voice; 2) acquired fluency: depth of discipline in the singing or speaking voice; 3) narrative hermeneutics: the application of language and musical modes; and 4) aesthetic substance: beauty without ornamental superfluity.
>
> *(2003: 190)*

Simply put, "*sŏngŭm* is the singer's celebration of the story via oral performance, the story's 'rebirth' through the vocal cords" (Park 2003: 190). For me, this metaphor does not adequately represent how I understand the relationship between voice and text. Text is not "the" story, an intact entity, like an infant, given life, or "rebirth," through the passage of an orifice. This seems to make text a much more stable thing than I think it is, and it seems to suggest that voice is the means by which "the" story, or "a" text is realized, positioning voice as carrier, perhaps interpreter, of text. The prefix "re" suggests "to do again," which seems to imply that "the" story is shaped again and again through voice, but ultimately remains its own, separate entity—voice and story text are ontologically separate. Instead, using Park's quote and my own experiences training in *p'ansori* as a departure point, I came to understand voice as "author" of text, creating, instead of re-creating. I will return to this discussion in Chapter Six when comparing the differences between training voice to interpret text in scripted material, a preoccupation of getting the story "from the page to the stage," and oral traditions that may have no written script but rely on voice as the authorial means to create text. In this way, I argue that voice is text, not simply the means by which text is realized. Ideally, voice and text in performance are necessarily collapsed—there is no ontological separation.

Um defined *sŏngŭm* as the sound/voice in *p'ansori*, which encompasses various elements, including techniques of vocalization, register, ornamentation, singing style, voice color, and vocal control (2013: 221). Voice color and vocal technique are characterized as "desirable," "acceptable," or "forbidden." She wrote,

> The most desirable voice colour for a *p'ansori* singer is *ch'on'gusong* (gifted voice), which combines *surisong* (husky voice) and *aewonsong* (sorrowful voice). *Ch'olsong* (iron voice) which has a resonant quality and dynamic, is also regarded as a good voice colour. In contrast, undesirable voice colours included *ttongmok* (tough voice), which lacks resonance, and *yangsong* (bright voice) which lacks *kip'unmat* (rich flavour).
>
> *(2013: 159)*

Like Um, Park also divided the "desirable" and "undesirable" vocal qualities into categories. Park referenced Pak Honbong's list of qualities from singers' circulating vocabularies from which she constructed four categories: desirable vocal qualities, undesirable vocal qualities, trained vocal qualities, and dramatically manipulated vocal qualities (Park 2003: 192). I will not go into a detailed discussion of these vocal qualities here because this would divert my discussion into a complex area deserving its own chapter. It is sufficient for now to understand that vocal qualities divided into desirable and undesirable categories evidence sound qualities that carry explicit aesthetic meanings. For my purposes later, contrasting the expected aesthetics of the "natural/free" voice approach with *p'ansori* aesthetics, the word "natural" hides, rather than reveals, the explicit expectations of a performance aesthetic. In the "natural/free" voice approach, there is no categorization of desirable and undesirable vocal qualities. The suggestion is that the "natural" voice is achieved when the "self" of the individual speaker is revealed. However, in training actors' voices for the conventions of different performance genres, I argue that the "natural" voice does carry with it desirable and undesirable vocal qualities that define how a "natural" voice should sound within a given context.

Training towards *sŏngŭm* in the studio

P'ansori training and performance methods have been used for generations and although the vocal product may differ slightly from one performer to the next, based on artistic license or the performer's school of training, the basic principles of breath and sound production are transferred from master to trainee using mimetic training techniques. Park wrote,

> As a rule, a trainee under a master does not deviate from what he receives to be the rhythmic, and melodic paths in the learning of narrative. Yet, after years of training, every singer has his own melodic, rhythmic idiosyncrasies noticeable by discerning ears, a delicate deviation from the acquired heritage but not from its tradition.
>
> *(1995: 263)*

In the *p'ansori* studios and classrooms in which I have studied and observed,[8] most *p'ansori* students brought a tape recorder, mini-disc player, or (later) smartphone to their lessons in order to record and, later during independent practice, imitate their teacher's voice exactly. Students may have a copy of the story/song text (lyrics) but generally do not have written music to help them adhere to a traditional vocal performance. *P'ansori* practitioner and Human Cultural Treasure, Ahn Sook Sun[9] explained,

> We have a written script. We have five notes to a scale and Western music has seven notes to a scale so later people wrote the music in Western scale but I don't think it's very good. *P'ansori* is a kind of theatre sound; to show the situation vividly we don't use the written music. We just teach the scene; how to express the scene vividly to the audience.
>
> *(Personal interview, Seoul, 2000)*

Using audio recording devices and the written *p'ansori* script for assistance, *p'ansori* students depend most heavily upon their master teacher to teach them the rhythmic and melodic paths. Occasionally they make notations above or below a word or phrase to help them remember how the vocal ornamentation looped around/through/over/under a word or to denote a syncopated rhythm. In my private lessons and during the classrooms in which I have trained and observed, students spend very little time during the lesson discussing vocal training techniques or questioning their teacher about ways to produce breath and sound, even though *p'ansori* has extensive terminology to discuss breath/sound production. Instead, students train their eyes and ears to the nuances of breath and sound production based on what they see and hear their teacher producing. From my observations and experiences it seems *p'ansori* students have devised learning strategies unique to their individual learning styles in order to teach themselves how to become keenly aware of breath and sound production.

The extensive training vocabulary of *p'ansori* used to talk about sound and breath production is not based on the anatomical and scientific terminology that dominates Anglo-American voice training for actors. Pihl writes,

> In the process of being trained by example, the disciple learned the *kwangdae's*[10] extensive technical vocabulary from his master. Appended to a recent anthology of biographical sketches of living *kwangdae* is a technical glossary of ninety-five entries divided into five categories: general, rhythms, singing modes, schools and vocal characteristics. The fifty-three vocal characteristics, in particular, give evidence of the close attention p'ansori singers have paid to the subtle details of vocalization. In addition to the expected "hoarse," "nasal," "muted," and "tremulous," we also encounter such qualities as "bent in the throat," "like a cracked cymbal," "ghostly," "pulled back then let loose.
>
> *(1994: 103)*

Video sample one—p'ansori *training*

The first video sample in this section is a clip from one of my *p'ansori* lessons. The purpose of beginning this section with this sample is to return to the site of personal learning strategies that would eventually evolve into a pedagogical approach to training actors' voices. For instance, on the recording, I point to the kind of "multi-tasking" I do in each lesson. This is similar to the kind of multi-tasking my KNUA students must perform in my classroom, as previously discussed in the Introduction. First, I am reading in a foreign language while listening to sounds I have never been exposed to before: the sound of the Korean language in the Cholla province dialect (I was taught Seoul dialect in my KFL classes) and the microtonal melodic paths of the *p'ansori* song. Second, I am notating what I think I hear into my own devised sound notation system written just above the *p'ansori* text. Finally, Sŏng Uhyang demonstrates through verbal and visual instruction how to follow her rhythmic and melodic path. The learning strategies I created during lessons like this relied on my ability to integrate new learning into my previously learned skills.

One of the previously learned skills I brought with me into the *p'ansori* studio was my training in the "natural/free" voice approach. In this training, I had understood one literal definition of text as the word in print and was taught training techniques to get the word "from the page to the stage," so to speak. I will return to this later in Chapter Six. Linklater wrote,

> Text implies the word in print, and once in print the word impinges first on the external visual sense. For the actor there has to be a conscious translation of the seen word into the heard and felt word. The word seen is inert; the word heard, moves.
>
> *(Linklater 1976: 186–187)*

During aspects of my *p'ansori* lessons, when using a kind of libretti, or written text, I was also learning how to consciously translate the seen word into the heard and felt word. Above the words on the page, I would self-design a kind of sound notation to remind myself of the rhythm and melodic progression, vocal ornamentation, breath marks, and specific vocal gestures needed to realize the text. In this way, part of the training necessarily separated text from voice. Text was the printed word and voice was the sound of the word performed. Then that sound was put into visual representation, or notated, above the word to help with memorization. I would eventually call this sound notation "vocal text" in order to differentiate printed text (word) from how text as word should be performed. I was not the only student to do this. All of the other students in both Han Nongsŏn and Sŏng Uhyang's studios used notation.

However, as I became more proficient in my lessons and no longer needed to look at my libretti, I participated more whole-heartedly in the oral/aural transference of the task(s) in the lesson. The ontological separation between text and vocal text that had existed for me in print, collapsed during transmission between my teacher's voice and my ear, and then between my ear and my voice when repeating back to her what I thought I heard, via mimetic training practice.

This is a fundamental difference between text-based learning and mimetic, aural/oral based learning. If, according to Linklater, the "heard word moves," as opposed to the word in print that does not move, then for me the question became when the "heard word moves" how does it move? What happens in the process of that movement from the printed word into its aural performance? For me, one benefit of this movement became the instability of "the" word, since it could morph into a variety of different aural/oral interpretations. Here, I was still thinking about text and voice as ontologically separate and the voice as vehicle, or interpreter of text.

But when immersing myself in the aural/oral transmission, between my teacher and me and then between my ear and my voice as I listened to myself, the heard word seemed to dissolve the stability of text and encouraged the collapse of voice and text so that the one could not be distinguished from the other. Voice was text and text was voice within the movement of sound at the moment of performance. There was a difference between the meaning of the words (their dictionary definition) and how that meaning changed through my performance of the word; performance of the word became the meaning of the word. There was no other meaning, no other "interpretation," in part because the performed word exists in the here and now and within an instant is gone.

"Interpretation" needs time for reflective comparison. Upon reflection, after the lesson, my teacher and I could discuss "interpretation," and artistic differences performers who sang the same or similar texts. But during the task there was a unison of voice/text in which there could be no other possibility than movement of this sound, in this way, in this time and place.

I began to unfold my relationship to sound within language and non-linguistic vocalizations and how these sounds carry storytelling meaning beyond the dictionary definitions of the text. First, I examined sound in the words on my printed libretti. I needed to understand the sounds of the Korean language within the written *hangul* script system. While studying Korean as a Foreign Language (KFL), one of my first lessons introduced the origins of the Korean language, sounds in the Korean language, and how those sounds were eventually written down as *hangul*, invented by King Sejong in 1443. There are several theories but the one I would like to examine for the purposes of this discussion suggests that *hangul* was not only a visual representation of vernacular sounds, but a visual reminder of the positioning of the vocal organs during articulation.

> In 1941, new historical evidence was uncovered in the form of a *hanmun* text discovered in North Kyongsang Province which spells out the pictographic cosmological nature of the symbol-shapes in no uncertain terms, and it is now clear that of the older writings, Hong Yang-ho was on the right track.
>
> *(Hoyt 2000: 157)*

According to Hong Yang-ho [1724], "the symbols used in the *onmun* are picto-graphic representations of the mouth at the time of articulation" (Hoyt 2000: 156).

> The notes state clearly that five of the original seventeen consonants were shaped according to the form of the organs of speech, "k" ㄱ representing the root of the tongue closing the epiglottis, "n" ㄴ representing the tongue touching the hard palate, "m" ㅁ representing the mouth, "s" ㅅ representing the tooth, and "Y" *(gamma) ㅇ representing the throat . . . In addition, some of the other consonants, including those formed by adding the aspira-tion stroke, are said to have been created pictographically as follows:

> | | | |
> |---|---|---|
> | ㅌ | "t" | "flapping of the tongue" |
> | ㅂ | "p" | "half-open mouth" |
> | ㅍ | "p'" | "open mouth" |
> | ㅈ | "ch" | "gums and teeth" |
> | ㅎ | "Y" (*gamma aspirate) | "throat and palate. |

> *(Hoyt 2000: 158)*

Hangul is a phonetic alphabet. Significant cultural understandings of sound are embedded in *hangul*, which frame the ways my students and I approach our various understands of sound in language. Embedded within *hangul* are understandings of *eum-yang* (*yin-yang* in Chinese), a fundamental principle throughout Korea and Asia. This principle permeates Korean ideology, society, and culture and is funda-mental to the composition of Korean traditional music like *p'ansori* (Chung 1998; Lee 2000). Speaking Korean is the act of experiencing the physical embodiment of the *eum-yang* principle. *Eum-yang* is a relative pair, an interdependent relationship, sometimes described as bright/dark or masculine/feminine: the *yang* principle is "bright" or "masculine" and the *eum* principle is "dark" or "feminine." In *hangul*, sounds are often characterized using these terms. For instance, 아 is considered a bright vowel sound and 어 is considered a dark vowel sound.

Sound helps define identity and is deeply connected to one's worldview. King Sejong wrote in *Hunmin Chong'um* [trans. *Correct Sounds for Teaching the People*, 1446: 6],

> The sounds of the language of our country differ from [those of] China: and [Chinese] characters do not correspond with the need. Therefore, the common people using the vernacular are unable to express their feelings completely. So having compassion, we have devised a new system with twenty-eight letters. It is our wish that they be used, since they are easy for everybody to learn and apply.

> *(Hoyt 2000: 161)*

Hangul was created not only as an accessible written form for mass education but also to differentiate Koreans from their neighbors, build nationalism, and express their unique identity. Sound is thus political. Also, Sejong linked sound in language with the ability to "express feelings completely." Sound carries with it emotional attachment, associations, memories, and cultural meaning.

During my lessons, I was not only trying to get the sounds "correct," position-ing my articulators in such a way as to be clearly understood, but to perform them in such a way as to trigger emotions, memories, and cultural meaning for the lis-tener. This was complicated by dialect variations. The standardized written *hangul* I had been taught in my KFL class corresponded to the Seoul standardized dialect. My *p'ansori* text was written in this standardized *hangul*, but the pronunciation of some of the words were in the Cholla province dialect. So the *hangul* that I had been trained to read and pronounce in KFL class was not suitable at times for the pronunciation of *p'ansori* text. To solve this problem, I rewrote the word using a more appropriate *hangul* character, even though this was "misspelling" the word. In this case, the standardized written word did not properly represent the sound intended, but because *hangul* is a phonetic alphabet, the "misspelling" could prop-erly represent the sound. Different dialects carry different cultural meanings and associations that can be read in performance.

What I was also creating during lessons, although I did not understand it explic-itly at the time, was a personal emotional association with these sounds that had at first seemed foreign and with which I had no previous emotional attachment. At times, during lessons or practicing alone, I would burst into tears because of the sounds of lamentation and the feeling of the vibrations traveling along the hard surfaces of my body. I would not be sad at the top of the lesson or the beginning of practice, but the act of vocalizing and listening to myself vocalize certain sounds began to trigger certain reactions. When I attended *p'ansori* performances, these same sounds would again trigger emotional reactions and I found myself tearing up during moments of others' performances. Sounds that previously carried no mean-ing for me early in my training, had now become embedded, embodied response through the repetition of listening and responding in training and as a spectator at performances. This was more than simply the act of making unfamiliar sounds familiar. Instead, these sounds felt personal and intimate. They were becoming physically and psychologically a part of my "self." Upon reflection, I began to understand my training in *p'ansori* as psycho-physical training. I will return to a discussion of psycho-physical and the role of "self" in training in Chapter Four. These experiences led me to investigate the larger territory of emotion and its role in training. Although such a topic could deserve its own chapter, I will only touch on a few ideas here.

The role of emotion, specifically *han*, in *p'ansori* training

As mentioned briefly in the Introduction, *p'ansori* is closely associated with *han* Heather Willoughby's 2002 PhD thesis titled, *The Sound of Han: P'ansori, Timbre and a Korean Ethos of Suffering and Lament*, is one detailed articulation of how *han* can function in off-stages spaces within Korean society and in on-stage performance spaces as an aesthetic within *p'ansori*.[11] Jeungsook Yoo, in her book *A Korean Approach to Actor Training*, quoted Willoughby in her discussion of the "sound of *han*" as having particular qualities of "harsh and rough vocalisations" (Willoughby 2000: 20; Yoo 2018: 98). In interview, Willoughby asserted, "*Han* (a Korean concept of deep anger or sorrow) is in fact a universal emotion. Such emotions embedded in the music will move listeners all over the world" (http://evoice.ewha.ac.kr/news/articleView.html?idxno=2206).

Yoo also discussed *han* in traditional Korean performing arts as a larger aesthetic (2018: 98). However, Yoo understood *han* as "one of the distinctive characteristics of Korean mindset and cultural ethos" (96). Instead of explaining *han* as a universal emotion, Yoo explained *han* through cultural psychologist Sang-Chin Choi's analysis (Choi 2012; Choi and Kim 2011). Choi categorized *han* in three modes: "*han* emotion," "*han* sentiment," and "*han* trait" and discussed *han* as a cognitive scheme.

> That is, Korean people have developed an underlying mental structure about what *han* is and what the cause or condition of *han* is . . . *Han* is both an individual emotional experience and a significant foundation of Korean culture. In spite of the particularity of any personal experience of *han* in specific contexts and situations, "the Korean people have developed a psychological mechanism, through which the individual can identify with his or her socio-cultural community."
>
> *(Choi and Kim 1998: 90, in Yoo 2018: 96)*

In this way, *han* as a particular emotion understood within Korean society is a kind of cultural construct. *Han* as an aesthetic in performance is equally complex.

Yoo suggested that *han* as an emotion distilled through training can become an applied technique. I am not suggesting that the emotions I experienced when practicing *p'ansori* was the development of *han*. What I am suggesting is that the emotions I experienced seemed to emerge from repetition during practice. This repetition created an embodied response to sound that eventually carried meaning for me. Upon reflection, perhaps I was developing an emotional response to sounds in *p'ansori* as distilled through training and applied as technique to my learning process.

Vocal techniques: Creating sound and meaning

I linked *p'ansori* "voice/sound" in performance as the *hangul* "word heard." Video sample two demonstrates one way in which the "word heard" is performed within *p'ansori* aesthetics. This sample is demonstrated by Bae Il Dong, *p'ansori* master performer, who was practicing at Sŏng Uhyang's studio during the same time I trained. He demonstrated for me the *p'ansori* vocal ornamentation of the word *sonsaengnim* [lit. "teacher"]. In the telling of the *p'ansori* story, vocal ornamentation is an important part of *p'ansori mehak* [aesthetics]. The way in which Bae *sonsaengmin* taught me was by first deconstructing the vowel/consonant arrangement in a word, using as his example the word *sonsaengnim* [teacher].

In the first syllable, *son*, of *sonsaengnim*, the first consonant, "s," is *ch'o sori* [first/beginning sound]. It represents the season of spring. Just as the farmer plants seeds in the spring, the performer plants the beginning of the sound. The vowel, "o," is called *joonggan sori* [middle/center sound]. It represents the season of summer. Just as the seed grows into the plant, the sound grows. The consonant, "n," is *gud sori* [pull/draw sound]. It represents the season of autumn. Just as the farmer harvests the plant, the performer harvests the sound. The vocal journey through this syllable *son* is a sung voice cycle like the cycle of seasons; "s"= plant + "o"= grow/push + "n"= harvest/pull in (Bae Il Dong, personal interview, 2004). The definitive meaning of *sonsaengnim* takes on additional meaning in performance through the sonic design of the vowels and consonants. In training, my relationship to sound and meaning was shaped by the imagistic way Bae Il Dong taught me to think about sound in language. Even if, during performance, the average audience member did not know this metaphor of planting, growing, and harvesting sound, they may still receive the benefits of the performer thinking about sound in this way because this teaching metaphor shaped the resultant performance through the way it developed technique in my body/voice. This reflects back to Spatz's observation (refer Introduction) of "direct and indirect uses of technique . . . that is, between what actors reliably do and what audiences reliably perceive" (2015: 125).

[Refer video sample: scanned image of my *p'ansori* text with sound notation.][12] The sound notation I wrote above my *p'ansori* text cannot document the kind of rich instruction I received from Bae Il Dong or Sŏng Uhyang. To the outside eye, my notation may look like loops, swirls, and scribbles, the written reminders of how to perform "techniques." Park observed,

> In receiving *p'ansori* one hand is placed on the recording equipment and the other maps the vocal route over, under, and through the written lines as the ear engages in auditory reception in preparation for oral reproduction. In the transmission of *p'ansori*, the learner's text strives to decode and document the teacher's vocal graphics . . . He or she emulates the teacher's basic consonantal differentiation of *ah* (velar), *sol* (lingual), *sun* (labial), *ch'i* (dental), and *hu* (glottal), and the teacher's style of what I term "vowel play" or "vowel navigation," the mellifluent diphthongal elongation of vowels that often stretches what is linguistically one to multiple oral-syllabic utterances.
>
> *(2003: 160)*

But my notation is also a visual aide that triggers memories of training. When I practice with my training text, I see the rubbed-out marks and remember/feel the frustration of trying to get the vocal ornamentation just right. I can retrace a swirl with my finger as I follow the words and remember my teacher nod and feeling relieved when I finally did perform the vocal ornamentation correctly. In this way, I relate to "technique" not as an "outside/in" approach, or an emotionless, technical skill executed with cold precision. Training technique in my body/voice is an emotional process. Embedded, embodied skills sets are not devoid of emotion.

Discussions in the "natural/free" voice discourse about the differences between British and American Method training (refer Chapter Two), characterize actor training as either "outside/in" or "inside/out," and set at odds technique from expression. I think there is a more subtle understanding of the relationship between technique and expression that such a binary cannot offer.

Technique can also be personal. Creating my own form of sound notation for my *p'ansori* lessons was a personal process, documenting my learning journey at different developmental levels and how I interwove different techniques from my various trainings. In order to create my own sound notation during my *p'ansori* lessons, I borrowed from several previously learned skills. First, I borrowed from my training as a classical violinist and vocalist with Western musical notation. I sometimes wrote down Western notes in the margins to denote melodic progression or beats to denote rhythm, but strict applications of time and key signatures were not helpful for representing rhythm cycles and microtonal progressions.

[Refer video sample: scanned image of IPA.] I also tried to use my acting training to help me devise a sound notation system. For instance, the International Phonetic Alphabet was invented to represent sound in a visual symbol and many actors use it particularly to train in accents and dialects. I found it extremely difficult to use as a notation device for *p'ansori*. First, the International Phonetic Alphabet is not international as it relies heavily on Romanized characters. Also, it was too cumbersome for me during the speed of the lesson to switch back and forth from reading the Korean alphabet with its phonetic vocabulary and writing a Roman-based symbol system.

[Refer video sample: scanned image of Labanotation.] Another acting training method I used to help me notate sound during my *p'ansori* lesson was based on my understanding of Laban Movement training for Actors. I brought Laban movement techniques as applied for voice with me to Korea, as a part of my US curriculum that explored the quality of sound gestures. Generally, I taught Laban for Voice using a combination of materials from Jean Newlove's *Laban for Actors and Dancers* (Newlove 1993) and the brief training methods I found in voice training texts, such as Michael McCallion's *The Voice Book* (McCallion 1988: 184). Both of these books were with me that first year in Korea when I began to search for better ways to train my KNUA students' voices.

Newlove wrote,

> Laban looked upon movement as a two way language process through which the human body could communicate by giving and receiving messages . . . Notation, or kinetography, as Laban called it, helps the observer to get a clear and exact recording of a movement, recalling all the subtleties of expression.
>
> *(Newlove 1993: 11)*

As a voice teacher, I understood sound as a "two way language process." Both movement and voice disciplines could write down these languages in written form using notation. The sound notation I was using in my *p'ansori* class was also used to "recall all the subtleties of [vocal] expression."

At times, I notated *p'ansori* sounds using my adaptations of Laban dance notation. Thinking of sound as three-dimensional movements helped me place sound in my body. The very physical understanding of producing sound in *p'ansori* seemed to work well with the physical nature of Laban. Also, both *p'ansori* and Laban use action verbs within the terminology to show how a gesture should be performed. I found Laban's "punch" and "press" gestures similar to *p'ansori's* "pushing/pulling" sound. Laban's "wring," seemed similar to *p'ansori's* "turning over" sound.

Over time, I could see that my sound notations were becoming more complex. Often, I would erase an old notation and rewrite it. Usually, my first learning experiences with a complex passage could not really reflect the vocal ornamentation of my teacher properly because my ear was still struggling to hear the microtonal progressions and rhythm cycles. Only when my ear could finally hear in more detail, could I rewrite a more exact notation to help me vocalize the progressions clearly. Notation and ear training were working together as learning tools to help me gauge my developmental process learning *p'ansori*.

Vocal techniques: "*Sankongbu*" [lit. 산/mountain 공부하다/to study, "mountain study"]

In a personal interview, Master Teacher Chung Hoi Suk, who teaches at the Korean National University of Arts, School of Traditional Arts, asserted that the unique sound of *p'ansori*, began with the training.

> Basically it is . . . the training . . . to have a louder voice because in older times we didn't have microphones. We performed *p'ansori* in the marketplace so we needed to have a big voice. That's why we train our voices this way. Still, one out of ten succeeded in training their voices. Nine others fail training their voice. Those who fail the training play instruments or do other things. Now when I go to a doctor, the doctor says I have wrinkles on my vocal folds . . . um . . . nodes. It is a very unique training method but it is not scientifically proved . . . "this is good or not good." It is true that we have to train our throat . . . or our "voices" to express a very dramatic voice. Also we can make a very pretty sound but we still need to express a very extreme sound. It is also good for *p'ansori* singers to train in nature. That's why they train themselves down by the waterfall. You have to penetrate the sound of the waterfall.
>
> *(Chung, personal interview, Seoul, South Korea, 2000)*

According to Master Teacher Han Nongsŏn,[13] *p'ansori* artists traditionally visited one of the many mountain retreats found all over Korea to study individually or in small groups for "one hundred days study" (Han, personal interview, 2000) Today, many *p'ansori* trainees usually study in the mountains for a month [August] during their school summer holiday. The majority of the training time for today's trainees is not spent training in the mountains but in the *p'ansori* studio. Of course, the difference in outdoor and indoor training environments has an influence on vocal training, but the extent to which this can be measured is undeterminable. Phonetician Dr. Moon Seung-Jae of Ajou University suggested that the vocal effects/affects of mountain training do not necessarily need to take place in the mountains (Moon, e-mail interview, 2003).[14] The tradition, however, is to strengthen the voice using natural obstacles, such as a waterfall, a grove of pine trees, or a canyon.

Chung's description of "penetrating the sound" is not the same as "release the call" that Linklater described,

> Set up a simple scenario in your mind's eye . . . You see your friend. What you see fills you with the need to call to him or her. You release the call. You relax, breathe, and wait for the reaction. Throughout the scene your body is acted on: first by the outside stimulus, then by the desire to communicate. There should therefore be no need to push or strain in order to call.
>
> *(Linklater 1976: 92)*

During mountain training, one tends to lose one's voice by extended use at extreme volumes in an effort to compete with the natural obstacle. Traditionally, losing and regaining the voice will create what Korean artists describe as "big" or "thick" voices. Indeed, this process could leave the vocal folds "thicker" literally because the elasticity of the folds may be affected and thus would have difficulty physically elongating, become "thinner" so to speak [thin fold action], when producing certain upper-range pitches. In contrast, Linklater's advice within the "natural/free" voice approach trains actors not to push or strain. The role of effort is noticeably different in each of the training traditions.

Pihl wrote,

> Chong No-sik's biographical sketches frequently tell of learners who not only sang themselves hoarse, but who vocalized in the wilderness or challenged the sound of a waterfall to produce voices of great power, often pushing themselves to the point of spitting up blood in the process.
>
> *(Pihl 1994: 105)*

Park quoted Pak Hon-bong in Pak's work *Changak taegang* [Survey of Vocal Music] detailing the process,

> First, for many days and months, scale the voice vertically from low to high, at the same time expand it horizontally. In time the voice turns hoarse and gets lost, until it becomes hardly audible even to a person standing next to you. Keep scaling your voice for years, even through occasional bleeding

from the vocal cords, until at last, the voice returns, reinforced and expressive and will endure singing for many hours at a time . . . the voice has entered the realm of mystery at last."

(1995: 70)

Some Anglo-American voice trainers might characterize the above description as "vocal violence" or "abuse" and be concerned about the vocal health of the performer. However, the husky *p'ansori* voice is part of what comprises the beauty of *p'ansori*. For a contemporary definition of "vocal violence," one might refer to an article published in *The Journal of Voice* entitled "Vocal Violence in Actors: An Investigation into Its Acoustic Consequences and the Effects of Hygienic Laryngeal Release Training."

> Actors, in rehearsal and performance, frequently engage in emotionally charged behaviors, often producing voice accompanied by extreme physical exertions (as in a staged fight), or sudden emotional outbursts, such as screaming, shouting, grunting, groaning, and sobbing. These vocally violent behaviors appear to involve extremes in pitch and loudness, increases of muscular tension in the circumlaryngeal area, and explosions of air across partially closed vocal folds. Such behaviors are generally accepted to be vocally abusive, and may contribute to vocal fold mucosal injury and voice mutation.
>
> *(Roy, Ryker, and Bless 2000: 215)*

P'ansori vocalists do not scream or sob on stage as many actors training towards Realism might because they do not embody character using the conventions of "naturalism." But the *p'ansori* artist, like the actor, must engage in "emotionally charged behaviors." Both types of performers must represent characters on stage in heightened emotional states. When representing characters in a heightened emotional state, the *p'ansori* artist, like the actor, engages in "vocally violent behaviours," which involve "extremes in pitch and loudness, increases of muscular tension in the circumlaryngeal area, (possibly) explosions of air across partially closed vocal folds." And like the actor, the *p'ansori* artist's vocally violent behavior may "contribute to vocal fold mucosal injury and voice mutation," especially because the *p'ansori* vocalist engages in these behaviors more frequently and for longer performance periods than most actors. According to Yi Po-hyong,

> The vocal technique of *p'ansori* generally resembles bel canto in terms of breathing from the stomach with pressure exerted on the diaphragm. It contrasts, however, there is [*sic*] the bel canto technique in which one constricts the throat in order to obtain a hoarse or husky vocal timbre. It is not surprising that many *p'ansori* singers develop a husky quality even in their normal speaking voices due to the tremendous demands made upon their voices.
>
> *(1982: 252)*

The *Journal of Voice* article continued,

> Although the professional voice literature is replete with references to vocal "abuse and misuse," there is little objective information defining what constitutes "abusive" sounds, how they are made and what frequency, intensity, and duration of abuse produces perceptible changes in voice or laryngeal tissue.
>
> *(2000: 215)*

If what constitutes vocal abuse cannot be quantified scientifically, then perhaps the term "vocal abuse" is more of a cultural understanding based on appreciated vocal aesthetics?

Traditional mountain study, *sankongbu*, and historical Anglo-American vocal training practice share certain similarities in practiced periods of extreme outdoor vocal use. Martin wrote,

> Great emphasis was placed on having a strong voice in the huge Greek and Roman amphitheatres and later in the nineteenth century, when it became necessary to speak to large crowds outdoors or in large auditoria. Even Quintilian's warnings against the ill-effects of vocal strain did not deter force and vigorous action of the voice from becoming popular well into the first two decades of the twentieth century . . . Diverse factors have contributed to the change in this practice today, as teachers have become aware of the abuse which unnecessary strain can cause and have begun to develop carrying power by other means, 'by breath control, openness of the throat and laryngeal areas, effective vowel formation and clear articulation' according to Anderson [V.S. Anderson, *Training the Speaking Voice* (66)].
>
> *(Martin 1991: 40)*

Contemporary actors and street performers have also cultivated a similar raspy quality to their voices through outdoor training and/or performance. Bim Mason wrote, "The voice is often strained to the limit and many [street] performers without training develop a rasp. It is said that Richard Burton developed his voice by shouting on the mountains" (Mason 1992: 185). However, mainstream voice training since the 1970s has been dominated by warnings against vocal strain with an increased interest in vocal health.

Influence of *sankongbu* in pitch range

One of the reasons actors avoid straining the vocal folds with resulting conditions of laryngitis, nodes, or polyps during voice training is because they believe these conditions limit the performer's vocal range. Of course, *p'ansori* artists must also have a considerable vocal range because a single vocalist is responsible for multiple character voices. To understand the effects of *sankongbu* on the voice's producible range, one must first keep in mind that the concept of pitch range is different to a *p'ansori* vocalist.

P'ansori has a moveable pitch range because there is no fixed tonal center. Therefore, pitches and pitch ranges are not categorized by such vocal categories as bass, tenor, alto, and soprano. A study done by Yonsei University Voice Research Center with *p'ansori* performer Cho Sanghyon determined that the moveable pitch range of *p'ansori* could be converted to reflect three and a half Western octaves. The study cited my *p'ansori* teacher's voice, Sŏng Uhyang, and suggested it could cover over three and a half octaves (Park-Miller 1995: 246). In a personal interview with Professor Ahn Sook Sun, she asserted that her own *p'ansori* vocal range was seven or, she roughly estimated, a pitch range of four to five Western octaves (personal interview, Seoul, 2000). Um wrote,

> According to Pak Honbong, the vocal range in *p'ansori* can be divided into seven registers (1966: 70–71). Chŏng Pyŏnguk considers these to be equivalent to seven octaves (which is physically impossible for any singer) while also suggesting that there is no distinction to be made between the male and female voice in *p'ansori* (1981: 69–70). According to Kim Kiryong, a medical doctor specializing in otolaryngology and the study of vocal dynamics, the *p'ansori* singer's physiological frequency range of phonation, which includes both a strong falsetto and breathing voice, is not nearly as wide as seven octaves.
>
> *(Um 2013: 77)*

In an interview, Han Nongsŏn, who performed an "Eastern-style" school of *p'ansori* (*Tongp'yŏnje*), stated that one *p'ansori* singer is expected to cover a range of pitches that would in Western music be divided into multiple categories of bass, tenor, alto, and soprano and be executed by various artists (personal interview, Seoul, 2000). The same pitch range is expected of male as well as female artists. Only the singer's tonal center or "starting pitch" for a song will vary from artist to artist. This "starting pitch" seems to be determined by one's preferred vocal pitch as well as where the student is developmentally in her vocal training. However, Um noted,

> [Kim Kiryong] (1986: 7) experiments on the vocal range of *p'ansori* singers suggested that a male *p'ansori* singer can produce up to 46 half-tones (80–1,000 Hz; D#-c3) ranging just under four octaves whereas the female counterpart can sing 38 half-tones (120–1,000 Hz; B-c3) covering just over three octaves.
>
> *(Um 2013: 77)*

In her doctoral thesis, Chan E. Park categorized the *p'ansori* voice as having seven vocal ranges: quadruple high (*choesangsong*), double high (*chungsangsong*), high (*sangsong*), middle (*p'yongsong*), low (*hasong*), double low (*chungsangsong*), and quadruple low (*ch'oehasong*)" (1995: 246).

Another difference is the Western concept of melodic progression measured in "half-steps" and "whole steps," which are discipline-specific terms not used in *p'ansori*. In my *p'ansori* lessons and observations, significant attention is paid to vocal ornamentation that includes microtonal slides that would be difficult to measure in a Western musical system of half-steps and whole-steps. For the beginning listener, the vocal ornamentation may at first sound improvisational but in fact is quite exact. Heather Willoughby wrote about her experiences learning *p'ansori* vocal ornamentation:

> In my own private lessons, taught by Yi Chu-un [Lee Chu Eun] the ability and need to master the movement between notes was a point which she continually stressed. She emphasized that even if the audience was unable to consciously perceive the microtones, they would certainly be aware if a singer's voice lacked the control to hit all "the notes between the notes."
>
> *(Willoughby 2002: 139)*

Once a song has begun at the performer's preferred "starting pitch," the melodic progression of the song simply adjusts to the "key" set by the tonal center. Please note, however, that *p'ansori* does not recognize a "key signature" as does Western music. In contrast to the *p'ansori* concept of "starting pitch," today's Anglo-American vocal training asserts that an actor's "natural" pitch level should be the foundation of her pitch range. Martin wrote,

> Scientists have determined that an individual's natural pitch level, which is often referred to as "optimum," lies somewhere near the third or fourth tone above the lowest which can be produced clearly. Many teachers now realize that locating this "natural" pitch level constitutes a basic step towards improving voice and a number of methods are easily available for its determination.
>
> *(Martin 1991: 39)*

Anglo-American voice practitioners might ask, if *p'ansori* artists must embody multiple character voices in a single *p'ansori* performance, performing a broad pitch range and creating the emotional intensity of the *p'ansori* drama, would *sankongbu*, which could "damage" the vocal folds, possibly limiting vocal range, not be antithetical to the demands of a *p'ansori* performance in which a wide pitch range would be advantageous? Park explained,

> For a singer to be equipped with a wide scale of pitch is clearly advantageous, for her voice has wider range of expression. But according to Chong Kwonjin, a singer must not insist on high pitch, but try to stay with middle and the low pitch. Sometimes motivated by erroneous notion that high pitch is always better-sounding, or driven by a desire to be showy, singers do pursue high pitch. But in so doing, they tend to lose the strong basic sound of the middle and the low pitch and sound rather flighty and flashy.
>
> *(1995: 250)*

Even if a *p'ansori* artist has access to her extreme upper register, the training culture and performance aesthetic shapes the vocal training by valuing middle and lower pitches.

In many mainstream voice training texts, pitch range is usually viewed as a vertical process, from lower pitches to higher pitches and back down again. Linklater's "resonating scale" follows a vertical process linking sound to different locations on the vocalist's body. Linklater and Berry have several exercises in their books that utilize "glide" to increase the student's pitch range. The "glide" exercises, which organizes sound from low to high and high to low tones, focus on expanding pitch range without straining the vocal folds. In a voice workshop held in Seoul, Korea (September 2000), Cicely Berry suggested using vocal "glide" exercises for actors concerned with "pitch break" problems (also refer Nelson 2015: 48). But *p'ansori* artists often employ "pitch break" to create sorrowful, melancholy sounds during emotional passages. "Pitch break" does not seem to be perceived as a problem resolved with training exercises but is instead cultivated as a means of vocal expression.

Also in *p'ansori*, pitch range is viewed not only as a vertical process but also as a horizontal process. Park quoted Pak Hon-bong's work *Changak taegang* when she wrote, "the aspiring singer works for months on end on strengthening her voice, by 'scaling up vertically from low to high as well as horizontally from narrow to wide'" (249). In interview, Chung Hoi Suk asserted, "Of course, we believe a big pitch range is important but we also in fact believe the wideness of the sound is important" (personal interview, Seoul, 2000). When asked what he meant by "wideness of sound," he demonstrated his meaning: he placed the sound towards the center or back of the chamber of the mouth and dropped his jaw. Placed there, the sound appeared to resonate within the chambers of the mouth, throat, and chest. In contrast, he demonstrated a sound that was not "wide" by placing the sound towards the front of the mouth allowing it to resonate in the mask of the face.

Aurally, in Chung Hoi Suk's demonstration, it seemed he was broadening the sound through placement and resonation. Visually, when he demonstrated a "widened" sound, the veins in his neck were straining under the pressure and his neck increased in width during the exhalation. When I watch myself in a mirror while mimicking this same technique during my own *p'ansori* lessons, it appeared that my neck widened because of the large capacity of air being channeled through the throat (e.g. air pressure). The throat tried to accommodate the large capacity of air by increasing in width. Simultaneously, muscular contraction is added to move the larynx during phonation. The stress caused between the throat's need to expand and the muscle's need to contract creates the visual and aural impression of excess tension added to the production of breath and sound during exhalation. Park identified this sound production as "laryngeal projection." In Laban terms, I would characterize this as "pressing." Chung Hoi Suk explained during his interview with me:

Q: So when you're seeking to produce this sound, it's not a sound that comes out of the front part of the mouth but actually a sound that is coming up from the neck and placed more towards the back of the throat?

A: (He nods)

Q: Is that, for the most part, where you want to always place the sound or are there instances in which you would want a more frontal placement?

A: We do have the frontal sound too demonstrated. But basically from the *dahnjeon* (center) we generate the sound.

Q: You produce the breath from the center? (I pointed to the area above my navel at my diaphragm) Or here? (I pointed to the area below my navel).

A: (He placed my entire hand over my navel and nodded. He sang part of a song I observed him teaching earlier during a class using *dahnjeon* breathing).

The start of the exhalation was recognizable as a combination of "punch" and "press" techniques from the *dahnjeon*, pushing the air past the vocal folds quickly and forcefully using the strength of the abdominal muscles. Park identified this technique as "tubular projection." She explained, "Tubular projection (*tongsong*), projected straight from the abdomen without interruption, has been revered for its beauty and strength . . . without the sturdy abdominal muscle developed over a long period of voice training, *tongsong* can rarely be projected" (1995: 252–253).

During Chung's demonstration of *dahnjeon* breathing, there seemed to be no visual tension on the inhalation, nor audible inhalation. In fact, during Chung's demonstration, his muscles appeared very released, allowing the air to simply fill his body. For me, this process of inhalation seemed to be a more muscular version of Berry's breath capacity exercise in which she encouraged the vocalist to wait for the need to breathe after the exhale and simply allow the air to fill the body, releasing any tension that might inhibit this process (Berry 1973: 23–30).

The way in which *p'ansori* vocalists shape the sound into tonal qualities depends heavily on the performance aesthetic and a worldview that conceptualizes sound in a particular way through *eum-yang* ideology. Chung explained:

A: Basically, we think in *Yin* and *Yang*. It's important. Do you know this word?

Q: Yes.

A: It is like this in shape [draws the *yin/yang* on the floor with his finger] and is like . . . female and male . . . so we try to express the *Yin* and *Yang* in our sound. *Yin* sound is like . . . um . . . suppressed, muffled sound. *Yang* sound is very bright. *Woojo* [*sic*] sound is bright [note to reader: think of the brightness of tones in a major key. Chung may mean *ujo*] and *kyemyonjo* is the other [note to reader: think of the tones in a minor key].

Alan Heyman wrote that the tension used to create the unique sounds of *p'ansori* was part of the cultural aesthetic of *yin-yang*.

> Known as the concept of *yin-yang* (*eum-yang* in Korean), the dual forces that govern the universe, this cosmology underlies the basic melody and rhythm in both contrast and tension-release structure . . . Distinction is made between a "continuing" voice and a "closing" or "blocked" voice; between

a "spreading out" voice and a "restrained voice" and between a high-pitched "lifting" voice and a low-pitched "descending" voice.

(Heyman 1993: 217; also refer Chung 1998)

A more complete understanding of pitch, tonal quality, and sound placement and their relationship to *eum/yang* can be understood through Park's work when she translated Pak Honbong's 12 different tonal qualities into five distinct vocal aesthetics.

First, Park categorized 12 different tonal qualities in *pansori*:

> *Tongsong* "tubular projection"
> *Cholsong* "metallic voice"
> *Surisong* "husky voice"
> *Sesong* "falsetto projection"
> *Hangsong* "laryngeal projection"
> *Pisong* "nasal projection"
> *Pasong* "cracky voice"
> *Palbalsong* "tremolo projection"
> *Chongusong* "clear spring voice"
> *Hwasong* "harmonious projection"
> *Kwigoksong* "grieving ghost tone"
> *Agwisong* "molar tone"

Park added,

> The desirability of *p'ansori* voice is directly related to *p'ansori* aesthetics, which requires the presence of both sides of cosmic gender, *yin* and *yang*. Insofar as the vocal narration of *p'ansori* is the portrayal of life's picture within, its artistic process must start with the selection and training of the kind of voice inherent with such qualities as capable of portraying different aspects of life: different moods, emotional changes, and multiple characterization.
>
> *(1995: 250)*

Park organized Pak's 12 tonal qualities into aesthetic groupings:

"Inherently ideal voice"="metallic voice," "husky voice," and a "clear, spring voice."

"Inherently undesirable voice"="cracky voice."

"Overall harmonious projection"="*hwasong*" or "harmonious projection" (refers to the voice capable of clear and correct differentiation of high, middle, and low pitches).

"Undesirable projection"="nasal projection" and "tremolo projection" (similar to the Western understanding of a tight vibrato).

"Projection for dramatization"="tubular projection," "falsetto projection," "laryngeal projection," "grieving ghost tone," and "molar tone."

In video sample two, 배일동 [Bae Il Dong] demonstrates several of these techniques. In these samples, he is demonstrating both 귀곡성 *kwigoksong* [trans. "grieving ghost tone"] and 새성 *sesong* [trans. "thin sound"] another vocal technique that uses a kind of falsetto voice pitched harmonically in the head resonators (personal interview, Seoul, 2004).

The role of resonance in sound production

Resonance plays an important part in shaping the tonal quality of the *p'ansori* sound. The sources of resonance for a *p'ansori* artist, according to Park, are "nape" for a high relative pitch, "thoracic cavity" for a middle relative pitch, "solar plexus" for a lower middle relative pitch, "centre of abdominal region" for a low relative pitch, "spinal column" for the highest relative pitch, and "occipital region" for a high falsetto relative pitch (1995: 265). Linklater too explored resonating areas in some similar regions of the body (i.e. solar plexus) but expanded the areas in her resonating "pyramid" (1976: 25). Certain resonating areas such as "nasal" or "sinus" resonation are avoided in *p'ansori* because of the "undesirable projection" in the performance aesthetic. The main difference between the two methodologies seems to be not only which resonating areas are used but also the amount of muscle contraction used in accessing these resonating areas.

For example, the amount of muscle contraction the *p'ansori* vocalist uses in the resonating area of the throat not only changes the throat's space for resonation but also the potential for the breath/sound to pass through the throat and fill resonating spaces above the throat into the head resonators.

> The vocalization of *p'ansori* utilizes the increased pressure on larynx resulting from not lowering it, thus confining the resonating area. Due to the pharyngeal tension, it is mostly larynx that does the amplification as well as resonation. It creates pharyngeal tension that in turn characterizes *p'ansori's sŏngŭm* as being hard pressed and husky, rather than elevated and smooth.
>
> *(Park-Miller 1995: 268)*

The *p'ansori* vocalist uses what Park called "increased pressure" or what may visually look like "tension," which prevents the larynx from lowering. This laryngeal positioning contrasts with Anglo-American voice training practice. Martin wrote, "More recently, research has indicated that optimum resonance is achieved by being able to lower the larynx during voice production" (Martin 1991: 38).

The "natural" in *p'ansori* and the "natural/free" voice approach

Students' vocabulary and questions within the tradition of Anglo-American voice training have been influenced by training developments that changed drastically after the mid-1800s when "naturalism" entered the classroom. According to Martin, "This has eliminated any attempt at using mimesis, or imitation, which is the foundation upon which the actor creates a character. In its place, he attempts 'to be' the character" (Martin 1991: 29). In my work, the difference between mimetic training and "becoming" the character is negotiating the difference between *p'ansori* embodiment of role and contemporary Anglo-American theatre understandings of inhabiting role in the genre of "naturalism." Voice students who choose to perform using the traditions of "naturalism" in an attempt "to be" the character using Stanislavski-style means of building a character, often train their voices in the "natural" or "free" voice approach.[15]

Natalie Crohn Schmitt pointed to the connection between the work of Kristin Linklater and the audience expectations for the genre of "naturalism" as "believable" or "honest" actor's vocal response. She wrote,

> The widely used physical exercises of Jerzy Grotowski and the vocal exercises of Kristin Linklater are designed to bring actors to precisely this state of self-renunciation . . . if self-renunciation provides a more direct, "honest," response to the material, a response that neither participant nor audience expects, the ultimate effect may not be "believable" (thus flouting the sine qua non of the Stanislavski method) – because believability is, after all, a function of our expectations.
>
> *(Crohn Schmitt 1990: 13)*

Schmitt pointed to the performer/audience relationship in developing a performance aesthetic. The "natural voice" could be understood as unnatural if audience expectations of "believability" are not met. In this way, what is considered "natural" in the "natural voice" approach is agreed upon by both performer and audience, not necessarily what the performer feels is her "honest" response.

Kim Woo Ok noted that *p'ansori* performers also strive towards their understanding of "reality" in the portrayal of characters and scenes. Kim wrote,

> For the *p'ansori*, reality is defined as an exact reproduction of life, including characters, emotion, actions, situations, and contexts. Nature is considered to be a model for the performer, his constant point of reference. There are many much-relished legends of performers making bird-calls so perfect that real birds were attracted and of other performers creating sounds so eerie that audiences were chilled with the fear that ghosts were present. This question of the reality of the performance depends on context, of course, and is related to the whole question of the nature of the presentation of reality in

Korean art—i.e. what aspects are chosen for emphasis, what are neglected, how perception of reality is a function of Korean psychology as embodied in its language and complex social structure.

(Kim 1980: 110)

In a personal interview with Bae Il Dong, we discussed one example of this difference in vocal "realism" between the way in which actors embody characters vocally and the way in which *p'ansori* artists vocally embody characters. During his demonstration of *kyemyonjo*, Bae instructed that the voice must "pull in" the sound for grieving. He said that it was "only natural" when one grieves the death of one's father, for instance, that one would contain the grief inside the body, unlike joyful times when one would release the sound out of the body. Bae thoughtfully added that perhaps when he said "natural," he meant "we" [Koreans] tend to contain the sound of grief within the body and so this is represented in *p'ansori* as "pulling in" the sound (Bae Il Dong, personal interview, Seoul, 2004). This discussion points to not only differences in understanding what is "natural" but also understandings of how culturally realized representations of the "natural" are transmitted through training into performance.

Kim Se-jong, the late 19th century master *p'ansori* performer and theorist, wrote,

Suppose that one is to cry. At that moment he should actually cover his face with a handkerchief and fall forward to cry, or cry with loud wailings. Whatever he does, he should show the action of crying realistically and be appropriate to the moment. If the singer remains composed and displays no sad emotion at all but simply sits absentmindedly without any movement, making only the sound of a lament, he will have failed in his craft by separating singing from drama. Has not p'ansori lost its spirit when the audience feels neither moved nor sympathetic at all?

(Pihl 1994: 104)[16]

In responding to Kim's comments, Pihl observed, "Kim Se-jong's advice brings to mind Hamlet's instruction to his players: 'Suit the action to the word, the word to the action; with this special observance, that you o'erstep not the modesty of nature' (*Hamlet* III.ii.20)." Hamlet's advice to the players, or Kim Se-jong's advice to *p'ansori* performers, demonstrates how the training and performance of the "natural" evolve over time. Contemporary actors following the tradition of the "natural" or "free" voice and contemporary *p'ansori* artists, such as Bae Il Dong, may not agree with Hamlet's or Kim's advice to the performer. They may have their own contemporary understanding of "natural" developed to please historical/culture/discipline-specific audience expectations.

Strategies for talking about voice

Because *p'ansori* and my UK students speak different vocabularies to talk about voice and sound, I use both vocabularies when integrating these two traditions. I find that often intercultural/interdisciplinary work develops a kind of shared vocabulary to help articulate respective training techniques in conversation. The very terms my students and I choose to use suggest the way in which we were thinking about sound or voice at any given moment during a class exercise or devising process. Not translating the terms from one language to another became important in shaping our unique understanding of, and approach to, training the voice.

In my KNUA classrooms, using a combination of Korean and English in class was a practical methodology for an English-speaking instructor teaching Korean-speaking students. When I took my developing pedagogy to the UK, I continued to teach portions of the training in Korean. For instance, I do not want my English-speaking students to misunderstand *p'ansori dahnjeon* by translating it into English as "center" because the term "center" has a culture/discipline-specific context.[17] One way in which I address Choi's concern about reducing a tradition to a "mere technique" (refer Introduction) is to keep the language as part of the cultural context for the tradition. Language shapes the way a student thinks and talks about voice training. In my classes at KNUA and in the UK, *p'ansori* terms remained in Korean and "natural/free voice" terms remained in English. This is how we approached conversations about breath and sound production and understood it in the body/voice relationship.

As with Chapter Two, certain principles and practices explored in this chapter could be adapted and integrated into an intercultural/interdisciplinary approach to training actor's voices. Specifically, I adapt the way *p'ansori* creates a relationship during training between text and vocal text, through mimetic training, aural/oral repetition, and sound notation. I also adapt the way *p'ansori* builds character voices using this text/vocal text relationship. Later, in Chapter Six, I will explain how I integrate the "natural/free" voice approach to building character with *p'ansori* character voice structures by considering vocal form and function along a continuum. Finally, I would like to adapt the relationship between sung and spoken voice as vocal forms that frame the meaning of the text/vocal text. Because Anglo-American vocal training usually separates musical singing voice techniques from training the speaking voice in many acting conservatoires, I find a great deal of potential in adapting this approach from *p'ansori* to help actors address this separation.

Of the basic principles in *p'ansori*, I adapt my understanding of *p'ansori's* use of *eum-yang* as realized in the contract/release muscular cycle for breath and sound production, and rhythm cycles. I also adapt my understanding of *dahnjeons*. I integrate my understanding of *p'ansori* resonating centers, the use of muscle contract/release cycle to shape the resonating chambers, and vibration as a physical manifestation of *ki* (energy).[18]

Finally, I adapt the way *p'ansori* talks about sound and sound production, using language that is highly descriptive, suggesting both the sound and the function of the voice within the word. In the next chapter, I build on the preparation work from Chapters Two and Three, detailing how I integrate certain principles and practices from these two different traditions, beginning with a (re)consideration of the role of breath in training actors' voices.

Notes

1 Yi divides the Choson dynasty into three periods, early, mid, and late: Early Choson: the period from the reign of King T'aejo (1392–1398) to the reign of King Myongjong (1545–1567); Mid-Choson: the period from the reign of King sonjo (1567–1608) to the reign of King Kyongjong (1720–1724); the Late Choson: the period from the reign of King Yongjo (1724–1776) to the reign of King Sunjong (1907–1910) (Jang 2014: xii).

2 www.barbican.org.uk/theatre/event-detail.asp?ID=4276. Accessed 17 April 2018.

3 For the purposes of this discussion, I will define "text" as the word in print that is read visually and "performance text" as the aural and visual information in and surrounding the performance that are "read" visually/aurally/emotionally by the audience in order to understand the performance on both a literal and symbolic level. For the purposes of these video samples, I will consider "text" to mean the words, which includes the *p'ansori* narrative as well as the subtitles. Part of the performance text is "vocal text" or the way in which the words (text) are performed vocally, subject to audience interpretation.

4 I will capitalize the character name, as well as the roles of Narrator and Performer to help denote when the *p'ansori* performer inhabits these various roles during the telling.

5 *Sugung-ga* is based on the story of the Dragon King, a tortoise, and a wily hare. This story is believed to have stemmed from a tale about a tortoise and a hare in the early period of the Choson Dynasty. A brief synopsis: The Dragon King of the Underwater Palace is suffering from an ailment that can be cured only with the liver of a hare. The King thereupon summons the tortoise to journey to a forest and return with a hare, which the tortoise succeeds in doing by luring the hare with the wonderful prospects of living in the palace. The hare, after discovering his dangerous situation at the palace, coaxes the King to allow him to return to the forest by explaining that his liver was so much in demand that it finally became necessary to conceal it in a secret place and that he has, therefore, come without it. Upon hearing this, the Dragon King grants the hare permission to go back to the forest with the tortoise after the hare promises that he will return with his liver. Once in the forest, the hare ridicules the King's and tortoise's stupidity and is never seen again. But the hare is actually quite moved by the tortoise's loyalty to the King (Yi 1982: 263).

6 In this scene, Tortoise arrives on land after swimming through the cold sea. As a result, his jaw is stiff, inhibiting his pronunciation. Thus, when Tortoise calls for the Hare, he mistakenly calls down from the mountain Tiger. The scene between Tiger and Tortoise is comedic and fast-paced, relying on a set of storytelling conventions and character voices to switch quickly between the characters of Tortoise and Tiger and Narrator.

7 For a more detailed analysis of the many ways in which yin/yang or eum/yang in Korean can be found in *p'ansori*, see Chung (1998).

8 This includes Han Nongsŏn's private studio, Sŏng Uhyang's private studio, and *p'ansori* classrooms at KNUA under Master teachers Pak Yun Cho, Ahn Sook Sun, and Chung Hoi Suk.

9 Ahn Sook Sun was awarded Living National Treasure status in 1997 and was Artistic Director of the National Chan-geuk [Ch'anggŭk] Company.

10 Pihl is using the traditional name given to *p'ansori* performers and referring to how the tradition was established historically.

11 Also refer Willoughby (2000).

12 Scan image taken from Sŏng Uhyang's text version of Chunhyangga with my sound notation above the text.

13 Han Nongsŏn in 1981 achieved the position to inherit "Living National Treasure" status from the Korean government. She passed away in February 2002 and was awarded Living National Treasure status posthumously.

14 Moon states, "I believe that the sound quality of *p'ansori* is basically due to the permanent change (or, damage, should we call it?) which is, in turn, caused by an extensive and prolonged training. 'Mountain training' doesn't have to be 'mountain' training. It doesn't

matter where, but the mountains probably offered the least distraction with nobody to bother with the training" (e-mail interview, 23 January 2003).

15 Refer to the Introduction in which I noted the "hypothetical four-year training program" found in the back of our class text at KNUA, Linklater's *Freeing the Natural Voice* (1976), which links her approach to a "natural voice" with a Stanislavskian-style acting approach.

16 Pihl (1994: 104). Pihl is quoting Kim Se-jong from Chong No-shik's work *Chosun ch'angguk sa* [trans. "History of Korean singing drama"]. Seoul: Chosun ilbo sa, 1940: 63–64.

17 I have found that students are quite accepting of *p'ansori* terms in class and eventually use Korean language themselves, as mimicked from my in-class instruction. The more commonplace the language becomes in class, the less exotic it seems to them. My intention here is to use the language to represent the experience of the training, not represent some romantic or exotic notion of foreign voice traditions.

18 I explain my understanding of "ki" in Chapter Four.

References

Ahn Sook Sun. (2000). Personal interview, Seoul, South Korea.

Bae Il Dong. (2004). Personal interview, Seoul, South Korea.

Berry, C. (1973). *Voice and the Actor*. New York: Collier Books.

Choi, S.C. (2012). *Korean Psychology*. Seoul: Hakjisa.

Choi, S.C., Kim, C. W. (1998). "'Shim-Cheong' Psychology as Cultural Psychological Approach to Collective Meaning Construction," *Korean Journal of Social and Personality Psychology*, 12 (2), 79–96.

Choi, S.C., Kim, K. (2011). *Cultural Psychology: Psychoanalysis of Contemporary Korean People*. Seoul: Jisiksanupsa.

Chong, P. (1998). *Ch'unhyangga rŭl T'onghaesŏ pon Sin Chaehyo ŭi Chakka Ŭisik* [Sin Chaehyo's Literary View as Reflected in his Ch'unhyangga Text]. Unpublished MA thesis, Seoul National University, Seoul.

Chong, N.S. (1940). *Chosun ch'angguk sa* (History of Korean singing drama). Seoul: Chosun ilbo sa (sections trans. Marshall Pihl in *The Korean Singer of Tales*).

Chung, H.S. (2000). Personal interview, Seoul, South Korea.

Chung, S.S.Y. (1998). *The Impact of Yin and Yang Ideology in the Art of Korean P'ansori Tradition: An Analytical Study Based on the Late Mme. Pak Nok-Ju Version of P'ansori Hungbo-ga*. Unpublished PhD—Ethnomusicology, University of California, Santa Barbara.

Creutzenberg, J. (2011). "Korean Literature on Created Pansori (창작판소리)." https://seoulstages.wordpress.com/2011/07/08/korean-literature-on-created-pansori-창작판소리/. Accessed 30 July 2017.

Crohn Schmitt, N. (1990). *Actors and Onlookers: Theatre and Twentieth-Century Scientific Views of Nature*. Evanston: Northwestern University Press.

Hahn, M.Y. (1990). *Kugak: Studies in Korean Traditional Music*. Seoul: Tamgu Dang Publishing in Cooperation with Korea Research Foundation.

Han, N.S. (2000). Personal interview, Seoul, South Korea.

Heyman, A. (ed.). (1993). "Pansori," in *The Traditional Music and Dance of Korea*. Seoul: National Center for Korean Traditional Performing Arts, 207–220.

Howard, K. (2006a). *Perserving Korean Music: Intangible Cultural Properties as Icons of Identity: Perspective on Korean Music Vol. 1*. Aldershot: Ashgate Publishing.

Howard, K. (2006b). *Creating Korean Music: Tradition, Innovation and Discourse of Identity: Perspectives on Korean Music Vol 2*. Aldershot: Ashgate Publishing.

Hoyt, J. (2000). *Soaring Phoenixes and Prancing Dragons: A Historical Survey of Korean Classical Literature*. Korean Studies Series No. 20. Seoul: Jimoondang Publishing Company.

Im, C.T. (1981). "Iyagi wa P'ansori" [Tales of P'ansori], *Silch'ŏn Munhak*, 2, 329–365.

Jang, Y. (2002). "Audience Response to P'ansori and its Impact on Contemporary P'ansori Performance," *Asian Musicology*, 2, 137.

Jang, Y. (2014). *Korean P'ansori Singing Tradition: Development, Authenticity and Peformance History*. Plymouth: Scarecrow Press, Inc.

Killick, A. (2010). *In Search of Korean Traditional Opera: Discourses of Ch'angŭgk*. Honolulu: University of Hawai'i Press.

Kim, A.J., Graves, R.B. (1999). *The Metacultural Theater of Oh T'ae Sok: Five Plays from the Korean Avant-Garde*. Honolulu: University of Hawai'i.

Kim, J. (2012). *Experiencing Korean P'ansori as a Western-style Singer: A Vocal Interpretation of Dongjin Kim's Operas Based on Kim's Shin-Ch'ang-Ak*. Unpublished PhD thesis, Ball State University, Muncie.

Kim, T. (1978). "P'ansorisa Yŏn'gu ŭi Che Munje" [Problems in the Historical Study of P'ansori], in Cho Tongil and Kim Hŭnggyu (eds.) *P'ansori ŭi Ihae [Understanding P'ansori]*. Seoul: Ch'angjak kwa Pip'yŏngsa.

Kim, W.O. (1980). *P'ansori: An Indigenous Theatre of Korea*. Unpublished PhD thesis New York University, New York.

Lee, C.E. (2000). *Sugungga* [video]. Seoul: KBS Media. www.kbsmedia.co.kr. Accessed 17 April 2018.

Linklater, K. (1976). *Freeing the Natural Voice*. New York: Drama Book Publishers.

Martin, J. (1991). *Voice in Modern Theatre*. London: Routledge.

Mason, B. (1992). *Street Theatre and Other Outdoor Performance*. London: Routledge.

McCallion, M. (1988). *The Voice Book: For Actors, Public Speakers, and Everyone Who Wants to Make the Most of Their Voice*. London: Faber and Faber.

Moon, S.J. (2003). E-mail interview, 23 January 2003.

Nelson, J. (2015). *The Voice Exercise Book. A Guide to Healthy and Effective Voice Use*. London: Nick Hern.

Newlove, J. (1993). *Laban for Atcors and Dancers: Putting Laban's Movement Theory into Practice, a Step-by-Step Guide*. New York: Routledge.

Park, C. (2003). *Voices From the Straw Mat: Toward and Ethnography of Korean Story Singing*. Honolulu: University of Hawai'i Press.

Park-Miller, C.E. (1995). *P'ansori Performed: From the Strawmat to the Proscenium and Back*. Unpublished PhD—Ethnomusicology, University of Hawai'i, Honolulu.

Pihl, M.R. (1994). *The Korean Singer of Tales*. Cambridge: Harvard University Press.

Roy, N., Ryker, K., Bless, D. (2000). "Vocal Violence in Actors: An Investigation into its Acoustic Consequences and the Effects of Hygienic Laryngeal Release Training," *Journal of Voice*, 14 (2), 215–230.

Taehan Min'guk Yesurwŏn. (1973). *Survey of Korean Arts Traditional Music*. Seoul: National Academy of Arts.

Um, H.K. (2008). "New p'ansori in Twenty-First-Century Korea: Creative Dialects of Tradition and Modernity," *Asian Theatre Journal*, 25 (1), 24–57.

Um, H.K. (2013). *Korean Musical Drama: P'ansori and the Making of Tradition in Modernity*. Farnham: Ashgate Publishing.

Willoughby, H. (2000). "The Sound of Han: P'ansori, Timbre and a Korean Ethos of Pain and Suffering," *Yearbook for Traditional Music*, 32, 17–30.

Willoughby, H. (2002). *The Sound of Han: P'ansori, Timbre, and a South Korean Discourse of Sorrow and Lament*. Unpublished PhD, Columbia University, New York.

Willoughby, H. (2006). "The Voice of Globlization Melding Past and Present Korean Identities in Contemporary Korean Performances," *3rd World Congress of Korean Studies*, http://congress.aks.ac.kr/korean/files/2_1358498465.pdf. Accessed 30 July 2017.

Yi, Po-hyung. (1982). "What is Pansori?" *Annotated Pansori*, trans. Bang-song Song. Seoul: Britannica Corporation.

Yi, U. (1984). *Ch'unhyangjŏn ŭi Yŏksa chŏk Pyŏnmo wa Kŭ Ŭimi [Historical Changes in Ch'unhyangjŏn and their Implications]*. Unpublished MA thesis, Ewha Women's University, Seoul.

Yoo, J. (2018). *A Korean Approach to Actor Training*. London: Routledge.

Yu, Y. (1990). "Posŏong Sori ŭi P'ansorisajŏk Ŭiŭi," in Ch'oe Tonghyŏn and Yu Yŏngdae (eds.) *P'ansori Tongp'yŏngje Yŏn'gu [A Study of the Eastern School of P'ansori]*. Seoul: T'aehaksa.

4

THE ROLE OF BREATH IN TRAINING ACTORS' VOICES

Chapters Two and Three offered a short introduction of the two source traditions. The aim of the remaining chapters is to critically compare the "materials" of training from each of these traditions, suggesting where they diverge but also where they might interact. This chapter specifically investigates the role of breath and consciousness. Using insights from phenomenology, I attempt to articulate my understanding of the practices within both traditions.

Breath, as a topic in training actors' voices, has had a recent resurgence of interest.[1] Throughout 2007 to 2008, several different international conferences hosted by major voice organizations in the US and UK[2] offered workshops and presentations combining Anglo-American voice pedagogy with Asian principles and practices. Although training approaches differed in combinations of practice, similar "problems" continued to emerge. This chapter proposes one principal reason for the difficulties: the different ways these modes of training link breath with the "self" of the practitioner. Through a systematic and self-conscious examination of current pedagogy, one aim of this chapter asks how Anglo-American voice pedagogy might better interface with Asian practice—specifically, concepts of breath as "awareness" and body/mind unity in training actors' voices.

Beginning with a very brief reference to the larger body of mainstream Anglo-American voice texts, I demonstrate the prevalence of certain ideas and practices in training the breath as a foundation for training the actors' voice. The "natural/free" voice has been instrumental in laying the foundation of this mainstream training. Then, I suggest that many of the key principles relating to breath-use in p'ansori can also be found in other Asian modes of training, as another way of understanding certain ideas and practices related to breath. In this way, the aim is to demonstrate that the "problems" of interweaving the "natural/free" voice with adaptations of p'ansori cannot be solved simply by opting for other, seemingly more "compatible," training practices. The intention is to open up a conversation about breath as a material of training that carries with it worldviews that must be negotiated within the voice studio.

The "problem(s)" interweaving breath

The role of self within practice helps determine how breath is conceptualized and trained. Modern voice pedagogy emerges from a tradition of understanding the self of the actor through a Western biomedical model,[3] which I suggest is viewed through the lens of Cartesian philosophy.[4] By conceiving of the act of breathing as the act of creating a thought (Berry 1992: 26; Carey and Clark Carey 2008: 39; Fitzmaurice in Hampton and Acker 1997: 247–248; Morgan 2008: 86), training is able to construct one kind of relationship between thought/mind and breath/body.[5] The body/mind dualism is realized on a muscular level; specifically, the action of the diaphragm during involuntary/voluntary lung function. Involuntary breath understood as unconscious response is associated with the actor's self as biological matter of the body. Mind, or the will of the actor, understood as conscious motor control, is associated with the voluntary act of breathing and is conceptualized as representing the thoughts and emotions of the actor/character. During training, the actor is taught to become aware, or conscious, of the involuntary breath so that this action can serve as the model for training the voluntary breath. The impulse to speak is associated with the kinesthetic feeling of the body's preparation to supply breath as fuel for voicing. Through this process, both actor and audience can realize immaterial thought as playable action. Conscious awareness of the breath and conscious motor control are essential parts of training through this conceptual model.

For Japanese philosopher Yasuo Yuasa, "conscious bodily movement" is a key difference between Eastern and Western practice (Yuasa 1993: 28). In Western practice, "the mind that is subject dominates and moves the body that is object," but in Eastern "body-mind oneness" there is no longer a felt distinction between "the mind qua subject and the body qua object" (ibid.). A level of body/mind integration is assumed at the beginning of training. The function of training, then, is not to *create* a body/mind relationship, but instead to train towards further levels of integration (Kasulis and Dissanayake 1993: 303; Sellers-Young 1998: 177).

The practitioner does not train the breath, but trains the body/mind through the breath, cultivating *ki*, or energy. For Yuasa, *ki* is "a function which cannot be perceived by ordinary consciousness in everyday life, but is a new function which consciousness (or mind) is gradually able to perceive through mind-body training in mediation and breathing methods" (Yuasa 1993: 75–76). The manifestation of breath into *ki* means that breath does not remain conceptually or literally at the diaphragm, but travels through *dahnjeons* (energy centers) via *meridians* (channels) in the body. *Ki*, *dahnjeons*, and *meridians* are a part of an Eastern understanding of the body integral to Eastern medicinal practice and fundamental to the way the body functions. This body knowledge becomes the foundation for the transmission of embodied practices. Breath/*ki* may first be experienced through the movement of the act of breathing. As the bodymind reaches further levels of integration, the breath into *ki* is experienced as "an energy flow" independent of the physical process of breathing (Nearman 1982: 347). Through long-term rigorous practice, the performer learns how to shift *ki* as "awareness" through the body/mind, thus contributing to a sense of the actor's presence (Barba and Savarese 1999; Zarrilli 2008). I will return to this in the next chapter, which focuses on the role of "presence" and "energy" in training actors' voices.

This understanding of breath as "awareness" is different from training towards conscious awareness of the breath. In mainstream Anglo-American voice pedagogy, breath is understood in relation to the physical and psychological self of the practitioner, remaining attached to self throughout the training; in Eastern practice, the actor can transcend ego-identification and form "one body" with the audience in which the practitioner's self is obliterated in favor of "absorption" and "communion" (Leder 1990: 171; Nearman 1978: 325).

Eastern understandings of breath and *ki* offer alternative ways of thinking and talking about breath in training actors' voices—indeed offer a (re)consideration of the role of breath in Anglo-American voice training. Integrating *dahnjeon* breathing and *ki* with voice exercises can help students mediate between body and mind, between the involuntary and voluntary breath, between objectivity and subjectivity. This would better nurture the body/mind relationship that many voice trainers work towards through psycho-physical practice, a Western term used occasionally to better articulate the way the mind (psycho) and the body (physical) work together.[6]

The role of self in Anglo-American voice pedagogy

As mentioned in Chapter Two, the opening to Rodenburg's video *A Voice of Your Own* (1994) begins by explaining her understanding of a "natural" voice using the footage of a crying baby. Similarly, many other leading voice training texts also use the metaphor of a baby (Barton and Dal Vera 1995, 2011: 6; Carey and Clark Carey 2008: 3, 99; Houseman 2002: 5; Lessac 1960: 4; Linklater 2006: 20; McCallion 1988: 3–4; Turner 1950, 2007: 1). The way a baby breathes, particularly when crying, exemplifies a "natural" responsive breath—or unconscious, involuntary act of the body. But as the baby grows into an adult, she learns negative habitual body use that interrupts the muscular efficiency of the breathing mechanism. Sometimes this is understood as a loss of "kinaesthetic knowledge" (Carey and Clark Carey 2008: 3) or "the wisdom of the body" (Linklater 2006: 3). From this, the student learns a basic premise of the "natural/free" voice, which is shared as a founding principle with many contemporary mainstream voice approaches: that the voice is intimately connected with the self of the actor (Barton and Dal Vera 1995, 2011: 6–9; Berry 1973: 11; Carey and Clark Carey 2008: vi; Houseman 2002: xiv; Lessac 1960, 1967: 4–5; Linklater 2006: 8; McCallion 1988: Introduction; Rodenburg 1992: 4). Experiences that affect the self also affect the voice.

From the baby example, the student understands that she enters the studio already influenced by environmental conditioning, sociocultural messaging, effects of illness, and/or lifestyle choices that result in negative habitual use, limiting the potential of her breathing and voicing ability (Barton and Dal Vera 1995, 2011: 7; Berry 1973: 7–8; Carey and Clark Carey 2008: 3; Fitzmaurice in Hampton and Acker 1997: 17; Houseman 2002, xiv–xv; Lessac 1960, 6–8; Linklater 1976: 1; McCallion 4; Rodenburg 1992: 8; Turner 1950, 2007: 1).

The student usually begins training by increasing her physical, or conscious, awareness of the effects of such influence; for example, how these influences have created extraneous "tension," or excessive muscular contraction, blocking effective breath/voice use. In this early stage, most training is focused on body alignment and breathing exercises, understood as the foundation for effective vocal use.

In training towards this physical awareness, the embodiment of breath is usually understood through two difference classes of experience. Anatomical drawings, plastic models, and mirrors used to assist with self-observation objectify the body, with a tendency to reduce breath to musculature and lung function. These training tools and methods are often taught in conjunction with subjective kinesthetic breath-training exercises exploring one's "own," "individual," or "natural" voice (Barton and Dal Vera 1995, 2011: 13; Berry 1973: 16; Carey and Clark Carey 2008: vi; Houseman 2002: xiv; Lessac 1960: xi, xii, 30–42; Linklater 1976: 185; Rodenburg 1992: 118). Subjective exercises cultivate an awareness of the body as acquired identity, or self-identity; in this way, the actor comes "to know his voice both subjectively and objectively at the same time" (Berry 1992: 17).

Objective training experiences tend to be assigned to the realm of the body, while subjective training experiences associated with self-identity tend to be assigned to the mind, or will, of the actor. Linklater wrote that "[t]he mind and the body must learn to cooperate . . . [actors] must educate the voice into a union of self and body" (Linklater 2006: 8). This notion of self, when separated conceptually from body, means a continuous shifting between objectification of the embodiment of breath (object-body) with subjective experiences of the self breathing (subject-body). This is one way that Cartesian dualism influences Anglo-American voice practice in many classrooms.

Approaches to mind, body, and awareness

Master trainers David Carey and Rebecca Clark Carey train students towards greater "kinesthetic knowledge," as understood within a larger "learning cycle." Houseman also referred to this process in her approach (Houseman 2008: 7, 311). This learning cycle links physiological awareness with consciousness. Carey and Clark Carey wrote,

> [t]he learning cycle begins when we move from unconscious incompetence (habitually using muscles in a way that is inefficient without realising it), to conscious incompetence (gaining an awareness of the inefficient pattern). From there we can work our way to conscious competence (introducing a new use of the muscles through exercise and focused attention), and finally

to unconscious competence (using the muscles in a more efficient way without having to think about it).

(2008: 7)

In this context, "awareness" means a conscious realization of, or focused attention on, the self as biological matter of the body. The goal is to work towards changing body patterns through conscious motor control or a new use of the muscles. Barton and Dal Vera advocate a similar "conscious" approach to training when they write, "You have been speaking all your life, but *unconsciously*. Your conscious vocal life begins today" (Barton and Dal Vera 1995, 2011: 6, italics in original).

Almost 50 years earlier, Lessac was teaching a similar approach. He wrote, "We cannot set out simply to break an established habit; through physical reeducation, we must create new habits to supplant the old ones" (1960: 7). This includes "becoming aware of the natural breathing process" (30) through "memoriz[ing] the action-sensation of the moments in these areas . . . repeat the feeling and you will repeat the action" (31). Lessac encouraged,

> gain mastery of your body . . . with practice you can gain such control over your body as a whole and over the individual muscle groups that you can choose the appropriate balance between action and rest in any act effortlessly and at will.
>
> *(1960: 44–45)*

Here mind/will trains towards "control" of the body as object. This act of "reeducating" the body is similar to F.M. Alexander's idea of "reeducation" in his practice, mentioned in Chapter Two. This way of training, although articulated slightly differently from one practitioner to another, has maintained its prominence in Anglo-American voice pedagogy over time despite the inclusion of Asian practices in some practitioners' methods, such as Chi Kung and yoga (Carey and Clark Carey 2008: xvi, 4) or shiatsu and tai chi (Houseman 2008: 20, 40). When interweaving Asian practice and mainstream voice training, the differences between body/mind dualism and bodymind are a perennial "problem."

This way of thinking about, and therefore training the body, is different from Eastern modes of training, as Yasuo Yuasa explains:

> [In Western practice] the mind that is subject dominates and moves the body that is object, and this is conscious bodily movement. In the state of body-mind oneness, the mind moves while unconsciously becoming one with the body. That is, there is no longer a felt distinction between the mind qua subject and the body qua object; the subject is simultaneously the object, and the object is simultaneously the subject. The movement of the object that is the body is such that it is wholly the movement of the mind that is subject . . . Zeami[7] calls this state "no-mind" [*mushin*] or "emptiness" [*ku*].
>
> *(1998: 28)*

In the final states of training, Zeami's "no-mind" and Carey and Clark Carey's (and Houseman's) "unconscious competence" are different, because of the way consciousness involves the distinction of mind, or will, of the practitioner.

Within Anglo-American voice training, levels of consciousness are assigned to different types of breathing. The involuntary breath can be understood as an "unconscious response by the diaphragm to a need for oxygen," an act of the body's autonomic system (Fitzmaurice in Hampton and Acker 1997: 248). Voluntary breath can be understood as "conscious motor control" (ibid.), an act of will [mind], because a kind of decision or choice is made in the quality and duration of the breath. When the involuntary and voluntary breath are separated and assigned to acts of the body or the mind, the body/mind split is actualized on a muscular level, specifically at the diaphragm.[8]

When mind, or will, interrupts the muscular efficiency of the system for breathing, voice exercises teach the student how to "get out of your own way" (Carey and Clark Carey 2008: 98–99) or "by-pass our will" in order to experience how "when the body needs breath it will breathe of its own accord" (Rodenburg 1993, 2001: 149). Linklater wrote that in order to "get to know our breathing process . . . we need to get out of the way" (in Boston and Cook 2009). For Michael McCallion, former master trainer at the Royal Academy of Dramatic Art (RADA), London, UK, the baby has "good use" of her body, because the baby "hasn't learned to *get in the way* of its own efficient functioning, it uses its body in the way it was designed to be used" (1988: 3–4, emphasis added). This approach assumes that mind and body are ontologically separate. *Who is in the way?* I am—me as self-identity seated in the mind/will of the actor. *What am I getting in the way of?* The body as biological matter, objectified as a breathing mechanism.

The site of the diaphragm is one area in which mind and body must learn to cooperate. Berry wrote,

> We have to see the breath not simply as the means by which we make good sound and communicate information; but rather we have to see it as the physical life of the thought, so that we conceive the breath and the thought as one.
>
> *(1992: 26)*

Similarly, Catherine Fitzmaurice, founder of Fitzmaurice Voicework, teaches that "'[i]nspiration' denotes both the physical act of breathing in, and the mental act of creating a thought" (Fitzmaurice in Hampton and Acker 1997: 247–248). Carey and Clark Carey teach, "We conceive with the in-breath, and we express with the out-breath" (Carey and Clark Carey 2008: 39). When in-breath and thought meet in one responsive act at the diaphragm, training can create a kind of body/mind relationship.

From my experience in working through this conceptual model, I understand this approach as helping to realize immaterial thought as physical action.[9] The beginning of a thought physically realized in the inhalation becomes the inception, perhaps conception, of a playable action for performer and audience. The breath/action continues throughout the exhalation as speech. When the breath/thought/speech ends, the action ends. But because the actor must take yet another breath or else suffocate, the end of one breath actually platforms into the next breath, which signals yet another playable action. For the audience, witnessing the actor/character breathing becomes part of meaningful storytelling. The breath, as seen and interpreted on the actor's body, is understood by the audience as thought. And so, the action of the performance journeys forward, literally and symbolically, on the breath.

In this way, both actor and audience perceive that "how we breathe is how we think; or rather, in acting terms, how the character breathes is how the character thinks" (Berry 1992: 26). Breath as a signifier of immaterial thought points to the body's role in thinking that is located, not in the brain, but in the diaphragm. In a sense, the student is "thinking" with the body.

This way of working has certain similarities with current, emerging philosophies of the voice.[10] Italian philosopher Adrianna Cavarero's work theorizing vocal expression asserted that before the Platonic view locating thought in the head, "the Greeks were thus convinced that thinking was done with the lungs, not the brain" (Cavarero 2005: 63). Building her argument in part on R. B. Onian's study (1988), she links this ancient Greek way of understanding breath with modern science:

> The affinity between thought and speech—or better, the derivation of the first from the second— situates the mind and the intellectual activities in the respiratory apparatus and the organs of phonation. It is, so to speak, the *phone* that decides the physiology of thought . . . In the final analysis, the strangeness of the ancient account depends on a single factor: the links that bind thought to speech and thus anchor it in the breast.
>
> *(2005: 63–65)*

The way Cavarero theorized breath is similar to the way modern voice trainers talk about breath. Linklater wrote that "[t]he actor's brain must *be* his or her body" (Linklater 2006: 9, emphasis in original) and thus instructed:

> Imagine that your mind (the impulse-dispatcher), your feelings (impulse-receiver), and your breath are all in the same place: the center of your body . . . Feel that your breath and your observing mind are both in the same place: the center of your body. Make sure that you are not split in two, with part of you sitting up in your head, commenting from above.
>
> *(1976: 28)*

Breath as thought "anchored in the breast" or located in "the center of your body" means that breath remains attached to the corporeal experience of lung function. Also, this way of thinking about breath heightens the importance of the diaphragm in training. In Fitzmaurice's approach, the diaphragm becomes the physical site for "healing the culturally prevalent body/mind split" (Fitzmaurice in Hampton and Acker 1997: 248). Training the diaphragm becomes central to the way the actor realizes the breath and thought as one. First, the actor must become aware or conscious of the way in which the diaphragm works during involuntary breathing, the kinesthetic awareness of the diaphragmatic "recoil" or feeling of the musculature springing into action that happens when the body needs oxygen (Berry 1973: 25–29; Carey and Clark Carey 2008: 47; Houseman 2002: 68; Linklater 2006: 46; Rodenburg 1993, 2001: 149, 2007: 270). This becomes the model for training the voluntary breath. The kinesthetic feeling for the need for oxygen is intertwined with an artistic concept of the "need to communicate" (Linklater 2006: 15) or "need for words" (Rodenburg 1993, 2001). Berry wrote that "[j]ust as breathing is a vital function, so the need to make sound to convey our needs is vital. Words came about because of the physical needs to express a situation" (1973: 16).

A good training example of this process, an exercise I have used in my own classroom, is Carey and Clark Carey's "breath and thought" exercise (Carey and Clark Carey 2008: 88–89). This teaches the student how to "practice joining the intent to speak . . . to the in-breath" (ibid.). Students begin this exercise by speaking words generated from their own thoughts. With a partner, the student is asked to "consciously engage your in-breath through the ribs as you think of something nice to say [to your partner]." Then, after several repetitions, students replace their own thoughts with "a line from a scene or speech." The goal is to continue engaging "your in-breath as you connect to the impulse behind the line, and then speak it" (ibid.). Through this process, students learn to transfer their own thought/breath impulse to a thought that is not their own.

Berry wrote that "[b]ecause you are dealing with words that are not your own, that come off a printed page, you have to be continually finding ways to make them your own" (Berry 1973: 16). The concept of making words your own underpins many practical exercises and is an intentional blurring of authorship. The breath/thought/word appears to originate from the actor, not the playwright. Perhaps more than this, the words do not simply *appear* "organic to what we are saying" (Berry 1992: 26), but in fact become "organ-ic," or from the organs—in this case, the lungs. Other approaches that teach ways of embodying the text sometimes characterize this process as "rooting" the spoken word into the breath (Berry 2001: 89; Rodenburg 1993, 2001: 150), or "the ability to breathe the word" (Rodenburg 1993, 2001: 89), or creating a "sense of speaking from the diaphragm area" (Houseman 2002: 100). In this way, "we have made the thought our own physically through the breath" (Berry 1992: 26). I will return to this later in Chapter Six when investigating the idea of the voice "authoring" the text.

By collapsing the need to communicate or the need for words with the need for oxygen, lung function becomes the literal and metaphoric fulfillment of all communicative needs. At the highest level of practice, "a perfect triangle [playwright/ actor/audience] of communication eventually forms with the word 'need' labelling each apex" (Rodenburg 1993, 2001: 96–97). "Need" is important to the teaching vocabulary of contemporary voice training; it not only suggests the kinesthetic origins of the breath, but insists that each breath/word is literally and artistically necessary. Working in this way heightens the actor's experience of speaking. By focusing on the experience of experiencing breathing/speaking, the actor creates afresh her/his relationship to a well-rehearsed play script, or "we begin to experience how the thought itself is moving" (Berry 1992: 26). This process also creates an aural difference to speech, a sense of urgency or purpose or importance. In this way, training gives "purpose to the breath" (ibid.).

This approach, however, also creates a way of training that perhaps focuses too much on the self of the actor. The actor is focused on her own experience. The training begins from the actor's experience as a social being and how that experience has affected the voice. The training continues into an investigation of the biological and psychological understandings of self, creating self-awareness. The breath is taught to respond to the needs of the self, both biological and artistic. The words become my own through literal embodiment. The origin of contemporary Anglo-American voice training is the self of the actor, and through this, breath training can be understood as "self"-centered.

Beyond Western biomedical models and understandings of self: Bodymind unity and breath as "awareness"

In contrast, Eastern arts practice does not necessarily teach the breath to respond to the needs of the self, service speech, or remain at the diaphragm. Through the breath, the bodymind is trained, cultivating *ki* (energy). At first, *ki* may be experienced through the movement of the breath, but later the student experiences "an energy flow capable of being directed independently of the physical process of breathing" (Nearman 1982: 347). There is a difference between voice that comes forth from the breath, and voice that comes forth from the *ki* (Nearman 1983: 60, 63). The breath/*ki* of the practitioner is trained towards harmonizing with the *ki* of the audience in order to "form one body [*t'i*]," a neo-Confucian concept that trains towards obliterating the self, or ego, of the practitioner, and connects with that which is outside of the self (Leder 1990: 156). Through long-term, rigorous practice, forming one body leads not only to better aural/oral communication, but also a sense of communion or togetherness.

The breath in Asian practice developed from classical Chinese metaphysics and it does not remain conceptually or literally at the diaphragm. The breath circulates through *dahnjeons* (energy centers) via *meridian* channels (*kyung lack* in Korean) traveling down the back of the body (*yang* energy) and up the front of the body (*eum* or *yin* energy) in a cyclical process, alternating between *eum*/*yang* polarities in the body (Yoo 2007: 87; Yuasa 1993: 75–76).

There are three internal and four external *dahnjeons*. The lower *dahnjeon*, also referred to as *tandien* or *tan-den* (Japan) or *nabhi mula* (Sanskrit, meaning "the root of the navel"), is located two inches below the navel and two inches inside the body. The middle *dahnjeon* is located two inches inside the body behind the sternum, and the upper *dahnjeon* is located roughly between and just above the eyes within the forehead (I have also heard this referred to as the "mind's eye," "inner eye," or "third eye"). There are four external *dahnjeons*: one is located in the palm of each hand where the center fingernail touches the palm while fisting (*jangsim* in Korean), and one on the bottom of each foot, just below the ball when the foot is flexed (*yongchun* in Korean).

Japanese actor/director Yoshi Oida wrote that "[t]here is an old saying: 'Ordinary people breathe through the chest [diaphragm], wise people breathe through the hara [located in the lower *tan-den*], and the skilled person breathes through the feet'" (Oida and Marshall 1997: 89). Oida's assertion that one can breathe through the *tan-den* or through the feet relocates the act of breathing away from the site of the diaphragm, defines breathing as a practice that involves more than lung function, and conceptualizes the role of breathing apart from its function as fuel for speech.

The way that breath can move around the body is not necessarily a metaphor, but a physical reality of the manifestation of breath into *ki* (energy). Breathing through the lower *dahnjeon* cultivates *ki* (Korean, Japan), *chi* (China), or *prana* or *pranavayu* (India), the "sensation of power" that results when training the mind through the body. According to Yuasa, *ki* is "a function which cannot be perceived by ordinary consciousness in everyday life, but is a new function which consciousness (or mind) is gradually able to perceive through mind-body training in meditation and breathing methods" (1993: 75–76). For Korean Dahnhak practitioner Lee Seung-Heun there are three types of *ki*: *Won-ki* is "inherited energy" the fetus receives from its mother in uterus, before breath as lung function is possible; *Jong-ki* is "acquired energy" from nourishment such as eating and breathing oxygen; and the third type is *Jin-ki*, "cultivated energy" through training processes such as meditation that develops mindful concentration of the breath (Lee 1999b: 33; Yoo 2007: 88). It is this third type of *ki* that I address here.

Through training, the performer learns how to shift *ki* as "awareness" in/through/ around the actor's bodymind, which is noticed by the audience and contributes to meaningful storytelling. Practitioner/scholar Phillip Zarrilli describes this state of awareness as "poised to act 'on the edge of a breath,'" allowing the actor to "ride an impulse through the breath/action/thought . . . what Herbert Blau calls 'the necessary'—the 'consciousness that must be seen, what would make the word come even if there were no breath'" (Zarrilli 1997: 103–116; Zarrilli and Boyette 2007: 71–72). This "consciousness that must be seen" is also a consciousness that can be *heard* and is a material condition of performance. When breathing through the lower *dahnjeon* is applied to vocal arts, the resultant sound manifests a sense of strength or energy that cannot be explained through the body's muscularity alone (Park 2003: 157). For example, in *p'ansori,* Chin Pong-gyu wrote that *tanjonsong* (*dahnjeon* voice) comes from the *dahnjeon* and can be identified by its sound as different from *poksong* (literally, abdomen voice), which comes from the abdomen (Um 1992: 128).

Part of this sound difference results from combinations of muscular usage and *ki* energy, in which various levels of *ki* as concentrated focus strengthens or manifests the resultant sound differently. *Ki*, combined with a muscular contract/release cycle of the abdominal muscles, is part of "the continuous alternation of tension and release" and creates "a common aesthetic feature of much [Korean] musical performance" (Lee 1999a). "This alternation may be present not only in the sonic design of the music, but also in the conditions by which the sound is produced, such as performance postures and some characteristic organological structures" (ibid.).

The way in which Zarrilli, through his work with Asian principles and practices, understands "discovering what is 'necessary' in the performative moment [is] not a decision of the mind, but one of learning how to embody a sediment decisiveness in space, through time" (Zarrilli 1997: 105). This understanding of what is "necessary" is different from responding to the needs of the self in Anglo-American voice pedagogy. In this context, breath is not a reaction to need, but instead is an action independent of biological and individual needs. Zarrilli quotes Blau: "Which comes first? The doing or the conceiving? What is the connection between the source of energy and the theatrical use you make of it? . . . Almost before thought, done" (ibid.).

Unification of *ki*/mind/breath must be achieved in order to execute a task well (Yuasa 1993: 76). This means that for many Asian modes of training, one does not train the breath only, but simultaneously trains *ki* and mind. Mind is essential to the process of training of the voice. As introduced in Chapter Three, Park wrote that "[v]oice is the acoustic reflection of the mind" (Park 2003: 189).[11] She described the function of *sori* in *p'ansori* via Son (Zen) master Wolgwang, teacher to *p'ansori* master Song Hungnok in the Paegun Mountain:

> *Sori* is the sound of all creations in the universe. It is the acoustic reflection of joy, sorrow, love, pleasure; of the four pains, birth, aging, illness, and death. It is the sound of the ocean that unifies into one salty tub all water flows . . . *Sori* exists outside *sori*.
>
> *(2003: 62)*

Breathing from the lower *dahnjeon* is fundamental to realizing the way that sound/voice (*sori* and *sŏngŭm*) is the acoustic reflection of mind and is understood as existing outside of itself, as being a part of everything. Returning to the quote I raised in Chapter Three, Park translates from the Confucian *Book of Rites*,

> Music rises as the mind is moved. First, the mind moves as it is touched by things external. The mind, touched, moves and it creates sound. Sound is distinguished in clear turbid, slow and fast, high and low, and these qualities interact with one another creating changes. The changes create melody, called *um*.
>
> *(2003: 189)*

Mind can be understood as a manifestation of breath. In Anglo-American voice, the breath, when "touched" or initiated, reacts to a situation or responds internally to a thought or emotion. Once touched, breath passes through the vocal folds and realizes thought/mind through sound/speech. This is an application of breath as fuel for speech via a biomedical model. In the above *Book of Rites* passage, there is a sense that the breath is not simply moving or passing through the vocal folds to generate vibrations understood as "sound"; instead, the notion of sound itself is a combination of the physical manifestation of breath, energy, body, mind, and consciousness that interacts with the world. Similar to Korean *p'ansori* principles, "recitation in Noh, unlike that customarily found in Western theatre, incorporates a vibratory theory that is fundamental not only to Zeami's discussion, but also to much of traditional Sino-Japanese practice" (Nearman 1982: 338).

If in Anglo-American voice pedagogy breath is trained to respond to the needs of the individual self, in the principle of "forming one body," the practitioner's needs are obliterated in favor of "absorption" and "communion" (Leder 1990: 171).[12] Within Japanese Noh drama, Zeami identifies the principle of one body as a fundamental component of performance and the best performers strive towards harmony between the audience's *ki* and performer's *ki*. A "level of rapport is reached where actor and audience are as one" (Nearman 1978: 325).

For philosopher and physician Drew Leder, forming one body is a process that creates a "profound interconnection between body and world [and] invites an ontology and ethics of interconnection" (Leder 1990: 161). Leder describes the practice as he understands it through meditation:

> The meditator finds that he or she "is breathed" as much as the breather. Watching the breath come in and go out for minutes or hours, one is saturated by the presence of a natural power that outruns the "I." Breathing simply happens and happens and happens. There is no need for wilful management; all is accomplished without effort on one's part. Thus breathing becomes the very prototype of Zen/Taoist *wu-wei*, literally translated as "non-action." This term refers to the effortless acting typical of one who has broken free from ego-identification.
>
> *(1990: 171)*

In contrast, Anglo-American voice, through constant referencing of the actor's self, has difficulty moving away from the ego of the practitioner. Berry wrote that "the voice is extremely sensitive to our own ego . . . it is tied up with how we think of ourselves—our self-image" (Berry 1992: 16). During training, breath remains attached to the self through the ownership of "your voice." According to Berry,

> [t]he breath goes in, and the sound comes out—you are touching down to your centre, you are finding the "I" of your voice. When you find this it is as though you belong, you are present in what you are saying. You will then find the breath touching off sound like a drum. You will find that you will not have to use a great deal of breath, because the breath will be made into

sound. It is economy of effort. When you find this absolutely right use of breath the voice will be effortless, it will impel itself. This is where your true energy is. This is what I mean by rooting the voice.

(Berry 1973: 22)

Leder's description of breath in Zen meditation and Berry's description of breath use in "rooting the voice" are compellingly similar. And yet, the position of the self within the practice is fundamental to their difference. In Leder's description, the "I" is obliterated; in Berry's, the practitioner is finding the "I." The self as ego-identification is maintained and the breath remains understood through a bio-medical model. Effortlessness is understood through economy of effort, a reference to the body's musculature. For Leder, "non-action" is accomplished without effort, understood as no willful management. Breathing as a prototype of *wu-wei* is a kind of breathing that in Anglo-American voice training terms has not been given a purpose, because there is no need invested in this act.

My training experiences in Zen meditation (Hwa Gye Sa temple, Seoul) as well as workshops with Cicely Berry have led me to experience breath in these different ways. Concepts of the breath are dependent on culture and discipline-specific concepts of the body. Breath is not a universally understood physiological process able to be reduced to lung function (object-body). Also, breath understood subjectively (subject-body) is equally problematic, in part because the "lived body" is heavily influenced by the sociocultural understandings of self and the place of body as self within practice. As argued in Chapter One within the discussion of "embodiment," the body is not a stable site for learning; I find, however, the fluidity within this instability creatively useful, because it gives me room to negotiate different conceptual models of training.

Benefits of integrating *dahnjeon* breathing and *ki* into the "natural/free" voice approach

Leder's and Berry's descriptions are examples of East/West differences in practice, but such differences need not be set in an oppositional relationship. By incorporating breath/*ki* with Anglo-American voice training into an intercultural approach that places both traditions along a continuum of training, students can shift between the "I" of the voice (focus on self) and towards the self that harmonizes with others (forming one body). This movement is possible through the "intercourse between mind and *ki*" (Yuasa 1993: 89). Yuasa translates this following from the Daoist book of meditation, *The Secret of the Golden Flower:* "When mind moves, *ki* moves. When breathing is subtle, the movement of the mind is subtle. This is because *ki* moves with breathing, affecting the activities of the mind" (ibid.).

When harmonizing with the audience, both practitioner and audience become present in what is being said. The audience is not only hearing the words, but listening. In fact, the act of listening to the actor's voice/speech becomes so involved at the highest level that "the speaking of words comes to an end and the mind's operations are extinguished" (Nearman 1978: 324). In other words, the audience "is no longer aware of the act of acting . . . the integration of actor, acting, and what is acted is complete. Its external mark is No-Mark" (ibid.).

"No-Mark" is different from "we perceive that . . . how the character breathes is how the character thinks" (Berry 1992: 26). The *perception* of breath is a kind of external mark or marking of the breath on the body of the performer in role. The differences can be negotiated by conceiving of these practices as part of a larger continuum of training: students can move between the perception of breath as mark and "no mark" by developing the means to shift their perception as "awareness" through breath/*ki*.

Could audiences also move between the perception of breath as mark and "no mark" along a continuum of listening? How audiences perceive breath that is marked and how that marking contributes to meaningful storytelling would depend, in part, on their familiarity with the conventions of the type of perfor-mance they are watching/listening to. Also, not all audiences at every performance achieve "forming one body" with the performer(s). Each performance in each culture/discipline-specific context is negotiated. In this way, the continuum of practices I am advocating is not perceivable universally to all audiences.

From the actors' position, I argue that a continuum of training that teaches various ways of perceiving thus places Eastern and Western traditions in a polar relationship, but I am not arguing that it is universally achievable in every class-room. Here I am borrowing Roger Ames' definition of polarity, who wrote: "I want to claim that mind and body are polar rather than dualistic concepts, and as such, can only be understood by reference to each other" (in Kasulis, Ames, and Dissanayake 1993: 158). For me, the process of interweaving the principles and practices of different training traditions inside of my body/voice can be understood in reference to each other; each tradition becomes an embodied context for learn-ing the practice of another tradition. Through trial and error as well as strategically designed interactions, the different trainings inside of me can interface. These combinations create different body knowledges from which I am able to develop alternative methods and models for training my voice.

In my experience, integrating breath/*ki* with the "natural/free" voice approach creates more than effective oral/aural communication; it creates a feeling of togeth-erness or "comunitas" that is a palpable, material condition of live performance. Um Haekyung equates Victor Turner's comunitas (Turner 1969: 96) with her under-standing of *p'an* in *p'ansori* as the "integration and interaction between performers and audience members" creating the "communicative performance space of *p'an*" (Um 2008: 41). Park suggests that *p'an* is the "flow" of the performance between the performer and audience resulting in an authentic experience (Park 2000: 272–273). The cultivation and use of *ki* through the breath is fundamental to creating this feeling of connectedness with others and to generate focus and shift awareness. I will return to this in the next chapter when discussing "presence" and "energy."

Perhaps in actor training, a feeling of connectedness might be described as "being in the moment," similar to Berry's description of the "I" of the voice as being "present in what you are saying." But being in the moment as I have understood it as both a professional actor and trainer of actors is an experience from the performer's perspective. Being present in what I am saying keeps the focus of the training on me. When my needs are physically represented in my breath I am tempted towards self-absorption, instead of becoming absorbed in the world around me.

Forming one body within non-Western paradigms as I have practiced and understood them is not an experience located in and generating from the practitioner's self. Not only is there no longer a distinction between mind (subject) and body (object), but there also is no longer a distinction between "me" and "you," "performer" and "audience." My aim in including Asian principles and practices with adaptations of the "natural/free" voice is to help mediate between objectivity and subjectivity. Integrating forming one body as a key principle helps the actor to use breath as the means by which she continuously connects with the audience.

By moving away from a biomedical model during training towards other models of experience, I am able to think and talk about breath differently, thus training towards different ways of using breath in the studio. Berry wrote in regards to her own international work:

> I have talked at some length about this work in other countries because with the increasing interest in cross-cultural exchange, I think it is important that we recognise and meet those differences, and we do not blur over them or pretend they are not there.
>
> *(2001: 63)*

This comparative study not only critically examines the differences in East/West practice, but does so to suggest one way that trainers can negotiate these differences in a creatively useful way. The next section offers an example of how this discussion underpins practical exercise. It also aims to demonstrate how *dahnjeon* breathing might be adapted and interwoven with Anglo-American voice training through a series of exercises I developed for my classrooms.

Dahnjeon breathing sequence

The overall structure of this sequence is an organized series of yoga asana positions that gradually "wean" the student from the floor to a standing position. Each asana uses the hardness of the floor, gravity, and the weight of the student's body to feel the breath/sound travel through her body, outside her body and across a distance to a listener. As she leaves the floor into a standing position, she must take responsibility for realizing the breath/sound production that gravity and the asana position was helping create moments before.

Aims: To train towards muscular efficiency in order to support the breath through the body, out of the body and across a distance to the listener. Through long-term, rigorous practice, an additional aim is to create further levels of bodymind integration, cultivating *ki* (energy), which will give the student's sound a sense of strength beyond muscular strength and contribute to vocal "presence," a feeling of being in the here and now.

- Directions:In each position, match each inhalation with a muscular release and each exhalation with an efficient contraction. This intertwines each breath cycle with a muscular contract/release cycle. During each breathe cycle, work towards realizing each asana position to discover how the body helps guide the breath as it travels through you, out of you, and connects with the world around you.
- Next, add simple counting, to the number ten perhaps, training towards listening and feeling the growing efficiency of the skeletal-musculature. When the student speaks the words, "one," "two," "three," and so on, ask the student to try to think of these words as simple vowel/consonant combinations that prepare her for more complex words. As she counts, she should focus on the feelings inside her body while also listening to the sound. This creates a heightened sense of these processes or perhaps becomes a "self" conscious process of the technique she is developing.
- Now, count again, only this time add an awareness of *ki* strength, working towards feeling and hearing a sense of strength or support for the voice that seems effortless or efficient beyond muscular efficiency.
- Finally, replace counting with a poem or other piece of text while realizing each position. This step introduces language and vocal expressiveness into the body/voice. The aim of this final step is to work towards combining technical proficiency with vocal expressiveness. When the student lives in each position or transitions between positions, she should notice how the body affects the voice, the sound, and her ability to breath. Ask her to work towards feeling and hearing how the words emerge from her body. Ask her as the words emerge, to try to link the feeling and sound of the words with the sense of what she is saying. Ask her to try to experience the experience of speaking, which should through repetitive long-term practice place her in the here and now as she says each word, sentence, idea. Once she is standing speaking text at the end of the training sequence, ask the student to continue speaking her text working towards feeling and hearing a "strength" or focus and concentration of the sound within her speaking voice that shows intensity and quality and encourages the listener to involve themselves in what is being said. Ask the student to work towards connecting with a listener and really communicating what she is saying.

Note: Remind the student that she must be attentive to the transitions between positions as well as live in each position itself. In this way, she can feel and hear how the architecture of the body shapes breath/sound production in motion and stillness, investigating the openness and closure of spaces in her body, which influences breath/sound quality. Most importantly, as she embodies the sequence, she must "taste" (Oida and Marshall 1997: 28) each asana position as she realizes it through the growing integration of her bodymind.[13]

Below, the brief description of each asana position, directions for realizing the position, accompanied by a photo, addresses *ki* cultivation, bodymind integration as well as muscular contract/release cycles within the lower *dahnjeon*. However, for a readership familiar with Anglo-American voice training biomedical models, the descriptions primarily address the skeletal-musculature. The directions refer to: spinal alignment for more efficient skeletal-muscular use and muscular contraction of the pelvic floor, transversus abdominis, internal obliques, (perhaps) external obliques, and rectus abdominis depending on position and intensity of the muscular action. Also included in the directions are questions to provoke a learning response. Ask the student to try her best to address each question with her bodymind, but do not expect an "answer" or immediate result. She must commit to long-term, rigorous practice as she would with any training in order to begin realizing integrations of bodymind and *ki* cultivation and their beneficial effects on her breath/sound production.

- Figure 4.1 demonstrates position one: a compliment to the "Death" pose [*savasana*] in Hatha Yoga. Aims: to use the hardness of the floor, gravity, and the weight of the body to feel the muscle groups of the lower *dahnjeon* during a contract/release cycle realized through resistance to the floor. To heighten the student's awareness of the relationship between the placement of the spine and the placement of the breath. [Note: Ask the student to place her "mind's eye," or focused attention, into her back and notice how the slightest movement of the tailbone provides different forms of support to the lower *dahnjeon*].

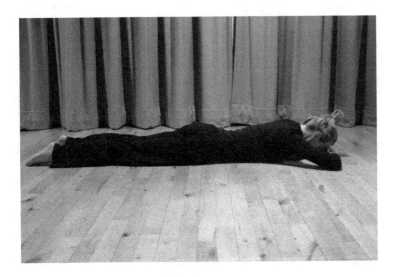

FIGURE 4.1[14]

- Figure 4.2 demonstrates position two (right and left legs): leg curls.

  Aims: With one leg at a time curled under the body on one side, the aim is to increase the awareness of the working musculature during a full contract/release cycle. [Note: Allow the abdomen to rest on the thigh of the curled leg when in a released position. During the inhalation, notice how the musculature pushes against the curled leg. Ask the student if during the exhalation, can she feel the musculature contract away from the thigh? The feeling against the thigh helps her determine if she is accomplishing the full contract/release cycle within the abdomen].

FIGURE 4.2

- Figure 4.3 demonstrates position three: "Half Lotus."[15]

  Aim: To create awareness of a "seat," or triangle of support for the lower *dahnjeon* and a feeling of lifting the pelvic floor to support the voice through the body, out of the body, and across a distance to the listener. [Note: The "seat" is comprised of three points—each buttock and the groin. You can feel the "seat" or pelvic floor release as it rests on the floor like a base for the spine. As the pelvic floor contracts, it lifts slightly away from the floor. This contraction will help create the intra-abdominal pressure the vocalist needs to travel the breath/sound through the body, out of the body and across the distance to the listener. The student should feel the muscles surrounding her anus engage during inhalation/exhalation and counting[16]]. A second aim is to help create further bodymind integration. [Note: Within this triangle of support floats the lower *dahnjeon/ki* "energy center." Ask the student to place her mind's eye, or awareness, into the breath. As she notices the breath come and go over a period of time she can let go of willful management of the breath and breathing should seem effortless. The breath will have a sense of strength and firmness apart from muscular efficiency].

FIGURE 4.3

- Figures 4.4 and 4.5 demonstrate either side of the "cat" position [*marjaravadivu*] adapted from my kalarippayattu training.

  Aim: Because this position lifts the pelvic floor off the studio floor, the student now must take responsibility on a muscular level for the support that the studio floor, gravity, and the weight of her body used to provide. [Note: This part of the "weaning" process gives the student's body the opportunity to teach itself the muscular adjustments it needs to maintain muscular efficiency and still complete the task]. Ask the student to focus her mind's eye on the placement of the spine and the placement of the breath in lower *dahnjeon* as she continues to notice the breath come and go.

FIGURE 4.4

FIGURE 4.5

- Figure 4.6 demonstrates position five: "sitting."
  Aim: To create an awareness of the muscle groups on either side of the lower *dahnjeon* through the position of the thighs as support. [Note: Ask the student to feel the breath as it is created in her, travels through her, travels out of her, and meets with that which is outside of herself. Ask the student to try not to "zone out," but focus on creating a connection with the world around her. Can she feel the space behind her back? On the top of her head? Ask her to shift her attention or awareness around her body, keeping herself "alive" in her developing bodymind.]

FIGURE 4.6

- Figure 4.7 demonstrates position six: kneeling—both knees on floor.

  Aim: By taking away the "sitting" support, the student's body must teach itself how to adjust and take even more responsibility for supporting the lower *dahnjeon* muscles. [Note: This transition identifies if the student is unable to tuck the tailbone beneath for support or if she has a tendency to clench her abdomen muscles when righting herself in a semi-standing position. Or, in this position she might be tempted to increase the natural curvature of the lower spine, collapsing into her body instead of building the spine as a means of support. Ask the student to take a moment to notice how her body shifts the support and takes responsibility for this task. Ask the student what part of her musculature can she let go of and still accomplish this simple task? How efficient can her use of the skeletal-musculature become in simply transitioning from "sitting" into "kneeling?" Where is her awareness as she accomplishes this task?]

FIGURE 4.7

- Figures 4.8 and 4.9 demonstrate right and left leg in position seven: Kneeling—one knee on floor.

  Aim: To increase an awareness of the muscles on either side of the lower *dahnjeon* by providing contrasting support during one-knee kneeling. [Note: Ask the student to place her awareness in the spine as if it were still rooted to the floor. Her kneeling leg should help her feel this connection between the floor and the lower *dahnjeon*. Even as her body begins to stand upright, ask her to continue to feel this link with the floor].

FIGURES 4.8 and 4.9

- Figure 4.10 demonstrates an adaptation of Patsy Rodenburg's "kabuki" position (Rodenburg, *A Voice of Your Own* [video]).

  Aim: To feel the appropriate position for the spine as it affects the tilt of the pelvic floor, helping to support the voice through the body, out of the body and across a distance to the listener. [Note: Ask the student to imagine she is about to sit on a tall stool, putting her awareness in the spine as if it is rooted to the floor. Ask her to focus her attention, or awareness, on the relationship between the placement of the spine and the placement of the breath in lower *dahnjeon*]. Another aim is to feel muscular and *ki* awareness in this position. [Note: Ask the student to place her awareness behind her, above her, in front of her. Ask her to feel *ki* extend through the soles of her feet into the floor and from the top of her head simultaneously. Ask her to strive towards a feeling of being present in this time and in this place, connecting to the world around her as she notices the breath come and go].

FIGURE 4.10

- Figures 4.11 and 4.12 demonstrate right and left leg positions for the "horse" [*asvavadivu*] adapted from my kalarippayattu training.

  Aim: To feel the *ki* extend from the top of the head and through the soles of the feet simultaneously. [Note: In this position, the student may be particularly tempted to bend her spine so that her chin tilts up and eyes are looking at the wall in front of her. However, she should align the spine, which will bring her external eye looking at the floor a bit away from her position. She should continue to put her mind's eye or internal eye into her spine, creating a relationship with the placement of the spine and the placement of the breath in lower *dahnjeon*.]

FIGURE 4.11

FIGURE 4.12

- Figures 4.13 and 4.14 demonstrate right and left legs positions in the "crane." Aims: To cultivate the feeling of a full contract/release cycle as gravity helps the lower *dahnjeon* muscles to release towards the floor and cultivate the feeling of *ki* as it circulates around the student's bodymind. Ask the student if she can feel *ki* extend off the top of her head and out through the soles of her feet simultaneously? Can she place her awareness behind her?

FIGURE 4.13

FIGURE 4.14

- Position eleven: Standing.
  Aim: to integrate muscular efficiency with *ki* strength during speaking. Also, to create a sense of speaking that connects with the world around the student in the here and now. Ask the student to feel inside her body a sense of ease as she supports the breath/sound through her body, out of her body, and across a distance to a listener. Ask the student if she can hear a focused energy in her sound, perhaps giving her sound a "strength" or purpose or direction?

Continue working through this sequence with a piece of familiar text. With regular practice, the student's bodymind will remember the sequence and the instructor will no longer need to repeat the instructions each day. In a classroom context, the students tend to find a way of doing the sequence together as a group without the instructor calling out the instructions each day. As the student works, ask her to remember "voice is the acoustic reflection of mind" (Park 2003: 189). As the voice moves so the mind moves, and as the mind moves so does the voice. One does not follow the other but both are together in the here and now, absorbed with the listener in the moment of speaking/listening.

Hopefully, this written exercise with accompanying pictures gives the reader a sense of how the theoretical discussion in the beginning of this chapter is integrated with the practice. Also, this exercise exemplifies one way to interweave Anglo-American voice training principles and practices with Asian modes of training, specifically focusing on the lower *dahnjeon* and the cultivation of *ki*. The next chapter picks up the discussion of lower *dahnjeon* and compares it with the idea and practice of "centering" in the "natural/free" voice approach. Through critical analysis, it investigates how breath and *ki* manifest into the actor's vocal "presence" and how "energy" exchange might be realized in the voice training studio, based on my experiences training with *p'ansori*.[17]

Notes

1 In addition to the 2007 to 2008 conferences, continued interest in the role of breath and training actors' voices includes the 2009 publication *Breath in Action* co-edited by Rena Cook and Jane Boston, an outcome of the RADA Breath conference; Sreenath Nair of the University of Lincoln was granted a Study Abroad Fellowship (2011) from the Leverhulme Trust (UK) to develop "a therapeutic application of breath for mental and physical wellbeing for actors, dancers and singers" (www.leverhulme.ac.uk/awards-made/awards-focus/restoration-breath-method-wellbeing-actors-dancers-and-singers). Also refer to Nair's monograph *Restoration of Breath: Consciousness and Performance* (2007), New York: Rodopi; and master trainer David Carey was asked to teach a workshop specifically addressing "Breath and Shakespeare" (2013) https://actorsandperformers. com/2013/10/breath-for-shakespeare1.

2 In January 2007, RADA in London hosted the "Performance Breath" conference (http://radaenterprises.org/summary_doc/summary_performance_breath.pdf), followed in March by the British Voice Association's (BVA) "Mechanics of Breath" conference (www.british-voice-association.com/reports_MechanicsOfBreathing2007.htm). In July 2007, the Voice and Speech Trainers' Association's (VASTA) conference in the US hosted "Practical Voice Science," which included an investigation of the role of breath (www.vasta.org/conferences/conf2007/index.html). Finally, in March 2008, the Center for Performance Research's (CPR) bi-annual "Giving Voice" conference offered "Breath Inspiration Voice" (www.thecpr.org.uk/news/index.php#43).

3 Refer to Jane Boston's introduction to the sixth edition of J. Clifford Turner's *Voice and Speech in the Theatre*, xii–xiii. Boston wrote: "Most of the main tenets of 20th-century voice theory can be traced back to [speech scientist] Dr. W. Aiken. Elsie Fogarty, founder of the Central School of Speech and Drama in London, first recruited him to the profession in 1912" (xii). Boston asserts that Aiken's work is the scientific foundation for Turner's voice practice. Boston wrote that the "twinning of science and practice within the modern tradition of voice work" was also influenced by the work of Manuel Patricio Rodriguez Garcia (1805–1906), who taught at the Royal Academy of Music in London and invented the laryngoscope in 1854 (xiii). Also refer to Jacqueline Martin's *The Voice in Modern Theatre*, who wrote that "[m]odern voice training has been based upon the finding of voice science which maintains that the act of voice production consists of an interplay between the following four areas: breathing, phonation, resonance, and articulation. These four areas have formed the basis of most textbooks written on voice training in the twentieth century" (37). Martin also notes Garcia's invention as significantly contributing to the way contemporary voice pedagogy trains the voice.

4 Here I am focusing on the particular ways a certain understanding of Cartesian philosophy has been integrated into mainstream voice practice. I understand that philosophical theories on body and mind are complex and ever-developing.

5 This model has different variations according to the particular trainer's approach. In an e-mail discussion with David Carey, this interpretation is overstating the connection; for him, the act of breathing is intimately linked to thinking and feeling, but the two are not the same thing (Carey 2008, e-mail discussion, 28–31 August).

6 Refer to Phillip Zarrilli's *Psychophysical Acting: An Intercultural Approach after Stanislavski* (2008). Zarrilli problematizes the way "psycho-physical" has been traditionally understood through Stanislavski's legacy within Western actor training and the challenges that arise from this understanding when integrating Asian principles and practices.

7 Zeami Motokiyo (1364–1443) wrote 23 Japanese treatises on Nō Drama, sometimes Romanized as "Noh," and is regarded as a central figure in the theoretical development of the ancient form of Japanese drama.

8 Also refer to Lessac breathing and relaxation exercises, specifically "Control and Consciousness" (1960: 45, 49), and his exercises for observing a "natural breathing pattern in supine position" (31) in contrast to "abdominal muscle strengthening" and "exhalation control" (41–42).

9 Leder, in *The Absent Body*, wrote: "The sense of the understanding as immaterial is suggested by the disappearance from awareness of the brain, the signifier, the body of the thinker" (1990: 151).

10 As Andrew Kimbrough notes, "The empirical pursuit of the voice intersects with the concerns raised in the philosophies and human sciences," and linking cross-disciplinary investigations "provides strategies for further research into the interrelationship of being and speaking" (2011: 2).

11 When asked during an interview to clarify what she meant by "mind," Park said that mind was "everything," including mind and body together (personal interview, August 2007, Columbus, Ohio).

12 Also refer to Mark J. Nearman's "Kakyo: A Mirror of the Flower [Part One]" (1982) and "Zeami's Kyui: A Pedagogical Guide for Teachers of Acting" (1978).

13 The process of doing these exercises is similar to Yoshi Oida's understanding of "tasting" the exercise. He wrote, "When doing all these exercises, it is important to remind yourself to 'taste' the movements. Doing them mechanically doesn't mean very much. You must try to notice the different sensations within the body" (Oida and Marshall 1999: 28).

14 The author demonstrates the positions in *dahnjeon* breathing exercise. Photos by Roberto Punzone, 2008.

15 In order to help the students realize this position, try using a teaching metaphor that was explained to me by Bae Il-dong during one of my *p'ansori* lessons: the spine should be "rooted" in this system of support like the roots of the lotus flower. The "stalk" or spine "grows" from the "roots" (through alignment), with the head floating on the surface of the water like the lotus floats on a calm pond (lessons throughout 2003 and 2004).

16 Refer to Yoshi Oida (1997: 8–9). "Even in performance, it [the anus] isn't necessarily held clenched all the time. But at the most important moments, when the person needs to strike a powerful blow, or has to use the voice with great power, the anus is held tightly shut" (8).

17 Long-term, rigorous studio practice is essential for this kind of exercise and brief descriptions and photos cannot begin to articulate the phenomenological experience of *ki*-cultivation.

References

Barba, E., Savarese, N. (1999). *A Dictionary of Theatre Anthropology*. London: Routledge.

Barton, R., Dal Vera, R. (1995, 2011). *Voice: Onstage and Off*. London: Routledge.

Berry, C. (1973). *Voice and the Actor*. New York: Collier.

Berry, C. (1992). *The Actor and the Text*. New York: Applause.

Berry, C. (2001). *Text in Action*. London: Virgin.

Boston, J, Cook, R. (2009). *Breath in Action: The Art of Breath in Vocal and Holistic Practice*. London and Philadelphia: Jessica Kingsley Publishers.

Carey, D. (2008). E-mail discussion with author, 28–31 August.

Carey, D., Clark Carey, R. (2008). *Vocal Arts Workbook and DVD: A Practical Course for Achieving Clarity and Expression with Your Voice*. London: Meuthen Drama.

Cavarero, A. (2005). *For More than One Voice: Toward a Philosophy of Vocal Expression*. Trans. Paul A. Kottman. Stanford: Stanford University Press.

Hampton, M., Acker, B. (1997). *The Vocal Vision: Views on Voice*. New York: Applause.

Houseman, B. (2002). *Finding Your Voice: A Complete Voice Training Manual for Actors*. London: Nick Hern.

Houseman, B. (2008). *Tackling Text [and Subtext]: A Step-by-Step Guide for Actors*. London: Nick Hern.

Kasulis, T., Ames, R., Dissanayake, W. (eds.). (1993). *Self as Body in Asian Theory and Practice. SUNY Series, The Body in Culture, History, and Religion*. Albany: SUNY Press.

Leder, D. (1990). *The Absent Body*. Chicago: University of Chicago Press.

Lee, B.W. (1999a). "Tension and Release as Physical and Auditory Signs of Affect in Korean Music," abstract presented at the Association for Korean Music Research Panel: Meaning and Emotion in Korean Music, Austin, 17–21 November.

Lee, S.H. (1999b). *Dahnhak*. Seoul: Dahn Publications.

Lessac, A. (1960, 1967). *The Use and Training of the Human Voice*. Palo Alto: Mayfield Publishing.

Linklater, K. (1976). *Freeing the Natural Voice*. New York: Drama Book Publishers.

Linklater, K. (2006). *Freeing the Natural Voice: Imagery and Art in the Practice of Voice and Language*. New York: Drama Book Publishers.

McCallion, M. (1988). *The Voice Book*. London: Faber & Faber.

Morgan, M. (2008). *Constructing the Holistic Actor: Fitzmaurice Voicework*. Saarbrucken: VDM Verlag Dr. Muller.

Nearman, M.J. (1978). "Zeami's Kyui: A Pedagogical Guide for Teachers of Acting," *Monumenta Nipponica*, 33 (3), 299–332.

Nearman, M.J. (1982). "Kakyo: A Mirror of the Flower [Part One]," *Monumenta Nipponica*, 37 (3), 343–374.

Nearman, M.J. (1983). "Kakyo: Zeami's Fundamental Principles of Acting. Part Three," *Monumenta Nipponica*, 38 (1), 49–71.

Oida, Y., Marshall., L. (1997). *The Invisible Actor*. London: Methuen.

Onian, R.B. (1988). *The Origins of European Thought about the Body, the Mind, the Soul, the World, Time, and Fate*. Cambridge: Cambridge University Press.

Park, C.E. (2000). "'Authentic Audience' in P'ansori, a Korean Storytelling Tradition," *Journal of American Folklore*, 449, 270–286.

Park, C.E. (2003). *Voices from the Straw Mat*. Honolulu: University of Hawai'i Press.

Park, C.E. (2007). Personal interview, August 2007, Columbus, Ohio.

Rodenburg, P. (1992). *The Right to Speak*. New York: Routledge.

Rodenburg, P. (1993, 2001). *The Need for Words*. London: Methuen.

Rodenburg, P. (2007). *Presence: How to Use Positive Energy for Success in Every Situation*. London: Penguin/Michael Joseph.

Sellers-Young, B. (1998). "Somatic Processes: Convergence of Theory and Practice," *Theatre Topics*, 8 (2), 183–187.

Turner, C.J. (1950, 2007). *Voice and Speech in the Theatre*, 6th edition. Ed. Jane Boston. London: Methuen Drama.

Turner, V. (1969). *Ritual Process: Structure and Anti-Structure*. New York: Aldine de Gruyter.

Um, H.K. (1992). *Making P'ansori: Korean Musical Drama*. Unpublished PhD dissertation, Queen's University Belfast, Belfast.

Um, H.K. (2008). "New P'ansori in Twenty-First-Century Korea: Creative Dialectics of Tradition and Modernity," *Asian Theatre Journal*, 25 (1), 24–57.

Yoo, J. (2007). "Moving Ki in Inner and Outer Space—a Korean Perspective on Acting Process in The Water Station," *Contemporary Theatre Review*, 17 (1), 81–96.

Yuasa, Y. (1993). *The Body, Self-Cultivation, and Ki-Energy*. Trans. Shigenori Nagatomo and Monte S. Hull. Albany: SUNY Press.

Zarrilli, P.B. (1997). "Acting . . . 'at the nerve ends': Beckett, Blau and the Necessary," *Theatre Topics*, 7 (2), 103–116.

Zarrilli, P.B., Boyette, P. (2007). "Psychophysical Training Physical Actions and Performing Beckett: 'Playing Chess on Three Levels Simultaneously,'" *Contemporary Theatre Review*, 17 (1), 70–80.

Zarrilli, P.B. (2008). *Psychophysical Acting: An Intercultural Approach after Stanislavski*. London: Routledge Press.

5

THE ROLE OF "PRESENCE" IN TRAINING ACTORS' VOICES

Chapter Four investigated the role of breath in the two source traditions, the "natural/free" voice approach and Korean *p'ansori*, touching on the way breath as "energy" is conceived and trained. This chapter picks up that thread and examines in detail relationships between "energy" and the voice in both traditions, embedded specifically within a comparison of two techniques: "Centering" adapted from the "natural/free" voice approach and "*dahnjeon* breathing" adapted from Korean *p'ansori* for training actors' voices. Using Rodenburg's fifth book, *Presence* (2007), as a departure point, and in comparison with my experiences teaching in Seoul and London, one aim is to reframe a discussion of "energy" and "presence" in contemporary voice training by displacing "universalism" as a primary explanatory position and offering instead an alternative paradigm to understand the interior/inner processes and potential of the voice as an embodied phenomenon and process.

The way in which "energy" is used in many mainstream Anglo-American voice texts can be confusing. For instance, master voice trainer, Sue Ann Park, student of Arthur Lessac, wrote about "voice and body and energy states" in Lessac's work (Park 1997: 108). This included the use of the term "energy" to name and describe "Vocal Energy States"; "Body Energy States"; "consonant energy"; "tonal energy"; "structural energy"; "leading energy"; and "exploratory energy" (Hampton and Acker 1997: 110–113). The "natural/free" voice has tended to use the word "energy" in a wide variety of different training contexts. For instance, Berry linked confidence with vocal "energy" (Berry 1973: 123) as well as discussing "energy through the text" (2000: 82, 178). Linklater wrote about activating "imaginative energies" in her voice work (in Hampton and Acker 1997: 3) as well as the "energy" of vowels and consonants (Linklater 1992: 99). Such different applications of the same term can confuse, rather than clarify the learning objectives of the exercises. Also, "energy," understood as a "universal quality" tends not to be discussed within a specific cultural context. For instance, Linklater wrote about the dynamics of the voice (pace, volume, pitch) as "built-in human energies" (Linklater 2017).

Voice trainer Elizabeth Mills critiqued Berry's use of the term "energy" as Mills attempted to apply it within her classrooms at the University of Cape Town, addressing "the South African English speaking student actor" (102). Mills wrote,

> [For Berry], all the foundational properties of voice become circumscribed predominantly by Shakespeare's texts and by the ethos of the RSC. For example, energy which is of major interest to Berry (1973, 1975, 1987) is described, in *The Actor and his Text* (1987), in terms of, among others, the metre, the structure of lines and rhyming devices. As such, it constitutes the daily linguistic fare of RSC life.
>
> *(Mills 1999: 102)*

Mills noted that when Berry discussed the energy of the line, meaning Shakespearian verse (iambic pentameter), this is "described as close to the rhythm of conversational speech," which "will be present as a consciously registered pulse for those [RSC] actors in a way that it would not be for the South African English speaking student actor, for example, whose tendency is towards more emphatic stress patterns" (ibid.).

Of the many ways the "natural/free" voice discusses "energy," the focus here is on an understanding of "energy" contributing to an actor's vocal "presence." As such, Rodenburg's book *Presence* offers a specific, in-depth study of how an understanding of "energy" emerging from the "natural/free" voice approach contributes to actors' "presence." Rodenburg, more so than Berry or Linklater, is associated with this particular area of training. Berry and Linklater have yet to publish as significantly on the topic of "presence" as has Rodenburg. Also, the wide-reaching influence of *Presence* as part of the "natural/free" voice canon of training texts is another reason why it deserves special attention here.

Presence has offered the field of training actors' voices a way of conceptualizing "energy" as "Three Circles of Energy,"™ the basis for training towards "presence." Rodenburg defined her understanding of "presence" through her experiences teaching in UK voice classrooms. She taught student-actors to become "audible, coherent and interesting to listen to, yet that wasn't enough . . . I couldn't understand why some actors did everything right yet didn't engage me" (Rodenburg 2007: xiii). When she discussed this with colleagues she was told that the thing she was seeking was "it," "talent," or "presence." She was told "presence" was something that could not be taught. However, she found the opposite to be true. She wrote,

> Once in a while, a student in one of my classes who initially didn't seem to have "it", would suddenly get "it." And if I acknowledged this transformation some would keep it . . . I had somehow enabled a student to find their true energy and this true energy was their presence.
>
> *(2007: xiii)*

Eventually, she

> began to know that presence is a universal quality that we all have but is somehow flattened out of us . . . What I discovered was that it wasn't a miracle that students found their presence, it was a tragedy that they had lost it in the first place.
>
> *(2007: xiii-xiv)*

For Rodenburg, "presence" is described through a lost/found, or absence/presence binary. Thus, the aim of her training is to "reinstate presence into your life" (Rodenburg 2007: 13).

Like Rodenburg, I have also had certain experiences in my voice classrooms that have led me to investigate the link between "energy" and voice. But there are key differences in our teaching experiences which inform differences in our approaches. While teaching at KNUA my students brought into my voice class other ways of thinking and talking about "energy" as *ki* based on mappings of body from Korean traditional medicine. As introduced in Chapter Four, Lee Seung-Heun understands *ki* energy as three types. The first type, *won-ki*, is vital energy received from the mother in utero via the blood through the umbilical cord before breathing is possible. After birth, the blood of your parents is part of the *won-ki* energy you "inherited." To this, a second type, *jong-ki*, is now possible through breathing air via the lungs. Lee wrote, "[*Jong-ki*] is acquired energy from nourishment. The energy source is replenished through diet and respiration." The third type, *Jin-ki*, is "accessed through deep mindful concentration of the breath . . . Wherever in the body that you focus that is where the Jin-ki goes" (Lee 1999: 33).

From this worldview, "energy" is not singular but plural. Also, *won-ki* and *jong-ki* cannot be "flattened out of us." Thus, the purpose of training is not to "reinstate" what has been lost. Because the materials of training (body, voice, breath, "energy") are not stable, universally agreed concepts, understandings of "energy" cannot be reduced to *a* universal "human" experience that we all share. This chapter investigates what can/should a voice do and how can/should it do "it" when working with "energy." Within this mix are varying understandings of what makes a voice "engaging," and how "presence" may emerge through different understandings of "energy."

Conceptualizing "energy" and "presence" through the "natural/free" voice approach

Rodenburg wrote that *Presence* was part of a "quest for positive energy started thirty years ago" (Rodenburg 2007: xi). Simultaneously, Rodenburg was developing her understanding of a "natural" or "free" voice approach. A quick comparison of key principles between her first book, *The Right To Speak* (1992), and her fifth book, *Presence* (2007), evidences the ways her concept of "presence" is intimately linked with her concept of a "natural" voice.

- The first premise in conceptualizing "presence" is that "the state of presence is your birthright" (2007:17), similar to the concept of a "natural voice," which is "what we came into the world with at birth" (1992: 19).
- The second premise is that the learner lost her "presence" like she lost her "natural" voice, in part, through the act of others or "life," for example, "life batters and restricts us" (1992: 19); "As life and its pressures infiltrate the infant and then the child, habits grow and take control. The natural voice begins to slip away" (1992: 23); "some people . . . don't want your presence, so it has been knocked out of you" (2007: 13); "[presence] is somehow flattened out of us" (2007: xiii–xiv); and "you are knocked out of your Second Circle presence by life's unwholesome forces" (2007: 97).
- Universalism remains a key principle. "Voice work is for everybody. We all breathe and the vast majority of us speak . . . 'the right to speak' is a right we all have" (1992: x–xi). In *Presence*, she wrote, "I began to know that presence is a universal quality that we all have" (2007: xiii–xiv).
- The fourth premise is that one's "natural voice" and "presence" can be regained through the exercises she offers in her training texts. Thus, the aim of the training is to "reinstate presence into your life" (2007: 13) or "reclaim what I have since called the right to speak" (1992: xiii).

Rodenburg's observations about "energy" in her first two books were organized into "circles of concentration" in her third book, *The Actor Speaks* (2000). Here "energy" was conceptualized as actors' "tools, placing you in the here and now" (2000: 226) in order to "help actors focus and energize their voices and place their imagination directly in service to the characters' words" (2000: 225–226). Seven years later, "circles of concentration" became "Three Circles of Energy"™ in *Presence*, and was marketed to a broader demographic, beyond actor-training, through her book, her TED talk, her workshops, and her website.

Similar to her concept of the First circle of concentration, the First Circle energy represents the "circle of self and withdrawal" (2007: 17), Third Circle energy, similar to Third circle of concentration, represents the "circle of bluff or force" (2007:19), and Second Circle energy represents "the energy of connecting" (2007: 21). This second circle is characterized as a state in which "your energy is focused . . . The art of being present is the art of operating from Second Circle" (2007: 21–22).

There is a noticeable shift of purpose from second circle of concentration to Second Circle energy. In *Presence*, "'staying in Second'" (2007: xvii) for non-performers is a means of "return[ing] to the positive presence you were born with" (2007: xi). But actors are told in *The Actor speaks*, "To sustain Second all day long would result in a breakdown!" (2000: 227). The aim shifts from "creating canny moments on stage" (2000: 226) to "make[ing] you more successful, more joyful and loving" (2007: xi).

Presence, released in the US under the title, *Second Circle*, makes no explicit attempt to delineate how "circles of concentration" for actors differs from embodying "presence" as a non-actor.[1] Current discussions surrounding "presence" point out the importance of conceptualizing "presence" specifically for theatrical representation (Fischer-Lichte 2012: 106–107, Goodall 2008; Jaeger 2006: 122–141; Power 2008: 142; Zarrilli 2012: 122).[2] Many of the exercises Rodenburg used to train actors' voices are similar if not the same as exercises used to train the voices of non-actors. This is not to say that voice exercises for actors cannot be adapted to train non-actors. However, a given context asks the voice to perform in a particular way. Also, the relationship to the listener changes, and this becomes especially important in performer/audience relationships.[3]

Universalism works in several ways here. First, it becomes the foundation of a pedagogical model to democratize voice training from the exclusivity of apprenticeships and conservatoires to "anyone who breathes and communicates sound to the world" (Rodenburg 1992: ix). As mentioned in Chapter One, this was part of a larger movement in voice pedagogy emerging from socio-political changes in the US and UK during the 1960s (Martin 1991: 171). Voice training sought to "free" the voice from social conditioning as part of a larger political act, giving voice to disenfranchised groups.[4] Rodenburg and Berry, among others, took their work into UK prisons. In *Presence*, the demographic includes "business people, teachers, physicians, police, politicians, even convicts" (2007: xvi). In teaching these other learners, *Presence* constantly refers back to Rodenburg's work with actors as the basis for conceptualizing "presence" for non-actors and is one of the main selling points of the book and her workshops[5]. Thus, universalism becomes not only a pedagogical model but also a business model, broadening the scope and application of her training. Finally, universalism is also the means by which techniques, based on *human* anatomy and physiology and training towards a "natural" or "free" voice, can be used to train towards "presence." Here, the human body is understood as the common denominator that links all of the learner demographics. However, anatomy-based exercises reinforce the assumed universal application of the practice without allowing for a more complex discussion of the ways in which different cultures understand body and voice within a specific cultural context.

Transmission of embodiment practices: Training towards "presence" using "natural/free" voice exercises

The supposition of Rodenburg's book *Presence* is that "presence" can be learned. Her position can be understood within a history of practitioners "for whom the lived phenomenon of presence still makes sense and is borne out in practical experience" (Jaeger 2006: 122). In order to understand how "presence" can be taught/learned, it benefits the reader to analyze the techniques offered in *Presence*, many of which are based on, or sometimes identical to, exercises used to train the "natural/free" voice. She wrote, "The natural voice is free and responds authentically to the feeling and thoughts we are experiencing in present moments of our life. It is built and designed to reach out and touch others in Second Circle" (2007: 84–85). A discussion of Second Circle will follow shortly.

Presence is divided into two parts: part one is concerned with "finding your presence" (2007: 1) and offers the bulk of the training exercises. Part two offers advice on "living with full presence" (2007: 199). Because I am interested in teasing out how "energy" in voice training "engages" (2007: xiii) the listener, or how "presence" works at the level of technique as "connection" (2007: 97), I focus specifically on the exercises found in part one of *Presence*.

Within part one, Rodenburg first offers exercises to train Body (chapters five and six) where the student "will relearn how to centre and place your body naturally, giving you access to your physical presence" (Rodenburg 2007: 39). These techniques alone will not create "presence" but are the necessary preparatory work: "You have now performed exercises preparing your body to feel presence" (Rodenburg 2007: 54). Then, the training continues to Breath (chapters seven and eight). Here the aim is "to rediscover the natural breath that marries to your presence" (Rodenburg 2007: 64). Next, the student progresses to Voice (chapter nine) with specific focus on "freeing the voice" (Rodenburg 2007: 90–97). Rodenburg notes that this point in the training is "first stage work" in which "you have exercises and techniques that can place our body, breath and voice into present connection to your world" (Rodenburg 2007: 97). The next chapters, Words (chapter ten) and Listening (chapter eleven) round out the practical exercises. The remaining 13 short chapters in the first half of the book offer fruitful commentary for the purposes of this chapter but very few training exercises. However, for the purposes of the discussion here I will briefly examine Mind (chapter thirteen).

Body

Regaining "presence" and regaining a "natural" voice both begin with the body, which is conceptualized as a "house" for the voice (1992: 115) as well as a "house" for energy (2007: 38). Eliot Deutsch points to the use of "container" metaphors as a traditional way of understanding the body in the West (Deutsch 1993: 6–8). This understanding of the body housing the voice is not particular to the way the "natural/ free" voice conceptualizes the body. Contemporary Western discourse surrounding theories of the voice tend to theorize the voice in a similar way. Mladen Dolar wrote that the voice "is a bodily missile which has detached itself from its source, emancipated itself, yet remains corporeal" (2006: 73). Brandon LaBelle reiterates this point of view when conceptualizing the relationship between the mouth (as body part) and sound, as it is projected from the body during sounding (2014: 1). The voice is "emancipated," trapped in the container of the body. The voice is of the body but it is not the body because it separates itself from the body during sounding. Sound then, functions like a "missile" (Dolar 2006) or a "projection [that] can be seen and heard as an amplification of . . . words" (LaBelle 2014), a projectile traveling a distance to the waiting listener.

The verb "to project" (Berry 1973: 139; Rodenburg 1992: 20), or "projection" (Rodenburg 1992: 223–224) is often used to help the actor travel the sound over a distance. The speaker is the departure point for the sound as it travels in an "arch" to "land" on the listener (Rodenburg 1994 video). In this way, the voice is understood as a kind of projectile and a popular exercise often used in voice training is to ask the student to toss a ball or some other projectile to a waiting listener while speaking text so that the act of throwing the ball and the support needed in the body is transferred to muscularly supporting the voice. There are versions of ball exercises in all three master trainer's approaches that are used to achieve a variety of different learning outcomes (Berry 1973: 41; Linklater 1976: 157; Rodenburg 1992: 213, 227). Such exercises physically embody a philosophy of the voice, a way of thinking about sound and how it should function between performer and listener.[6]

Based on this tradition, Rodenburg trains towards developing "presence" also using an exercise in which the student throws a ball (Rodenburg 2007: 75–76). A "First Circle throw" is one in which "you are throwing without any power leaving you so you are unable to connect with the world." A "Third Circle throw" is one in which "there is no fluidity or readiness—the resulting throw is one of force and over control" (2007: 76). The quality of the throw comes to represent not only the amount of muscular support the body provides to help the sound leave the body and travel a distance, but also represents how the "self" interacts with "the world." Rodenburg wrote,

> Imagine throwing a ball underarm. Inhale as you swing your arm back. Your arm will suspend with the natural suspension of your breath and as you throw the imaginary ball your arm moves forward with exhalation and the breath throws the ball. This breath supports the projection of the ball, your voice or a movement. The support projects you and everything in you out to the world. It effectively connects you to the world and in this way is Second Circle breath.
>
> *(2007: 75–76)*

In Second Circle, one's voice leaves the body but does not leave "you." This relates back to a key principle of the "natural/free" voice in which the voice is linked with self-identity. Instead, the voice as "you" is projected out to the world and in this way "connects you to the world." This is a particular understanding of the "self," both as material body and identity, as it interacts with that which is outside of the "self." Cartesian dualism helps here to conceptualize this moment of separation: the material body is the point of departure for the sound and the voice is self identity, or the "mind" of who "you" are that connects with the world. This is similar to previous exercises found in her first book, used to train towards "placement of the voice." Rodenburg wrote,

> All placing means is to release the power and sound to the world, to place sound outside yourself. Sound, like a word, must be placed as far forward in the mouth as possible in order to leave us and have an effect. Think of the image of a dart being launched, no longer part of us but finding its place on

a target. With our voice, however, a part of us stays with the sound dart when we place it. We make our mark with sound when we release it.

(Rodenburg 1992: 211)

In the exercise that follows, she advises, "Let the sound flow from you, let the energy go" (212). The voice, like the dart, leaves the material body, or is no longer "part of us." But "a part of us" as identity remains within the resultant traveling sound to make its "mark" once released, or after physical separation. "Energy" simply follows the pattern of voicing. There is no difference between how communication is conceptualized between performer and audience and how "energy" might function in that relationship. Voicing and "energy" have been collapsed into the same role. Where the sound goes, so too "energy" goes. But in Asian understandings of breath into *ki*, *ki* can exist in silence and is not reduced to the sounding voice.

Thinking about "energy" and "presence" as an extension of the "natural/free" voice paradigm re-inscribes assumptions underpinning the "natural/free" voice approach as universal truths about "human" energy. This is where an intercultural approach to training actor's voices can benefit the multi-cultural, multi-linguistic voice studio. One advantage it offers is other ways of thinking and talking about "energy" and "presence," refreshing a conversation about voice and "presence" and displacing "universalism" as the primary explanatory position for training. For instance, an understanding of the way "energy" functions between speaker and listener in the theatre is different from an Eastern worldview embedded within modes of training that work towards bodymind oneness (Yuasa 1993), "no-mind" (Nearman 1978: 324–325), and the principle of "forming one body" through "absorption" and "communion" (Leder 171). "Energy" is also different from the way *ki* functions in training and performance, creating *p'an* in *p'ansori*, what Park characterized as the "flow" of the performance, or how Um described *p'an* through Victor Turner's concept of "communitas," mentioned in the previous chapter.

Breath

After discussing the body/voice relationship and training towards "presence," Rodenburg then focused on breath. "The more you breathe naturally, the more present you will be" (Rodenburg 2007: 77). She brought into her understanding of "presence" a similar concept of breath used in training towards a "free/natural" voice: "The body houses the breath. The breath powers the voice" (Rodenburg 2007: 83). As argued in Chapter Four, this is a popular way many contemporary voice trainers understand breath as being anchored in the body, specifically at the diaphragm, so that breath remains attached to the corporeal experience of lung function. Certain exercises she offered for finding oneself in "Second Circle," or a state of being present in the body, are similar exercises used for "rooting" the breath as a means of rediscovering one's natural voice (Rodenburg 2000: 150), or "the ability to breathe the word" (Rodenburg 2000: 89). In *Presence*, the exercises offered in "exercising the natural breath" (71–77) are similar if not the same as exercises she offered in her previous training texts.

Breath exercises also help establish an understanding of the Three Circles of Energy™ in terms of geographical locations outside the body surrounding the speaker. Rodenburg instructed,

> Place your hand in front of your face, about a foot away. Look and fully concentrate on your hand and breathe to it. You will feel the moment the breath touches and connects to your hand. You are now touching your hand in Second Circle. Now breathe half the distance to your hand and you will feel immediately closed down into First. Now breath past your hand and you will feel the extra distance and your energy shift into Third Circle . . . First Circle will have the breath dropping off before it reaches that point. Third Circle will have you breathing beyond the room, maybe even drilling through the wall. Now breathe the whole room with the connected Second Circle. When you feel this you are now in command of the whole room. All great performers and speakers breathe the whole space they are in. They don't breathe half the room or over breathe it as this disengages them and they would lose their charisma.
>
> *(2007: 78–79)*

Through this breathing exercise, the learner comes to understand that energy is connected to breath and that breath-fueled energy is able to be located outside of the speaker's body in geographic proximity between speaker and listener. The function of the breath, whether it reaches its target (e.g. the hand or the listener's ear) determines if the speaker's energy also reaches its target. In this way, energy (here described as "charisma" or sometimes interchangeably "presence"[7]) is intimately linked to breath and the way one breathes.

The idea of "breath[ing] the whole space" is built on her earlier work (1992: 226) within a larger conversation about "Volume Control, Level and Projection" (223). The hand exercise above is very similar to an exercise in her first book. She wrote,

> Notice how the breath changes, becoming shallower as you limit your awareness. Hold your hand close to your face and breathe towards it, move it further away breathing to reach it. Look at your feet and breathe. Each focal distance requires a different breath. Look at a seat close to you and breath. Now at one further back and further back still. The breath and support needed to touch a close point will not be enough to fill the whole. Once you embrace the whole space in your imagination and breath accordingly you will be taking sufficient breath to fill the space and find the right vocal level.
>
> *(1992: 226–227)*

Here the exercise is about "awareness" as "focal points" offering multiple distances to understanding the "self" in space and the actor's proprioceptive awareness of self and space in relation to sounding and the acoustic properties of the performance hall. This exercise offers more possibilities between "self" and connection to that which is outside of the "self." At the Royal Central School of Speech and Drama and East 15 Acting School, part of my remit is to "fit the voices to the space," a colloquialism used to describe the sort of work the above exercise aims to accomplish. I have found such exercises as Rodenburg's "breathe the space" useful to introducing young actors to the different acoustic properties of various indoor and outdoor performance spaces, helping them determine how to "project" their voice, within this tradition. This is different from limiting the distance to three proximities, or circles, and privileging one circle (second circle) as the most desirable.

"When you talk about 'centering' the breath, do you mean using the *dahnjeon*?"

Within the School of Drama at KNUA, breathing from the *dahnjeon* was one of several *p'ansori* techniques considered beneficial to Korean actor training. Park wrote, "A trained *p'ansori* voice is typically husky, resonating with *ki* (strength) and subtle expressiveness simultaneously" (Park 2003: 157). Here the "strength" of the voice is not muscular strength alone but also the *ki* (energy) of the sound which resonates in the lower abdomen.

The lower *dahnjeon* is intimately linked with the production of voice in *p'ansori*. Jang wrote,

> The ideal voice used in *p'ansori* singing is *t'ongsong* (literally 'whole sound'). It is a powerful and dignified voice, which originates from *tanjon* . . . *T'ongsong* has been considered to be the fundamental voice among mastersingers, at least since the late nineteenth century . . . Achieving *t'ongsong* requires several years of training and producing a *t'ongsong* demands solid and concentrated strength within one's abdomen.
>
> *(Jang 2014: xix)*

Although sometimes *dahnjeon* as a word and concept is translated into English as "center," Korean *dahnjeon(s)* includes a system of knowledge that is different from an understanding of "center" or "centering" in the "natural/free" voice approach.

As introduced in Chapter Three, in the practice of *p'ansori*, the lower *dahnjeon* can be understood through a biomedical model as the musculature that prepares the breath for sounding, a part of intra-abdominal support. *P'ansori* scholar Um Hae-Kyung wrote,

> The principal technique in vocalization is *t'ongsong* (lit. straight voice) or *chungangsong* (lit. central or principle voice), which the pressure is exerted on the diaphragm in combination with *dantian* respiration to push out the vocal

sound more powerfully. The *dantian* respiration makes the most of the breathing energy supported and controlled by the abdominal muscle around the umbilicus and lower abdomen.

(Um 2013: 76, italics in the original)

Um's description of *dantian* details intra-abdominal pressure exerted on the diaphragm to create a well-supported breath stream, part of "*dantian* respiration." But her description also includes "breathing energy" cultivated in the lower *dahnjeon*. This "energy" is integral to an understanding of the way the *dahnjeon* functions, not only in *p'ansori* but through other Asian modes of training.

As an embodied practice, the term *dantian* in *p'ansori* describes not only the process of breathing ("abdominal muscle" + "breathing energy") but the resultant sound itself. As mentioned in Chapter Four, Chin Pong-gyu asserts "*tanjonsong* (*dantian* voice)" comes from the *dantian* and can be identified by its sound as different from "*poksong* (lit. abdomen voice)," which comes from the abdomen (1984: 42–45; Um 1992: 28).

Voicing from the *dahnjeon*, not only for performers but also for the drummers who accompany them and the audience when offering *ch'uimsae*, helps create the performative "energy" of *p'an* in *p'ansori*.[8] In describing *p'an*, Park and Um reference Abraham Maslow, Victor Turner, and Mihaly Csikszentmihalyi (Park 2003: 233; Um 2008: 41). These leading figures are also often referenced in discourses surrounding "presence." Park's and Um's descriptions could be understood as the beginnings of theorizing "presence" in *p'ansori* performance. Like Csikszentmihalyi's idea that total immersion in a task places the doer of the task in a state of "flow," Jang wrote that some *p'ansori* performers

> describe such experiences as *soriga aengginda* (Jang trans. "sound hugs me" or "I am hugged by sound"). In Korean, *aengginda* means someone clings tightly to one's body, and I understand that a singer experiences this when he or she is totally immersed in his or her performance. According to Song Ch'angsun, she experiences it as an entry to a trancelike state when her performance is going extremely well.
>
> *(Song 1995: 219–227 in Jang 2014: xxii)*

During the 19th-century gentrification of *p'ansori*, Shin Chaehyo "expound[ed] the essential elements of *p'ansori* performance: *inmul* (appearance), *sasol* (narrative composition), *tugum* (vocal attainment), and *norumsae* (accompanying gesture) . . . [Marshal] Pihl reconstructs *inmul* (appearance) as 'fashioning a presence,' to dispel the 'commercial overtones' in the notion of physical appearance" (Park 2003: 72). Lee Cheol Yoo (Cheol-u I) suggested the "art of *pan*" creates a relationship between "drama and *p'ansori*" through "the benefit of presence as a principle of art," although noting the differences between the ways actors embody character and "the character of [the] singer in *p'ansori*" (2003: 35–36).[9] There seems to be some development in *p'ansori* scholarship towards an understanding of what makes the *p'ansori* voice "engaging," which includes discussions of "presence." However, there is little explicit, detailed discussion in English publications about the relationship between *ki* as "energy" and the *p'ansori* performer's "presence."

In comparison with *dahnjeon*, "center" can be understood through a biomedical model as the body's center of gravity (Benedetti 1990: 28–29). But as a concept used in the transmission of embodied practice, "center" is understood differently between disciplines and/or practitioners within disciplines. Linklater wrote, "Center means one thing to Martha Graham, another to Michael Chekov and other things to others and to me" (Linklater 1976: 136). "Center" shifts between biomechanical functions (center of gravity) and more conceptual functions. Linklater conceptualized both a "center" and multiple "centers" with the additional understanding of "center of energy." Linklater wrote,

> I want to suggest two paradoxical approaches to the center. One is to pin down more precisely where it is, and the other is to say that it can be any-where . . . Thus, pragmatically, it must be stated that the center is moveable. As a purist, however, I would argue that there is an immutable center, one primary center of energy from which all movement and sound springs.
>
> *(Linklater 1976: 135)*

This paradox set up a kind of oppositional relationship in which she ultimately chose "as a purist" the idea of "one primary centre." I argue that using both "center" and multiple "centers," like *dahnjeons*, do not have to be seen as paradoxical or oppositional but instead can co-exist on a continuum of training, allowing the student to shift how she sees her body by applying different mappings to her body.

Unlike a moveable center, the *dahnjeons* do not move around the body but are specifically located either inside or on the body. What does move around the body, in/through/between the *dahnjeons*, is *ki* [Korea], *chi* [China] *qi* [Japan], *prana*, or *pranavayu* [India]. But like *dahnjeon* breathing, "centering" as a technique also has an effect on the resultant sound. Linklater wrote, "The strict, physiological benefit of centering the voice is that the more economically the breath plays on the vocal folds, the better the tone" (Linklater 1976: 136).

In *Presence*, Rodenburg began the practical training towards "presence" with a centering exercise (2007: 49–50). She wrote that the student "will relearn how to centre and place [their] body naturally, giving you access to your physical presence" (2007: 39). Her centering exercise in *Presence* is based on earlier exercises found in her first book training the "natural" voice. Rodenburg instructed,

> Stand with feet directly underneath the hips taking the full weight of support, knees unlocked, spine up, back unbraced, shoulders unheld and head balanced on top of the spine. As you gently rock in this position you will feel the weight of the body find and return to its center.
>
> *(1992: 126)*

Commenting after the exercise, Rodenburg added, "Being centred (and what is more and more coming to be called 'in the zone') is fundamental to concentrated expertise in sports and martial arts" (Rodenburg 1992: 127). Breathing into the center is part of her understanding of "rooting" the breath in which the "lower part of the body has to be balanced" with "proper even distribution of the weight over the feet" (ibid.: 129). This sense of balance (through a kinesthetic feeling of ones center of gravity) gives the practitioner a "state of readiness . . . You are standing alert and ready to begin" (1992: 129). In the same exercise in *Presence*, Rodenburg noted, "Do this and you will begin to feel more alert and on your toes! More ready for life" (Rodenburg 2007: 50). What Rodenburg has described is a kinesthetic awareness in which proprioception enables the practitioner to sense the body in relation to itself and the space around it. The description of "centering" in Rodenburg's exercise in *The Right to Speak* (Rodenburg 1992: 126) as well as its adaptation in *Presence* (2007: 50) instructs the learner using an anatomical description—it tells the student what to do with her (object) body—then follows with an explanation of what this experience aims to accomplish. Like many training texts, Rodenburg's instructions are written in an order; once the act of finding one's center is accomplished, then another task, the idea of "readiness," is possible. This suggests that the body as object is instructed to complete an action, following from which mental preparation, "readiness," results. This could be read as another example of Cartesian body/mind dualism in Anglo-American voice practice. The limits of written instruction do not capture an understanding of the kind of "energy" voice trainers identify with the experience of "centering." Linklater asserts that, "working from it [center] clears the mind and focuses energy" (Linklater 1976: 136).

Placing "centering" and "*dahnjeon* breathing" on a continuum of training

The overlapping interests between scholars and practitioners and between voice trainers and *p'ansori* artists in cultivating a relationship between voice and "energy" or more specifically "presence," helps me place techniques from different traditions in the same voice studio. Citing my own experiences with the help of others who also think and talk about voice and "energy," I will try to explain what I think happens in my classrooms when I teach side-by-side techniques adapted from "centering" and "*dahnjeon* breathing."

In my experience, the bodymind task of finding one's center is the act of "readiness." It is not necessarily a "state" but an ever-becoming, emergent process. For many of my beginning students this feeling of "centering" as "readiness" comes and goes as they struggle with mind wandering and/or "zoning out." When my beginning students first train towards "readiness" it helps teach them how to be present physically and mentally in the "here and now" to perform a task, whatever that task might be. "Presence" and being "present" are different but related.[10] Being "present" makes the transference of skills possible between the bodily co-presence of teacher and student.[11] In this way, being "present" could be understood as the necessary condition for cultivating "presence." From student feedback, I sometimes learn that their experiences of being "present" means, for them, that their senses are augmented. For instance, they become keenly aware of sounds in the room they had not noticed before.

Eventually, through repetition, the student begins to understand that this "readiness" creates a heightened state of awareness in the studio that focuses both teacher and student on task(s). This level of "readiness" can be understood as the necessary foundation from which the sounding voice emerges, or a kind of "pre-expressive" energy, which "renders the [body/voice] theatrically 'decided,' 'alive,' . . . attracting the spectator's [listener's] attention before any form of message is transmitted" (www.odintheatret.dk/ista/anthrogpology.htm; Barba and Savarese 1991).[12] However, collapsing "energy" with the sounding voice means that the "state of readiness" is only a place from which sound alights, a "container" for energy which will be ready to use for the purpose of sounding. In contrast, "readiness" as process cultivates *jin-ki*, which is part of *won-ki* and *jong-ki* already manifest, active, and moving. *Ki* is not held in a "state" nor is it awaiting purpose. Energy, in this "readiness," is communicating without sound so that when the voice sounds it is adding to communication already in progress. Barba suggested that pre-expressive energy attracts the audience's attention *before* any form of message is transmitted but this act of attention gathering is a message: pay attention. Not sounding could be understood as "silence" but what if "silence" is not the absence of sound, but a form of voice that is communicating without sound, through breath/*ki*?

Alice Lagaay, in conceptualizing a philosophy of the phenomenological voice and its "presence," wrote,

> Most recent theories of voice tend to focus on the acoustic, embodied, actualised, speaking/uttering sound of voice (e.g. Meyer-Kalkus 2001; Cavarero 2005; Dolar 2006). But do we not experience on a daily basis the reality and power of voices that are withheld, voices that refrain from actually speaking, silent voices? I expect that a voice that were only ever in an active mode of actual speaking performance, a voice that knew no silence, could not be a real voice nor even identified as an hallucination.
>
> *(in Kendrick and Roesner 2011: 65–67)*

Thus, in her search "for a theory of voice that does not reduce voice to mere sound" or "a concept of sound that allows it to be stretched beyond the actual moment of is resonance," Lagaay looks to the "performative turn" that has led critics and philosophers to concern themselves more intensely with the specific materiality, embodiment, and temporal liveness. She wrote,

> and this is what the prism of voice certainly appears to reveal, that an intense preoccupation with that which is present/presence necessarily leads to an increased attentiveness towards that which is not yet fully there, but might

be, could be on the brink. Stated bluntly: a conscious focus on sound sharpens the listener's ears to the surrounding pregnant silence.

(in Kendrick and Roesner 2011: 65–67)

I argue that this concept of voice, of sound and silence, is not the "absence/presence" binary Cormac Power criticized as typical ways scholars and practitioners have thus far thought of "presence." He wrote, "An understanding of presence in theatre must take into account that the complexity of the stage forbids a simple presence/absence binary (142)" and he called for "a different approach to understanding theatrical representation in terms of how presence is put into play" (ibid.). Instead of collapsing sound and "presence," and characterizing silence as the "absence" of sound, what if sound and silence were conceptualized as forms of voice, connected in part through their use of *ki*?

Similar to other practitioners, I understand *ki* to be connected to breath but also to physically manifest itself in the body of the performer as heat or vibrations in the body (Da Liu 1986: 50–51; Yoo in CTR February 2007: 81–96). From Lee Seung-Heun's understanding of *jin-ki*, I understand *ki* as concentrated focus and heightened awareness in the performer that can be "read" on the actor's body by the audience. The audience's *ki* can also manifest itself as a similar concentrated focus or awareness, and can be observed or felt by the performer while she is performing, what Fischer-Lichte theorized as part of an "autopoietic feedback loop," which is "generated and kept in motion not just through visible and audible actions and attitudes of actors and spectators but also through the energy circulating between them. This energy is no phantasm . . . but is physically perceptible" (2008: 59). In this way, the performer does not have to look at the audience (directly or through peripheral vision) to understand she has the audience's attention. Instead, the performer can "sense" the audience's attention. Through a Cartesian model of experience, it might be described as a physical sensation as well as a mental awareness. This is part of my understanding of the way in which the performer's *ki* "harmonizes" with the audience's *ki*, what Yuasa discussed in the context of the Japanese "bushi" tradition.

It is important that the student understand the difference between focusing with the external eye to create a visual connection with a stage partner and using one's "internal eye" to focus concentration of *ki* between oneself and one's stage partner or spectator. During the exercises, students are repeatedly asked to build bodymind through focused awareness via the "mind's eye." The "mind's eye" or "inner eye" is differentiated from the "external eye" that supplies one's vision. In one sense, the "inner eye" is imagination, but for the most part, I use the "inner eye" to develop tactile awareness and concentrated effort. The "inner eye" helps shift *ki* round the body. When *jin-ki* is generated the physical manifestations of that energy can be felt as heat or vibration.

This exchange of focus or awareness during the performance between the performer and the spectator is part of what I understand to be the exchange of *ki*, or "presence," and is at the heart of live performance. Lagaay argues that the "transcendence" of performance is not one that takes the performer or audience member beyond the material or out of the body but "it is a transcendence, if you like that relies centrally on the human senses to the extent that these are capable, essentially, of sensing beyond themselves and the moment—towards the silent yet resonant potential *within*" (in Kendrick and Roesner 2011: 67, italics in original). Perhaps, then, "presence" could be characterized as a kind of "pre" + "sense," an awareness that something is about to happen, "a potential within," but has not yet affected the traditionally understood five senses, specifically in this case, hearing/listening.

As a performer, I have trained myself to become aware of the audience by feeling the heat and vibrations from their bodies. The vibrations from their bodies tell me how concentrated their focus is through a kind of "tempo-rhythm" of vibrations. The physical presence of their body that issues these vibrations may be affected by their breathing patterns, but not necessarily. I am not listening for the way they breathe to gauge the concentration of their focus; I am sensing the rhythm of the vibrations in their body.

As a teacher, I use this experience to determine my students' progress in developing *ki* in voice training. When I teach *tai chi*, *dahnjeon* breathing or vocalized *om*, my students tend to listen to their breath as an external gauge of their focus; "focus" is misunderstood as the external signs and sounds of breathing through the nose at a slow pace, or "om-ing" a low pitch with chest resonance. But I am not listening to their breathing to understand the concentration of their focus. I am physically feeling the heat and vibrations as the rhythm of the vibrations reaches a kind of "tempo" of focus. Sometimes I sense a feeling of "heaviness" like a Laban "press" as the tempo of the vibrations slows down and other times the concentration of *ki* can be "light" as the tempo of the vibrations quickens, a kind of Laban "float."

Sometimes, the focus on task can become intense, in part through a kind of mindful repetition that asks the learner and teacher to constantly reinvest in this focus through an ever-becoming embodied awareness of the task. At times, this co-created "awareness" can lead to an energy exchange in which the teacher and learner become so involved, or using Drew Leder's term "absorbed," in the task that they may forget about time and place; they are able to feel "connected" not only to the task but to each other in the doing of the task. The doing of the task becomes a nuanced level of understanding action between teacher and student in which stepping out of task to give instruction and reflection would interrupt this "flow." If this "flow" and "connection" is understood as a kind of emerging "presence" in studio, then it is founded on being "present" in the exchange of learning/teaching for both student and teacher.[13]

Perhaps such experiences in studio become the embodied reference points for young performers as they perform for audiences? If the student during training was able to create with her teacher this feeling of "connection" then this could become a guiding experience used to try and "connect" with an audience in performance. In this way, moments of "flow," in studio during the training of technique can possibly become employable moments of "flow," with an audience, reliant on the deployment of technique in performance. I am not arguing that "presence" can be reduced to technique but instead I am interested in teasing out how "energy" as actors' "tools" (Rodenburg 2000: 226) in voice training "engages" (Rodenburg 2007: xiii) the listener, or how "presence" works in training to develop "connection" (Rodenburg 2007: 97). Also, I am interested in how different techniques can interact to create "connection" and how, perhaps, doing so creates different kinds of "connection" or understandings of "presence." I am not arguing that this exchange of "energy" in studio between student and teacher can or does happen universally.[14] I will return to this later.

The way the "natural/free" voice understands the location of "center" differs from *dahnjeon* but the larger notion that working through a center can "clear the mind and focus energy" (Linklater 1976: 136) or suggests a way to prepare the body to be "ready" (Rodenburg 2007: 50) offers the potential to place "center" and *dahnjeon* on a continuum of training practice within the same voice studio. Strategic interactions, and sometimes unplanned happenings, between the two techniques have created fruitful learning moments for me and my students as we access different ways of understanding and cultivating "energy" and voice.

"Mind" and "energy"

In working towards ways to "clear the mind and focus energy" (Linklater 1976: 136), it is important to first understand what "mind" and "energy" mean in the traditions of the "natural/free" voice approach and Asian modes of training. Breath training is fundamental to both traditions. Both share an interest in training the breath towards some kind of relationship between *bodymind*[15] and using a kind of "energy" in training/performance. Despite shared interests, different ways of understanding the body/voice give rise to pedagogical differences.

In *Presence*, Rodenburg's chapter thirteen, Mind, briefly discussed her understanding of "mind." Here, "mind" is a place of reflection, "idea" (2007: 127), and "thought" (ibid.). A Second Circle mind is "listening and connecting to new ideas" (2007: 128). In this way, "mind" is understood through a traditional Cartesian split in which "mind" is located in the head and is the source of logic and reason.

In contrast, Chan Park wrote, "Cartesian dualism falls short of explaining the conceptual mind-body collaboration in the materialization of . . . *sori*" (2003: 199). When she asserted that "voice is acoustic reflection of the mind" (2003: 189), her understanding of "mind" encompassed "everything" (personal interview, Ohio, 2007). "Mind" is not ontologically separate from body and is not located in the head. In Park's translation of the *Book of Rites*, introduced in chapter three, "mind" is essential to the process of training of the voice. Other writings of Eastern practice also refer to the importance of "mind."[16] What this suggests goes beyond the idea of training the actor's body as one might train an athlete, embodying a set of skills well-executed during performance (Berry 1973: 44). The muscles of the body are not simply being trained through "conscious bodily movement" (Yuasa 1993: 28) but the bodymind is being trained.

The mind and the body become one through the practice of training the body—through the process of embodying a practice. In my various experiences training in *p'ansori*, cultivating seated meditation at *Wa gye sa* [temple] or "moving" mediation in martial arts, the set of skills being developed are dependent upon bodymind oneness. It is the fundamental means by which other skills in each of these various practices can be accomplished.

The "problem" with "presence" in conceptualizing the relationship between "energy" and voice

In the introduction of *Presence*, Rodenburg wrote,

> Here's the problem with the word "presence." Many people believe it is something you have or don't have . . . I don't agree: you might not have the make-up, clothes and lighting effects that enhance the stars but you can learn to find your full charisma. All it is, is energy. Present energy—clear, whole and attentive energy.
>
> *(Rodenburg 2007: xi)*

Although she rejected the idea of "presence" as a thing one does or does not "have," she offered in substitution other binaries, "to be or not to be" (xii), and a few pages later lost/found binaries (xiii and xvii). Such absence/presence binaries are difficult to integrate with understandings of *ki*; *won-ki* and *jong-ki* are linked to blood inheritance and diet/respiration that cannot be "lost" in the way Rodenburg means. "Presence" is also essentialised as a human quality outside of a given cultural or discipline-specific context.

When placing different traditions within the same studio, often I ask the student to see and hear her voice from different perspectives, different mappings of body, different value systems. This creates within one student, many possible voices and other possibilities for understanding what makes a voice engaging or how "presence" might function in relation to voice. Instead of emphasizing a singular, "natural" voice, I am interested here in students investigating multiple voices.

For Rodenburg, "presence" is singular. However, I argue there is no one "presence," but many different kinds of "presence," even within the cultivation of *jin-ki*. If *jin-ki* is cultivated through "mind," then the state of perceived "presence" varies according to the development of "mind" or level of concentrated awareness. Within a performer/audience relationship, the perception of "presence" within the performer by the performer is as important as the perception of the performer's "presence" by the audience. I will return to this argument when discussing the idea of *kwimyongch'ang*, or the "informed listener."

Zarrilli argued for a notion of "multiple presences." For him, "presence" is "an emergent state of possibility" in which,

> from the performer's perspective inside the performance 'presence' should only exist for the actor as a question—is it possible on *this* night with *this* audience to attain an optimal mode of engagement of awareness,

deployment of energy, and embodied consciousness appropriate to the aesthetic and dramaturgy of *this* performance score?

(2012: 120–121, italics in the original)

This "emergent state of possibility" (2012: 121), from moment to moment, can be understood as manifesting "multiple presences." The conditions under which multiple presences emerge rely on

the quality, valence, and intensity of the actor's ability to generate an inner "energy," to engage one's entire embodied consciousness in each performance task, to command space and hold attention is always shaped by one's training/experience, as well as the dramaturgy and aesthetic of a specific performance.

(2012: 122)

If the ability to "hold attention is always shaped by one's training/experience," can multiple "presences" also result from multiple trainings? When multiple trainings are placed along a continuum of ways of doing they may offer different results in sounding. As the sounding voice is heard, does a perception of voice as it becomes "present" also lay along a continuum of ways of listening to and eventually perceiving "presence?" And how does the ability to "hold attention," or a voice that "engages" the listener, develop in training?

If "presence" is understood, in part, through spectator/listener perception, then perhaps audiences, perhaps even specific audience members educated to appreciate a particular kind of "dramaturgy and aesthetic," will have a different understanding of what makes a voice "present" than others.

Listening

Rodenburg's eleventh chapter in *Presence* is "Listening." She wrote,

Like speech, listening is an extension of the breath. When you listen properly, you do it through the breath. Sound and words flow through your breath and touch you just as your sounds and words flow on your breath to others.

(2007: 116)

The practical exercises she offered in pages 120 to 121 prepare listening by "stay[ing] in Second Circle body and breath. Keep the jaw released, breathing calmly and deeply throughout" (120). The learner is then asked to listen to "silence," to "nature," and "to your own body" as well as to "music" and people the learner comes in contact with. These exercises focus on the individual's act of listening but not necessarily the way audiences are in role as listeners in a performance. Discipline-specific listening asks the audience to listen for something particular.

The act of listening to music, for instance, within a performer/audience relationship in *p'ansori*, is structured in a particular way. Within a performer/audience relationship, the perception of a performer's "presence" is understood differently by the "informed listener," or *kwimyongch'ang* in *p'ansori* from other audience members.

At a *p'ansori* performance, there may be a member of the audience in attendance who has such a highly skilled level of listening to the nuances of the *p'ansori* performer that she is called a *kwimyongch'ang* [trans. "great singer (critic) who sings with an ear"].[17] This is the term for an "informed listener" of *pansori* whose "'text' is oral/aural, requiring its own set of 'competences'"(Park 2003: 208). Park argued, "As manifest in the term 'great singer of the ear' (kwi-myong-ch'ang), locating the 'interior dimension' in *sori* is not for singers only, but for listeners reciprocally" (Park 2003: 208). The "connoisseur" (Park 2003: 208) or "discerning ear" (Park 2003: 204) can readily identify and appreciate the *sori* beyond that of other audience members, the "interiority" of the *sori* or *imyŏn*, what Park characterized as "the vocal reflection of the semantic interior of what is sung and is received by the discerning ear" (Park 2003: 204). For Park, the degree in which *p'an* in *p'ansori* can be created depends "not only developed via 'telling' but also tuned in 'listening'"(Park 2003: 233).

I argue that such "informed listeners" are placed to identify and appreciate "presence" in the voice as it emerges during performance in ways that are not accessible to a novice listener. When the audience is mixed with "informed listeners," "presence" exists on a variety of different levels. This is not to say the novice listeners do not feel the "presence of a great performer." Ethnomusicologist, Heather Willoughby described her first attendance of a *p'ansori* performance, a pre-demonstration activity before a student protest in 1986. She described seeing/hearing Kim Sohŭi, one of the greatest *p'ansori* performers of the 20th century (although she did not know this at the time), as "mesmerized by her voice, her presence, and her strength," although she "did not understand many of the actual lyrics in the story she related, I knew that her message was powerful and was producing a profound effect on all those in attendance." She wrote,

> I did not immediately understand why it had that affect on me, but began to concentrate more fully on the sounds themselves, the apparent bitter cries of lamentation. I had studied Western classical vocal music since I was twelve, and could not comprehend how a performer could produce the raspy tones, with such ease and delicacy.
>
> *(2002: 25–26)*

Within the dramaturgy of this performance, I read Willoughby's description of Kim's "presence" as emerging through the becoming performance on several levels. She is affected as much by Kim's powerful voice as she is by feeling the effect it has on the other students around her. She does not have access to certain levels of the performance, perhaps because of her level of Korean fluency at that time, perhaps because of the structure of the telling that may be in verse form, or maybe because "many words in *p'ansori* texts are Sino-Korean. Without understanding the characters, which are inserted, it is hard to comprehend the text thoroughly" (Jang 2014: xvi). Instead, Willoughby accessed listening through another embodied practice, her years of classical Western vocal music.

This would mean that "presence" is not a phenomenological event everyone can see/hear and has access to—it is not one, "universal" human experience. Instead, it is an ever-becoming experience between performer and audience member that exists in multiple ways, in other words "multiple presences." Thinking about "presence" as a relationship between performer and listener is useful for my purposes because it opens up a way for me to integrate a key principle of Korean traditional arts aesthetics, *mŏt* and *mat*, into my intercultural approach. One aim is to offer another way to work towards "the unification of subject and object [which] is central to the perception of *mŏt*" (Hwang 1978: 30).

An application of *mŏt* and *mat* to training actors' voices towards an understanding of "presence" in the voice

As an aesthetic of *p'ansori*, Jang defined *mat* as "taste" (its literal translation) and *mŏt* as "aesthetic taste." She wrote,

> These terms are used in the same sense as in everyday life. The former is, for example, used to describe tasty food, while the latter is used in, for example, admiring someone's dress sense or tasteful style. However, when speaking of a *p'ansori* performance, these terms denote that the performance is full of artistic charm. Elderly *p'ansori* singers, for example, say *soriga masiitta* ([someone's] song is tasty) when complimenting a singer's performance.
>
> *(2014: xxiii)*

Jang's last example also locates *mŏt*/*mat* within a listener/singer relationship. This is necessary, in part, because in *p'ansori*, the training of the voice does not start with the voice but with the ear. "In the process of acquisition, 'the learner's ears should open before his or her mouth'" (Park 2003: 202).

There is a heavy emphasis during *p'ansori* training on aural/oral feedback, listening first to the teacher and repeating back what you hear. This relationship augments to include the listening ear of the audience who offers *ch'uimsea* (trans. "calls of encouragement"), which, in its own way, "teaches" the performer how to meet audience expectations. In this way, the aural/oral relationship between teacher and student in the training studio is realized on stage through the oral/aural relationship between performer and audience during performance.

The "inner dimension of the ear" or "drawing the inner dimension" (2003: 205) that Park referred to as part of *imyŏn* can not only be understood through *p'ansori* but "in such related genres as the instrumental *sanjo* and *salp'uri* dance," and Park asks, "Considering their kinship with the native ritual process of healing and purging, could 'drawing the inner dimension' signify kindling the spirit of the performance itself?" (Park 2003: 205).

From discussions of the "inner dimension," Park offers her perspective and interpretation of *mŏt* and *mat*, concepts used to discuss the "flavour" of the voice in *p'ansori* aesthetics. For Park,

> *Mat* is the taste that the audience experiences, whereas *mŏt* is the quality or flavour that causes good taste that the performer exudes. "Flavour" is the subjective expression, while its "tasting" is the objectified reception by the audience. Then, again, the performer's expression is also an objectified outcome of subjective thought, while the audience's objectified reception is a collective of multiple subjectivity.
>
> *(2003: 210)*

Mŏt and *mat* exemplify the close relationship between ear and voice, or vocal characteristics with perceptual characteristics.

Hwang Byong-ki asserts,

> We can say that an object has *mŏt* or that we have become conscious of the *mŏt* within it, if, when we come in contact with the object our spirit by some means seems to enter into the spiritual rhythm of the object . . . The joy of life experienced in the unification of subject and object is central to the perception of *mŏt*. It is this life-joy to which importance is attached.
>
> *(1978: 30)*

The "unification of subject and object" is similar to Drew Leder's "forming one body." Leder asserted that there is a "correlativity of world and subject" in which "the world is an experience world, its character dependent upon our powers of apprehension . . . as the world exists only in relation to the experiencer, so the experiencer exists only in relation to the world" (Leder 1990: 158). Leder quoted Wang Yang-ming, "The eye has no substance of its own. Its substance consists of the colors of all things. The ear has no substance of is own. Its substance consists of the sound of all things." For Leder, this means "As subject, I do not inhabit a private theatre of consciousness but am ecstatically intertwined, one body with the world" (ibid.).

If, from a Neo-Confucian understanding of "one body," the performer and audience are already connected, then the aim of "presence" is not that it connects audience and performer, but that it increases this pre-existing connectedness. Hwang notes that the unification of subject and object is not available to every listener,

> highly refined *mat* cannot be easily understood by the ordinary listener . . . there are cases in which things that would commonly be said to have no *mŏt*, can be found upon examination on a higher level to have a *mŏt* which was

at first not readily discernible. This *mŏt*, called *songmŏt* (lit., "deep or inner mot") is something for which Korean artists, and particularly folk musicians, strive.

(1978: 30–31)

Marcus Cheng Chye Tan in his book, *Acoustic Interculturalism*, addressed the "concept of an 'intercultural voice' and extend[ed] the question of (re)sounding to one of listening in/to Asia" (Tan 2012: 136). He specifically addressed the use of *p'ansori* in Ong Keng Sen's *Desdemona*, with special mention to *mŏt* and *mat* in endnotes (146). Tan wrote,

> In Chinese thought the origin of the universe was realised through the two universal spirits of *yin* and *yang*. This principle is prevalent in Chinese music as well and has unmistakably been appropriated by Korean *a'ak* . . . It follows, then, that the Korean aesthetic principles of *mŏt* and *mat* are adapted notions of *yin* and *yang* applied to art and culture.
>
> *(2012: 224)*

As mentioned in previous chapters, *yin* and *yang*, or in Korean *eum-yang*, are in polarization. In this way, *mŏt* and *mat* denote an interdependent relationship (like *eum-yang*) between those who exude "flavour" and those who "taste," or between the performer and audience. One could argue that the relationship between performer and audience can be understood as a relative pair, a polarity, or as a *eum-yang* relationship. Could one, then, understand *mŏt* and *mat* as part of the mechanism that generates a speaking and listening model (feedback loop) which generates and perceives "energy" perhaps characterized as "presence?" This way of conceptualizing *p'ansori* training and performance offers other ways of thinking about "presence" for my voice students. Instead of "presence" being a thing one has, "presence" could be conceptualized as an interdependent relationship embedded within speaking/listening models, characterized as "feedback loops." The vocalist and listener construct ever-becoming "vocal presence" together. Juxtaposing Fischer-Lichte's understanding of the body as "becoming" with my understanding of the voice as "becoming" within the context of Park's concept of *p'an* results in the ever-becoming voice finds "presence" in the presence of an informed listener.

If there is a "problem" with "presence" (Rodenburg 2007) in training actors' voices, perhaps it is because voice, too often, has been conceptualized separately from the ear. Within oral art forms, like *p'ansori*, and especially those that train mimetically, the training of the voice explicitly understands voice in relation to the ear. I would argue that under these conditions one cannot theorize the voice alone. If one accepts this premise, then understanding the role of "presence" in voice pedagogy could benefit from investigating the aural/oral feedback loop in a similar way in which Fischer-Lichte theorized the performer/audience autopoietic feedback loop.

Feedback loops

In explaining his understanding of an aural/oral feedback loop, Alfred Tomatis wrote,

> We think of energy as something you expend in activity, or we believe we feel it circulate in us, something like electricity. Some say it descends, while others say it rises. For some it is a fluid circulating through the body. Others feel it localized at "focal" points or chakras. The perception of energy is quite subjective. Some people feel "flows of energy" that fill them with mental and physical vitality. When we are feeling fine, we sometimes like to sing; and if we do, the more we sing, the more energy we get, and the better we feel. What I have just described is a feedback loop, or cybernetic circuit. The activity feeds itself, and enhances the mental and physical state brought about by singing.
>
> *(2005: 5)*

From this aural/oral feedback loop within the singer, Tomatis continued to the aural/oral feedback loop between the singer and the environment in which she is singing.

> The act of singing permits us to open a dialogue with space so that we become flooded by its vibrations and merge with it, acoustically speaking. As soon as you sing you get feedback from your surroundings . . . The interactions between the singers' physical body and the acoustic environment create a proprioceptive image of the body, and they structure a sensory-motor experience of the surrounding space in a perpetual dialogue. We create the vibration and are in turn affected by the space we have set in motion.
>
> *(2005: 6–7)*

Although Tomatis concerns himself primarily with sung voice, he does address his theories towards spoken voice, but only to the degree in which sung voice and spoken voice share similar areas of performance (2005: 5).

Applying Tomatis's explanation to (re)conceptualize "presence" in voice training for actors, the actors' voice and ear are relational and can be understood as participating within an aural/oral feedback loop first produced within the body/voice of the actor. In this way, the actor listens to herself speak and guides that speech with the ear towards the desired performance.

[Refer to video clip of my learning *p'ansori* in Sŏng Uhyang's studio in Chapter Three.] In this video clip, I attempt to explain what I think is happening in my lesson with Sŏng Uhyang in terms of feedback loops. Noticeably absent from this description will be visual clues I gather from watching my teacher as well as my kinesthetic understandings of this sounding event, such as the feeling of vibrations in my body telling me where sound is placed, the feeling of muscles contracting and releasing at appropriate times with appropriate levels of support and breath capacity, and the feeling of articulation relationships during speech.

Sŏng Uhyang embodies an aural/oral feedback loop within her body/voice as she delivers *Sarang-ga* to me. Her ear guides her voice to perform certain sounds into a certain structure. This structure carries meaning for her. A second oral/aural feedback loop is created when she sings and I listen. She sings in a particular way for a learning situation—not a performance situation—which means perhaps she is singing more slowly or pronouncing her words more carefully or over-emphasizing where the sound happens on which beat. I listen to all of this and attempt to decipher meaning from it as I am memorizing it, because I know I will need to repeat back to her exactly what I hear. A third aural/oral feedback loop is created within my body/voice when I attempt to sing back to her. My ear guides my voice to try and repeat what I think I heard moments before. The entire lesson is made up of a series of these kinds of aural/oral exchanges. In this way, embodied skills are delivered from her body/voice into my body/voice.

In this clip you can hear that I am not successfully repeating what Sŏng Uhyang is singing. I am not only struggling to hear the melodic progression but I am also stumbling over the pronunciation of Korean words. There are several reasons for this.

First, my aural position: the melodic progression in *p'ansori* contains microtonal slides and my ear has been trained to understand pitch through a 12-tone chromatic scale while studying violin and voice for my music degree. My ear is trying to hear whole-steps and half-steps—I am trying to find a musical structure based on my previous music training. If I can anticipate the musical structure I can better follow what my teacher gives me. The problem arises because this musical structure is unfamiliar to me. Thus, the process of learning *p'ansori* begins through deep, attentive listening so that I not only hear the sound correctly (aural) in order to repeat it correctly (oral), but also I am simultaneously learning to understand that sound in relation to the other sounds around it, for example, the overall melodic progression. In doing this, I am trying to find the musical "key signature" but *p'ansori* does not have a Western-style "key signature" so my expectations have been thwarted. Instead, *p'ansori* has a moveable tonal center, which means that this lesson might begin this song on a different note than during our lesson yesterday, not wildly different but enough to disrupt the expectations of my ear. So in musical terms, my "ear-training" needs work, in other words, I need to train my ear to identify what I am hearing and give it meaning within another, very different musical structure to what I have previously learned.

Second, my oral position: the Korean language is also a problem during this lesson, not only because of my developmental level of Korean but also because I have learned the Seoul dialect in my Korean as a foreign language classes and this particular pronunciation is in Cholla province dialect. Because I am having difficulty hearing the difference between /o/ and /au/ I cannot position my articulators to create the aural difference. I do not know what these combinations should feel like in my mouth. The role of the ear is to help guide these new relationships as I create a greater kinesthetic awareness of these articulatory patterns and my habitual oral setting. I struggle to use my voice to create my teacher's sounds, not only because my voice is not yet conditioned as hers is but because my ear is not yet conditioned to listen to sound in this new way.

These feedback loops become the means for embodying skill sets and can be understood as the foundation for developing "technique," or a set of highly developed skills used when executing a task. These skill sets are structured to realize certain aesthetic principles. Also, the training is structured to presuppose certain audience reactions. The feedback loops during training rely on a set of assumptions about audience expectations. So then, when the training is ready for performance, the performer's embodied aural/oral feedback loops participate in yet another aural/oral feedback loop between performer and listening audience.

Like the *p'ansori* studio, the *p'ansori* performance has a series of aural/oral feedback loops. Again, my description of this event is purposely simplified in order to focus on this one aspect and momentarily disregards the participation of the drummer in order to conceptualize what I think is happening between performer and audience. The performer vocalizes (oral) and the audience listens (aural). Through *ch'uimsae*, the audience can shout calls of encouragement to the performer (oral). The performer receives these calls (aural) and responds (oral) sometimes through direct address to the audience or by heightening her level of performance, or both.

For the young performer, the aural/oral feedback loop in studio, which was the basis for studio training, continues as performance training during the aural/oral feedback loops with a live audience. The audience picks up where the teacher left off and continues to "train" the performer to meet audience expectations through audience response. If the seasoned performer is understood to exude "presence," it is in part because her developing younger self and her audiences have been creating together the conditions for "presence" to eventually emerge within the seasoned voice and the seasoned ear. Thus, technique is not embodiment training only realized in studio but also in performance. And it is not a process embodied only by the performer but also by the listening audience. The listening audience learns how to listen as much as the performer learns how to vocalize with the aural/oral feedback loop.

Feedback loops, *mŏt* and *mat*, and detailed descriptions of listening/speaking models (both connoisseurs and novice listeners), are ways I try to articulate to my students how "energy" might be cultivated in studio between teacher and student. Techniques such as "centering" and *dahnjeon* breathing, when practiced rigorously over time, offer my students embodied skills that work towards this energy exchange. If a student can experience an exchange of "energy" with her teacher as "flow" or "forming one body," she could use this experience as a template for cultivating "energy" exchange between herself as performer and her audiences. Depending on how such exchanges are perceived within the dramaturgy and aesthetics of the performance, the ever-emergent "energy" of the performer could be characterized "presence(s)."

The investigation here between performer and audience will continue in the next chapter, specifically located within the context of "text" and "vocal text." Chapter Six investigates the role of sound with the text, how sound contributes to meaning beyond dictionary definitions, and how the training of voice contributes to meaning-making with the text/vocal text relationship. This investigation is situated within a series of original devised projects, called the Namdaemun Market Projects, which take voice training out of the studio and "back to the mat."

Notes

1 When addressing non-actors, which includes a wide range of vocal users, there is also no explicit attempt in the training to address the unique ways these learners use their voices within a given context and how that context might influence access and implementation of "presence" for the voice user as well as the receiving listener.

2 "The question arises as to who is present and perceived by others– the actor or the dramatic figure?" (Fischer-Lichte 2012: 106).

3 I will return to this when discussing *kwimyongch'ang* in *p'ansori*.

4 Also refer McAllister-Viel (2009: 432–433).

5 www.patsyrodenburg.com/PatsyRodenburg.com/Teaching.html. Rodenburg three-day workshop in Portugal emphasizes a connection between her theatrical background and training participants' voices in other areas such as presentation skills and leadership along with "presence." Her website advertises, "Patsy Rodenburg's intensive 3-day course on voice, presence and ethical leadership is based around her extensive knowledge of classical texts. The aim of the course is to engage in not only connected speech and presence, but to provoke meaningful debate on the good use of power (a concept which lies at the heart of all Classical Greek and Shakespearean text) and to reflect upon how these principles should be applied today."

6 There is a correspondence between this training model and "the standard folk-psychological notion of language use" that supports "all the dominate theories of speech production" that are "part of the comparator family of models, and share the assumption that speech starts with a clear preverbal conception of what to say, which is then translated into an utterance through successive levels of linguistic and articulatory encoding" (Lind, Hall, Breidegard, Balkenius, and Johansson, *Frontiers in Human Neuroscience*, March 2014: 3–5).

7 Rodenburg interchangeably uses "charisma" and "presence." She wrote, "you can find your full charisma. All it is, is energy. Present energy – clear, whole and attentive energy" (Rodenburg 2007: xi).

8 Refer Jang (2014: 153). "According to Kim Yongja, *ch'uimsae* must come from one's abdomen, and should not be made with a light, 'flying' voice. This is why *ch'uimsae* from drummers who have previously learned *p'ansori* is the best" (interview with Kim, Yongja, 23 April 1997, Seoul).

9 It is not my aim here to argue that *p'an* = "presence" and then attempt to merge Rodenburg's understanding of "presence" with an understanding of "presence" from *p'ansori*. Instead, I am interested in how two techniques (specifically *dahnjeon* breathing and centering), which already concern themselves with different understandings of "energy" from within their different traditions can bring their shared interest in "energy" as a material of training and performance, finding a relationship within the same voice studio. How "energy" works to cultivate what might be understood as "presence" in *p'ansori* or "presence" in Western-style theatre performance would need an extended discussion not possible here.

10 For larger conversations about the relational difference between "presence" and "present" refer Power (2008: 3) and Fisher-Lichte's "weak concept of presence" in Giannachi, Kaye, and Shanks (2012: 106).

11 This understanding of "present" may shift in future as more conservatoires are under pressure to devise ways of training through "distance learning"; live or recorded workshops offered online to enrolled students who are not or cannot be physically in the classroom, disrupting understandings of "present" as being in the same place at the same time.

12 Fischer-Lichte critiques Barba's assumption that there are universal laws that "underlie these practices, developed and actualized by performers of diverse cultures in order to conjure up energy within themselves and let it circulate through space, so that it can be transmitted to spectators, who in turn also generate energy" (in Gainnachi, Kaye, and Shanks 2012: 110). My assertion is NOT that pre-expressive energy stems from a universal principle underpinning practices. I am attempting to move away from universalism as a primary explanation for training. I think there are areas of overlap between "centering" and *dahnjon* practice that allow for the transference of skills.

13 I understand that the power difference between student and teacher in many classrooms may make this kind of "connection" difficult or impossible. Also, I am not arguing that this is achievable at every class or during every lesson. However, I have experienced this with my students on a fairly regular basis as to suggest that this model of interaction is not extraordinary or profound but can be understood as a cultivated happening, initiated through the transference of technique in studio training.

14 The power relationships in the studio as well as time, the space of the studio, and resources enabling training are all factors helping to determine if both teacher and student can be "present," allowing for an intensive focus on task and "energy" exchange, as conditions for "connection" or emerging feeling of "community." This is similar to the necessary conditions by which "presence" may emerge through the conditions of performance; here I am adapting Zarrilli: "is it possible in *this* [class] with *this* [student(s)] to attain an optimal mode of engagement of awareness, deployment of energy, and embodied consciousness appropriate to the aesthetic and dramaturgy of *this* [training task]" (Zarrilli 2012: 120)? I will discuss Zarrilli's quote in the next section, the "problem" with "presence."

15 Voice practitioners, as least since the early 1900s, have been interested in creating a better relationship between mind and body. F.M. Alexander was interested in ways of addressing mind wandering through his Alexander Technique. He argued in his 1924 publication, "I would remind my readers that I do not separate 'mental' and 'physical' operations (manifestations) in my conception of the manner ('means-whereby') of the functioning of the human organism. For how can we prove that the response to any stimulus is wholly 'physical' or wholly 'mental?'" (29–30).

16 Refer Zeami Motokiyo (1364–1443), in his treatise *Kakyo*, trains the Nō actor's voice using *ki*, "First the Key; Second the Activating Force [*chi*], Third, the Voice," Nearman (1982: 343–374, 347).

17 I am using Chan Park's translation and understanding of this type of *p'ansori* audience member (2003: 306).

References

Barba, E., Savarese, N. (1991). *A Dictionary of Theatre Anthropology*. London: Routledge.

Benedetti, R. (1990). *The Actor at Work*. Upper Saddle River: Prentice Hall.

Berry, C. (1973). *Voice and the Actor*. New York: Collier Books.

Berry, C. (1987). *The Actor and the Text*. New York: Applause Books.

Cavarero, A. (2005). *For More Than One Voice: Toward a Philosophy of Vocal Expression*. Stanford: Stanford University Press.

Da Liu. (1986). *T'ai Chi Ch'uan and Meditation*. New York: Schocken Books.

Deutsch, E. (1993). "The Concept of the Body," in Kasulis, T., Ames, R., and Dissanayake, W. (eds.) *Self as Body in Asian Theory and Practice*. Albany: State University of New York Press, 6–8.

Dolar, M. (2006). *A Voice and Nothing More*. Cambridge and London: MIT Press.

Fischer-Lichte, E. (2012). "Appearing as Embodied Mind—Defining a Weak, a Strong and a Radical Concept of Presence," in Giannachi, G., Kaye, N. and Shanks, M. (eds.) *Archaeologies of Presence: Art, Performance and the Persistence of Being*. London: Routledge, 103–118.

Giannachi, G., Kaye, N., Shanks, M. (eds.) (2012). *Archaeologies of Presence: Art, Performance and the Persistence of Being*. London and New York: Routledge

Goodall, J. (2008). *Stage Presence*. London: Routledge.

Hampton, M., Acker, B. (1997). *The Vocal Vision: Views on Voice*. New York: Applause.

Hwang, B.K. (1978). "Aesthetic characteristics of Korean Music in Theory and in Practice," *Asian Music, Korean Music Issue*, 9 (2), 29–40.

Jaeger, S.M. (2006). "Embodiment and Presence: The Ontology of Presence Reconsidered," in Krasner, D. and Saltz, D.Z. (eds.) *Staging Philosophy: Intersections of Theatre, Performance and Philosophy*. Ann Arbor: University of Michigan Press, 122–141.

Jang, Y. (2014). *Korean P'ansori Singing Tradition*. Toronto: Scarecrow Press.

Kendrick, L., Roesner, D. (2011). *Theatre Noise: The Sound of Performance*. Newcastle upon Tyne: Cambridge Scholars Publishing.

LaBelle, B. (2014). *Lexicon of the Mouth: Poetics and Politics of Voice and the Oral Imaginary*. London: Bloomsbury.

Leder, D. (1990). *The Absent Body*. Chicago: University of Chicago Press.

Lee, S.H. (1999). *Dahnhak*. Seoul: Dahn Publications.

Lind, A., Hall, L., Breidegard, B., Balkenius, C., and Johansson, P. (2014). "Auditory feedback of one's own voice is used for high-level semantic monitoring: the "self-comprehension" hypothesis," *Frontiers in Human Neuroscience*, www.frontiersin.org/articles/10.3389/fnhum.2014.00166/full. Accessed 13 June 2018.

Linklater, K. (1976). *Freeing the Natural Voice*. New York: Drama Book Publishers.

Linklater, K. (1992). *Freeeing Shakespeare's Voice*. New York: Theatre Communications Group.

Linklater, K. (2017). LinklaterVoice.com. www.linklatervoice.com/resources/articles-essays/item/1143-the-art-and-craft-of-voice-and-speech-training. Accessed 30 March 2017.

McAllister-Viel, T. (2009). "Voicing Culture: Training Korean Actors' Voices through the Namdaemum Market Projects," *Modern Drama*, 52 (4), 432–433.

Meyer-Kalkus, R. (2001). *Stimme un Sprechkunste im 20 Jahrhundert*. Berlin: Akademie Verlag.

Mills, E. (1999). *Theatre Voice as Metaphor: The Advocacy of A Praxis Based on the Centrality of Voice to Performance*. Unpublished MA thesis, Rhodes University, Grahamstown.

Nearman, M.J. (1978). "Zeami's Kyui: A Pedagogical Guide for Teachers of Acting," *Monumenta Nipponica*, 33 (3), 299–332.

Park, C.E. (2003). *Voices from the Straw Mat: Toward an Ethnography of Korean Story Singing*. Honolulu: University of Hawaii Press and Center for Korean Studies.

Park, S. (1997). "Voice as a Source of Creativity," in Hampton, M. and Acker, B. (eds.) *The Vocal Vision*. New York and London: Applause, 107–119.

Power, C. (2008). *Presence in Play: A Critique of Theories of Presence in the Theatre*. New York: Rodopi.

Rodenburg, P. (1992). *The Right to Speak*. New York: Routledge.

Rodenburg, P. (1994). *A Voice of Your Own* [video]. New York: Applause Books.

Rodenburg, P. (2000). *The Actor Speaks: Voice and the Performer*. New York: St. Martin's Press.

Rodenburg, P. (2007). *Presence: How to Use Positive Energy for Success in Every Situation*. London: Michael Joseph.

Song, C. (1995). *Nŏn sori todungnyŏniyŏ [You are a Song Thief]*. Seoul: Ŏnŏ munhwa.

Tan, M.C.C. (2012). *Acoustic Interculturalism*. London: Palgrave MacMillian.

Tomatis, A. (2005). *The Ear and the Voice*. Toronto and Oxford: Scarecrow Press.

Um, H.K. (1992). *Making P'ansori: Korean Musical Drama*. Unpublished PhD thesis, Queen's University of Belfast, Belfast.

Um, H.K. (2008). "New P'ansori in Twenty-First-Century Korea: Creative Dialectics of Tradition and Modernity," *Asian Theatre Journal*, 22 (1), 24–57.

Um, H.K. (2013). *Korean Musical Drama: P'ansori and the Making of Tradition in Modernity*. SOAS Musicology Series. Farnham: Ashgate.

Yuasa, Y. (1993). *The Body, Self-Cultivation, and Ki-Energy*. Trans. Nagatomo, S., Hull, M.S. Albany: State University of New York Press.

Zarrilli, P.B. (2012). "'Presence' as a Question and Emergent Possibility: A Case Study from the Performer's Perspective," in Giannachi, G., Kaye, K., and Shanks, M. (eds.) *Archaeologies of Presence: Art, Performance and the Persistence of Being*. London: Routledge, 120–152.

6
TEXT/VOCAL TEXT

The role of voice/sound and text

How the actor gets the text "from the page to the stage" is a preoccupation of many mainstream Anglo-American voice texts. Chapter Four offered a brief look at how making "the words your own" (Berry 1973: 16) emerges from the materials of voice, in this case, the role of self and breath in practice. This chapter builds on this link between breath and text and develops an understanding of text from other materials of voice, specifically how sound behaves in language. To recap the basic premise from chapter four from which this chapter builds, the "natural/free" voice approach aims to "embody" the words (literally putting inside the body/voice) via techniques that create an impulsive and spontaneous emotional and psycho-physical response to words, such as Linklater's "Sound and Movement: Embodying Language" workshop offered through The Kristin Linklater Voice Centre, Orkney, Scotland (Linklatervoice.com 2017). Rodenburg wrote in her second book, *The Need for Words* (2001),

> When we need a word—really connect with it and release it in a brave, physical sense—the experience is not just an act of intellect but a feeling act felt throughout our entire being ... Words that respond to need flow through us, practically becoming part of our circulatory system.
>
> *(2001: 3)*

For the actor-in-training, the ideal result would be the assimilation of technique as a response on a muscular level so that technique is no longer marked on the body/voice and the playwright's words "feel" like the student's own thoughts. Sometimes this is called colloquially "owning" the language. For the audience, the ideal result would be that they "forget" they are listening/watching an actor and instead momentarily believe, through willing suspension of disbelief, that the words the actor speaks are not the playwright's words but are the character's original thoughts, spoken for the first time in the presence of the listener. The way the actor speaks, indeed the sound of the voice, should not remind the audience that the text has been memorized and rehearsed for several weeks before performance. The goal is to sound spontaneous and impulsive so that the actor's experience of "impulse" is collapsed with the character's impulsive behavior.

In order to train towards spontaneous and impulsive vocal performance, some voice texts divide into separate books the technical, basic training of the voice (breath support and capacity, resonance, pitch, articulation patterns, etc.) from the expressive elements of interpreting spoken text. An example is Houseman's *Finding Your Voice* (Houseman 2002), which focuses on practical voice work and *Tackling the Text*, which emphasizes learning strategies for text interpretation (Houseman 2008). Berry, Linklater, and Rodenburg compile the majority of their basic voice training into their first texts, with a heavier emphasis on text work in subsequent texts. All three have written specifically on the expressive elements of Shakespearian text in particular. In general, the basic training of the voice, often found in the first book, is organized in a linear process, beginning with alignment and breath and finishing in the final chapters with speech. In this way, practical voice training services speech. If the speech act suffers, then the practical voice training that preceded the speech act must be changed. Ideally, towards the end of the process, the technical and expressive elements of the voice are interwoven so that the speech act and text interpretation become one. The goal is to hear what is said (the text), not the technical markers that point to the voice itself as a vehicle for speech. Jeannette Nelson, Head of Voice at The National Theatre, London, UK, and a student of Patsy Rodenburg instructs, "Your listeners should be listening to what you are saying, not how you say it" (Nelson 2015: 24).

The model for speaking contemporary, psychologically based play text is usually off-stage models for voicing but the model for voicing "heightened text" such as verse forms (e.g. poetry, Shakespeare, Restoration, or other period dramas) tend to be models set by particular master teachers, such as Cicely Berry, voice director for The Royal Shakespeare Company. Within voice training texts focusing on both classic and contemporary play texts, authorial intention is of primary importance. Privileging of the author within voice training has been heavily criticized (Knowles 1996 in Bulman; Werner 2001). Knowles and Werner argue that within the training texts of Berry, Linklater, and Rodenburg, which focus specifically on the texts of Shakespeare, the ideology of the training is hidden behind assumptions of "universal truth" that authorial intention supposedly reveals. At times during training, the student's experience and the character's experience are intentionally collapsed. For instance, in Stanislavsky-based approaches to teaching voice, students are encouraged to ask "What do I want" as if she were speaking as the character (Linklater 1976: 204). The paradox of the "natural/free" voice approach is that the practical voice work supports one's individualism (e.g. freeing one's own natural voice) but only to a point. Once the practical voice work is folded into speaking text, one's individual interpretation of text must meet a larger, implicit set of criteria that is a combination of teacher expectation and vocal performance tradition.

In contrast, *p'ansori* evolved from an oral art form that has a very different relationship to the written word and performing text. *P'ansori* stories as literature and the performance of *p'ansori* stories sometimes offer very different understandings of the same story. As mentioned in Chapter Three's overview of *p'ansori* history, *p'ansori* texts have been edited and changed over time. Modern *p'ansori* performance texts have been written down in part to preserve a particular performer's version, part of the Korean government policy to "preserve" *p'ansori* as a traditional art form. In this way, there is no one story but many versions by different "authors." Arguing authorial intent in this context would be difficult for performers.

Although *p'ansori* students may learn in studio with text, the nature of *p'ansori* training still relies on a oral/aural model in which mimetic devises shape vocal technique, expression and text interpretation. As mentioned earlier, the "natural/free" voice approach rejects mimesis because it was one of the hallmarks of an earlier training approach called "Voice Beautiful." The *p'ansori* student trains in an environment in which teacher expectation and oral performance tradition are made explicit through the mimetic process.

Also, *p'ansori* is an oral storytelling form in which the storyteller is ever present as performer. The storyteller goes in and out of many different roles without collapsing one's "self" with the character. To portray a character "truthfully" is not dependent on a "correct" way of embodying authorial intent, or the "feeling" of "truth" a student actor has when intentionally collapsing her own experience with that of the character.

According to Park, *p'ansori* rises to its own understanding of "truth," but of critical importance is how the audience identifies a performance as "truthful," particularly in the idealized relationship between performer and aficionado audience members, *kwimyongch'ang* (2003: 3). Park suggests (quoting Fredrick Turner) that in order to "view the interior as well as the exterior of orality, on must enter the oral tradition, for performance radically transforms the 'text' while simultaneously 'actualizing it into a single unique reality or manifestation'" (2003: 19). The position of author within the text is less secure in *p'ansori* than it is in script-based voice training and I argue that in *p'ansori* the storyteller's voice "authors" the text.

My students at East 15 train their voices for both text interpretation, when working on script-based projects, as well as training their voices as "text" when working without a script, for example, devising original material. In my classes, particularly when working with aural/oral storytelling forms in devised pieces, I often ask students to place sound and voice within the center of a creative project so that sound/voice become the foundational "textual" reference before adding language in further developing the story. Although there are learning strategies that cross-over between training the voice towards text interpretation and training voice for devised, voice/sound-based projects, at times, the training necessarily diverges. When the practical voice training prepares the student for text interpretation, I adapt "natural/free" voice exercises. When the training prepares the student for oral/aural messaging, I adapt my experiences training mimetically in *p'ansori*, offering strategies that view the voice itself as text. My long-term goal, which I continue to work towards, is to better interweave the trainings so they do not exist as separate entities but can be called upon by the student according to the task in a more joined-up way.

Here, I introduce a practice-based project that attempts to demonstrate how these trainings interact with various notions of text. Chapter Four introduced the idea of a text/vocal text relationship when creating sound notation in my *p'ansori* script during my lessons. This chapter investigates an adaptation of this relationship through a practice-as-research methodological approach within a set of original, devised projects exploring how sound/voice functions as "text." In these projects, oral history interviews were compiled from multiple visits to outdoor sites. These visits also introduced the notion of site-specific vocal training and performance. By returning to the marketplace environments that first fostered *p'ansori* training/performance techniques, students re-examined certain aural/oral training/performance relationships. Students combined these aural/oral training/performance relationships with Western "street" theatre aesthetics, producing several research performance projects across four years (2000–2004), which I have called the "Namdaemun Market projects," developed by me and my postgraduate students at KNUA. I also created market-place projects each year with my Central students as a part of their first-year voice classes. Both KNUA and Central projects functioned as in-class learning and were not developed into public productions. Later, I taught marketplace projects at the National Theatre School (Spain), visiting an open market in Valladolid's center, and for The Actor's Centre in Madrid, as well as the Centre for Performance Research at the covered and open market in Cardiff's town centre, Wales. Here, I focus on the original investigation within the Namdaemun Projects at KNUA.

The *p'ansori* techniques I adapted for my approach, such as supporting the breath/sound from lower *dahnjeon*, come from a tradition of training the voice outdoors for outdoor performance. The marketplace was one of the first training/performance grounds for the voice of the *p'ansori* performer. In order to reach my *p'ansori* lessons at Han Nongsŏn's studio, I had to walk through an outdoor neighborhood market. Sometimes I would notice similar sounds and certain vocal gestures, specifically vendor calls, with sounds I was learning in *p'ansori*. At this point in my development, I was possibly influenced by my previous voice training that encouraged me to look at vocal function in off-stage sites as models for training and on-stage vocal performance.[1] Later, I explicitly began visiting open-air markets after my *p'ansori* lessons in an attempt to understand the possible performance conditions that may have historically affected aural/oral training/performance rela-tionships in *p'ansori* and may continue to influence contemporary *p'ansori* performers who choose to train and perform outdoors. From these experiences, I formulated learning strategies for my developing pedagogy. By asking my students to also visit such outdoor sites, the students had the opportunity to research empirically the aural/oral training/performance potential of the market and eventually devised student-led, original in-class projects.

In the first section of this chapter titled, "A return to the market and street," I attempt to unpick some of the influences of my previous training; I am drawn to this way of working because I have been already exposed to a tradition of artists from the US and UK that have looked to the streets as sites of "performance." In this section, I briefly explain how the traditions of outdoor marketplace/street performance in Korea and the UK have influenced contemporary artists. I also introduce the idea that the market/street is a site of other kinds of vocal "performance," such as vendor calls, laying the groundwork for the projects detailed later.

The next section, "Re-examining aural/oral training/performance relationships in the market/street", I discuss how some Korean and UK artists return to the market/street linking themselves with a performance past that shapes current performance practice. I specifically link contemporary *p'ansori* performance with the "performance" of vendor's voices in Namdaemun Market, suggesting how similarities between the two aural/oral training/performance relationships might be used in combination for the in-class projects. I also argue a return to these sites is an alternative way to understand sonic "text" and oral histories as performance "text."

The next section in this chapter introduces the specific integration of *p'ansori* character and performance structure with the interview/storytelling techniques of oral historian, Studs Terkel, as another set of methods employed for these projects.

The fourth and final written section, "Performance project details," articulates how my KNUA students used the methods discussed in the previous section to develop their in-class projects. I use video performance samples and analysis to demonstrate how the training prepares the actor's voice for devising such a performance.

A return to the market and street

It has been useful in setting up the marketplace projects at KNUA and Central to draw some similarities between Korean and Anglo-American history so that students begin to understand how their work emerges from or is linked to the work of other artists and previous artistic developments across cultural contexts. Our work at times implicitly references these influences and at other times explicitly borrows or adapts methods for our own purposes.

In Chapter Three, I discussed outdoor training traditions in *p'ansori*, such as "*sankongbu*" [lit. "mountain study"] and traditions of performance in the marketplace. Pihl wrote of *p'ansori* traditional performance,

> Most traditional kwangdae[2] performed alfresco, setting up shop in a farmer's marketplace or a fishing village. Some of the better singers, however, would be invited to perform in private homes or in government precincts . . . P'ansori was sung to any audience that would pay: fishermen or farmers in the markets, rich men at their banquets, or successful state examination candidates celebrating their good fortune . . . The event that brought p'ansori from a mat in the marketplace to the proscenium stage was the 1902 erection of Korea's first national theatre, the Huidae.
>
> *(Pihl 1994: 4–5, 10)*

European countries also have a tradition of outdoor marketplace arts performances. Marvin Carlson wrote that in European cities, "The late Middle Ages and early Renaissance constitute the major historical period when theatre existed as an important part of urban life without any specific architectural element being devoted to its exclusive use" (Carlson 1989: 14). Artists were able to produce performances in various outdoor locations in the city, taking advantage of "already existing connotations of other spaces both in themselves and in their placement within the city" (ibid.). According to Carlson, "Often a particularly favored locale was the marketplace, which like the encompassing city could be seen as a symbol of the stage upon which Everyman played his earthly role" (Carlson 1989: 17). Similar to *p'ansori* history, European street performance eventually left the streets of the city in favor of indoor venues. "[In European cities] the institutionalized theatre of polite society, once having left the streets, generally abandoned them to this sort of popular entertainment, and this division remains generally alive today" (Carlson 1989: 27).

More recently in the 20th century, Korean and Anglo-American artists returned to the markets and streets, placing the aural/oral audience/performer relationship at the center of certain kinds of aural/oral contemporary performance. In general, their return was prompted by a political or artistic response to events in the latter half of the 20th century. In England and the US, artists turned away from "the institutionalized theatre of polite society" in part as a rejection of the capitalization of art, and a rejection of "the theatre building as a symbol of the 'cultural industry'" (Carlson 1989: 33). By returning to the streets, these artists made art more accessible and affordable to the average citizen in venues not traditionally thought of as performance spaces. Art developed on the street was their attempt to cultivate a more democratic or socialized form of theatre.[3]

For many Korean artists, a return to the streets was one way of discovering and asserting their cultural heritage and making traditional Korean arts more visible and accessible to other Koreans through free or government subsidized performances.[4]

In the summer of 2004 on Insadong street, I attended a Choson Dynasty reproduction play, which is a good example of a Korean government subsidized street performance intended to demonstrate Korean cultural heritage. Although this performance happens during the July tourist season and takes place in Insadong, a well-known tourist area, the primary purpose does not seem to be to entertain foreign visitors, but it is directed towards fellow Koreans. While non-Korean visitors may appreciate the visual spectacle, the play text is only performed in Korean, using Sino-Korean words and specific vocabulary that offers cultural "insider" jokes, unassisted by aural or visual translation.

In this performance, one of the actors in role as a military Captain, repeatedly uses traditional Sino-Korean terms that are contrasted with the contemporary term "*gunggi*", a joke for cultural insiders that the adults in the audience could probably appreciate. Through the use of language and culture, this street performance is designed to function on a cultural level. This example challenges the idea that streets as "public" domain offer greater accessibility of performance for the "Everyman," or a kind of democratization of performance culture. "Public" space, and in this example the public performance in this space, is culturally constructed and not necessarily accessible to all.

Further along Insadong was a street vendor selling a traditional kind of Korean taffy. His costume and scissors, along with the rhythmic performance, is a representation of a traditional Korean taffy vendor. From my observation, this businessman links himself with Korea's past traditions for commercial reasons. This vendor could sell the taffy without the costume. The scissors act more as a percussive instrument to entertain than simply to cut the taffy. They also act as a prop signifier for the role of a traditional taffy vendor. This vendor is performing a "role" and his rhythmic taffy cutting is a kind of street "performance."

Further down the street is a comedy pair playing guitars and joking with the audience. One performer leads the crowd with a chant, made popular when Korea-Japan hosted the 2002 World Cup. At that time, thousands of Koreans lined the streets of Jongno-3ga, the district where Insadong street is located, to watch huge outdoor television screens and cheer as their football team advanced to the finals, chanting in unison. According to Dr. Kim, Seong-kon, Professor of English at Seoul National University,

> Traditionally, the Korean people gravitate toward public gatherings to throw a party, stage a play or hold a conference. Traditional Korean folk arts such as Pansori [sic], and "open theatre" performed at the village square, and even the huge crowds cheering the 2002 World Cup games are a good example of this.
>
> *(Kim 2003)*

For Kim, modern Korea's use of outdoor space is still connected to the way pre-modern Korea had traditionally used outdoor spaces, like the marketplace, as sites for performance.

Like Kim, Pihl suggested that Korean culture was intimately connected to a use of outdoor space as site for performance when he wrote, "We should be looking for the survival of the art of *p'ansori*, not on stage but, rather on the 'mat' again, where the narrator is still master of all he conjures up for us" (Pihl 1994: 12). Site and voice have a symbiotic relationship. The site demands certain kinds of vocalizations that will travel an outdoor distance and grab the passing listener. The voice and the sounds it produces shape the site through the performance of culture.

(Re)examining aural/oral training/performance relationships in the market/street

If historically in Europe the marketplace and city streets had always contributed a political element to performance, then it is no surprise that artists like Brecht who returned to the streets and marketplaces to inspire their own work, would engage with the political messages inherent in street performance.[5] Brecht's return to the streets[6] helped European, UK, and US political artists cultivate their own work from the streets in the 1960s and 1970s.[7]

Another reason artists in the 1960s and 1970s were drawn to the street for training and performance was to cultivate a different kind of aesthetic or theatre experience. Street performance develops a certain kind of performance aesthetic, in part because it takes place outdoors; the natural lighting, weather, and environmental noises make outdoor performance look, feel, and sound different from indoor performance. Outdoor performance replaces the well-trained, well-informed indoor audience with a bustling crowd that might not normally visit institutional theatre venues and might only be watching a street performance out of curiosity or chance. In this setting, the performer's voice must grab the passing listener and probably needs to overcome ambient sounds that may be acoustically difficult for the aural/oral relationship. The performance space requires different performance objectives, which requires a different training of the voice.

Simply by training in an outdoor space, body/voice will have the opportunity to teach itself how to solve the problems of performing outdoors. The vocalist may not even be able to articulate exactly how this training happens because in fact her body/voice is responding to the vocal performance demands through a series of very quick experiences. This is not to suggest that responsive training does not have a reflective component. I am simply pointing out that this kind of experiential learning happens so quickly that it asks body/voice to make sudden adjustments.

I suggest that the distance created by the proscenium stage between performer and audience has led to an expectation of how sound should function, an idea of what sound does; this creates a certain kind of role for sound in training and performance. Refer to the idea of "projecting" the voice discussed in Chapter Five. From the crowd/audience, the vocalist learns immediately when their vocal tactics worked or did not work, when the audience felt included or walked away.

Could my student actors benefit from "a return to the 'mat?'" I train actors' voices for a contemporary marketplace (e.g. film, television, voice-over, etc.) but could I train modern actors' voices in a literal marketplace? What additional benefits might there be when taking voice training for actors out of the studio and into the streets?

Finding "text" in outdoor sites

During the 1970s, a return to the streets not only cultivated a particular aural/oral training/performance relationship but developed an understanding of the kinds of stories and characters that could be found in this environment. Studs Terkel's collection of oral histories from Division street in Chicago, published in his book *Division Street: America* (Terkel 1967) is a good example of the way American artists returned to the streets for these narratives.[8] The political nature of Terkel's work is obvious in his borrowing of Brecht's work, quoting a Brecht poem "A Worker Reads History," in his book *Working*, to link the book's primary investigation with Brecht's political theatre:

> The books are filled with the names of kings.
> Was it kings who hauled the craggy blocks of stone? . . .
> In the evening when the Chinese wall was finished
> Where did the masons go?
>
> *(Terkel 1972: 15)*

One aim of Terkel's work is to showcase personal histories that may have been written out of history books, offering an alternative understanding of history as individual experience. When each individual experience is placed in strategic juxtaposition to create a larger, collective narrative, patterns form a kind of "meta-narrative" that can be understood through the artist/author. Terkel's work would later influence such contemporary artists as writer/performer Anna Deveare Smith,[9] renewing a trend in storytelling as political theatre (sometimes referred to as "verbatim theatre" in the UK). US theatre companies, such as Tetonic Theatre, have had great success with productions like *The Laramie Project* (2000), and in the UK, productions such as *Talking to Terrorists* (2005) and *London Road* (2011) have cultivated unique mainstream audiences.

Terkel has been called, "a unique treasure of our [American] culture" (Ayers 2001: 143) and his work has been understood as cultivating a national voice (Burkman 2002). The "sound of a nation" (ibid.) recorded in Terkel's work is sometimes understood as developing an American "archetypal" character, to which Terkel has responded,

> Each of the subjects is, I feel, uniquely himself. Whether he is an archetypal American figure, reflecting thought and condition over and beyond himself, is for the reader to judge, calling upon his own experience, observations, and an occasional look in the mirror.
>
> *(Terkel 1967: 22)*

Korean government institutions also look to build a national voice, or look for an "archetypal" sound, through indigenous "cultural treasures." The characterization of Terkel's work as the "sound of a nation" is similar to the characterization of the *p'ansori* voice as the "voice of Korea," introduced in Chapter Three. I was interested in investigating this idea of how a voice/sound could come to represent a community's collective "voice." Here, I was negotiating the "natural/free voice" emphasis on the individual with the individual voice in a socio-cultural context.

What if the "sound of a nation" could be found in any market or street? This might include the training of the literal voice in the outdoor space of the market/street as well as the metaphorical "voice" of a nation by creating a community of narratives among the people who occupy the site. The relationship between sound, voice, and culture are central to investigating this idea of the "sound of a nation" or the "voice of Korea."

Sounds of culture

One of the first aspects of sound, voice, and culture my students and I explored were our experiences relating to each other in the classroom. Although I taught through in-class translators, we depended heavily on developing our ability to interpret meaning apart from language translation, particularly during performance when the juxtaposition of text to subtext or body to voice gesture created a more complex understanding of the staged situation. Examining these initial strategies became the foundation for developing research strategies when visiting the market and later when exploring the ways performers communicate to audiences.

The first learning strategy depended on our ability to listen to sound in language and decipher the intended meaning of sound. Certain sounds carried no meaning because they existed outside of our respective cultural/linguistic contexts. Even certain non-language sounds were difficult at times to understand because meaning existed in the many components of sound: pitch, resonance, placement in the body, amount of breath support and breath capacity, amount of muscular contraction within the gesture, intensity, duration, and so forth. The meaning would change with each subtle shift in production of sound. The longer we worked together the better our ear-training became in recognizing these shifts and deciphering the components of sound in the larger communicative context. My students and I were carefully "reading" each other's voices, or vocal text.

Living outside of my own culture and language helped me to develop a greater awareness of the way sound behaves as a kind of sign-system both on- and offstage. This growing awareness made me question one of the primary assumptions behind current voice practice already explored in previous chapters: that socio-cultural vocal training fosters habits not useful to discipline-specific voice training.

As introduced in Chapter Two, the "natural/free" voice approach, like much contemporary mainstream voice training, begins with the premise that the student enters training with negative vocal habits learned through environmental and sociocultural influence. These habits manifest themselves in muscular tension, or body/voice misuse that blocks vocal function. Exercises are designed to release the body/voice from this tension (e.g. excessive or unnecessary muscular contraction). This is the necessary preparatory work that lays the foundation for discipline-specific voice training for many American and British actors.

This premise creates particular ways of approaching the relationship between vocal function and culture, that cannot be applied universally. Yet within the writings of voice practice, phrases like "living in the world," the "condition of life," and "humanity all over our planet" suggest that every culture affects the voice in the same way. Examples from writings on voice training can be easily found:

- Linklater asserts, "The second assumption is that the tensions acquired through living in this world, as well as defenses, inhibitions and negative reactions to environmental influences, often diminish the efficiency of the natural voice to the point of distorted communication" (Linklater 1976: 1).
- Berry points to the way "the condition of life conditions the speech" through one's "environment" and "experience," which may include how one is "conditioned by education" (Berry 1973: 7–8).
- For Arthur Lessac, "Humanity all over our planet is immersed in chaos" and as a result, we must "recognize and perceptualize [sic] how the present outer environmental and social influences can destructively condition, pollute, and erode our inner natural capacities and creative potential" (Lessac 1968: 17).
- Rodenburg focused on the way "background [and] gender . . . taint the sound we make," and argues that society has created a conspiracy against one's "right to speak" (Rodenburg 1992: 8).
- Michael McCallion wrote that during "all of that living time he [the adult] has been learning, and choosing how to adapt himself so that he can feel reasonably well adjusted to cope with the pattern of his life" (McCallion 1988: 4). He goes on to suggest that such adaptations, in the long term, can have "perverse" effects (ibid.).

The similar ways these five master voice trainers discuss culture and voice is not a coincidence, but part of a larger tradition in 20th-century actor training. As early as the turn of the 20th century, F.M. Alexander wrote that bad, inefficient habits were learned through social training. He asserted that if one applied his "psycho-physical guidance by conscious control," as "a universal principle to 'living,'" one could prevent the negative conditions brought about by the "evils of civilization" (1902: 109). The rhetoric shaping phrases like "universal principle to 'living', and "evils of civilization" is startlingly similar to the language used in modern voice texts. Other similarities with contemporary voice training include practiced approaches to identifying bad "habits" as embodied excessive muscular contraction or "tension," inhibiting the habit through conscious awareness, via "introspection and analysis" then substituting "new and correct" habits.

Throughout the 20th century, this tradition of voice practice usually referenced culture in a particular, limited way, focusing almost exclusively on negative cultural influences that resulted in vocal "misuse" or silenced the voices of the oppressed. Sociocultural influence has been positioned, at times, within voice discourse as a kind of bad habit that needed to be resolved before the actor, or layperson, could effectively train the voice.

What if one began voice training with the assumption that sociocultural and environmental influences prepare the body/voice with certain skills necessary for discipline-specific actor training? In this way, voice pedagogy could strategically use culture as one of the material conditions of training and performance.

While both Korean and Anglo-American voice pedagogy have used the training of the voice to address social change, noticeably different is the way KNUA linked voice and culture to rebuild a sense of nationhood after Japanese colonialism, the Korean civil war, and the consequences of Western influence. Unlike Anglo-American voice training, which focuses on the negative effects of culture, KNUA seemed to explore ways to address the changing notion of culture by questioning what Korean culture is in a time of change.

For instance, within the Korean performance traditions my students followed, explicit investigations of Korean culture were the center of artistic experimentation. Korean avant-garde director and playwright Oh T'ae-Sok examined Korean daily life for examples of "Koreanness," which he staged in his performances. Oh investigated how social vocal training might be used as a resource for the vocal user in performance:

> In attempting to define Koreanness, [Oh T'ae Sok] insisted that his actors adopt peculiarly Korean modes of behaviour and expression. Oh has said that "Koreans traditionally do not look into each other's eyes when they speak; our communication is inherently indirect." Thus his characters often do not answer each other directly, and in staging his plays, he often asks actors, even in confrontational scenes, not to look at each other but to pretend to be pre-occupied with something else (such as scratching the floor with a fingernail) or to face toward the audience throughout the scene.
>
> *(Kim and Graves 1999: 11)*

In this instance, the way the voice had been socially trained provided this Korean artist with the tools to examine his culture and society. At KNUA, my students and I also explored culturally understood vocal behavior and its representation in both offstage and onstage performance spaces in order to develop a voice training approach that addressed certain ways culture, as social vocal training, communicates with the audience on a cultural level.

My ability to create new learning strategies as a foreigner living in Seoul depended on previous embodied learning. The comparison of my social vocal training as practiced response, or habit, to the responsive vocal gestures of my students made me more aware of my habitual attitudes towards voice and ear. My habits were the point of origin for understanding difference. When my habitual vocal responses did not get me what I wanted, or the expectations of the ear were not fulfilled, my habits then served as a point of departure for creating new strategies. I could then build other vocal and listening patterns in order to satisfy my wants and needs. As Patrice Pavis wrote,

> Actors simultaneously reveal the culture of the community where they have trained and where they live and the bodily [vocal] technique they have acquired, be this rigorously formalized by an established tradition (as in

Peking Opera, for example) or camouflaged by the ideology of the "natural" (as with the western naturalistic actor). Training does not do away with the choice of form; it presupposes it. The elaboration of a form developed from existing forms, but yet altered, characterizes all intercultural theatre.

(Pavis 1996: 17, brackets added)

As Pavis suggested, social vocal training is one means by which cultures reveal themselves in the voice and the ear. If training "does not do away with the choice of form but presupposes it" could social vocal training itself be useful in creating new forms for our intercultural approach? We needed to investigate further what previous social training was embedded in our bodies in order to better understand mood or intention. Then, we needed to devise a way to use this knowledge to train voices, develop voices for performance (e.g. character voices), and communicate with each other and the audience by paying attention to the cultural "readings" inherent to the performance text.

After we reflected on the learning-teaching dynamic in our own classroom, I addressed the students as experts[10] on the subject of their own cultural voice existing in an already skilled body/voice. In this way, I hoped to encourage students to stop perceiving their voices as having been damaged by society and voice training as a way to fix what was wrong. Through class discussion and journal reflection, students began to understand that social vocal training had already provided certain skills that allowed them to read vocal and sonic meaning.

Through ear-training assignments in class, I attempted to help my students increase their awareness, which could, through critical examination and devising processes, develop into a sound sign-system in performance. I applied my understanding of Elaine Aston's and George Savona's *Theatre as Sign System: A Semiotics of Text and Performance* (Aston and Savona 1991) to explore what I believed was a kind of sound sign-system that existed between performer and spectator in the making of meaning for sound. I began exploring theatre semiotics as "a methodology: as a way of working, of approaching theatre [voice] in order to open up new practices and possibilities of 'seeing' [hearing]" (Aston and Savona 1: brackets added).

Once we had developed a self-made sign-system, we used it as a part of our training language and as a tool to create character voices. Phillip Zarrilli wrote that although an actor "cannot act on the basis of understanding theatre as a semiotic system," the actor could understand building a character from "not only the relation between semiotics and acting but also what is required in productions where one plays moments which are not motivated psychologically—moments in which an actor's action/gesture/posture [voice] might be said to 'stand on their own'" (Zarrilli 2002: 16–17; bracket added).

With this I incorporated the work of Elizabeth Mills, who had been exploring the possible meaning of voice and sound within the performance text. She argued,

The voice as sonic image signifies meaning in performance. When the making of vocal meaning and the signifying of vocal meaning are held central to the act of theatre, then the voice can be conceived of as having multiple sonic possibilities. The term sonic is used here to suggest that the voice is present as a sound image as well as being present as spoken text or vocal gesture.

(Mills 1999: 3)

The voice present as sound image is part of what I am calling "vocal text," and which includes the sound of the way the words are spoken. In class, this was explored separately from text, which was either words in print or a narrative lifted from an oral storytelling experience. Within the training we created ways of linking vocal text with text. For instance, when using printed text, we notated the vocal text above, around, over, and under the words to represent quality of gesture, volume (including crescendo and decrescendo), stress (via accent marks), pitch, and pauses/silences. I based this approach to notation on my experiences notating p'ansori during my private lessons. In this way, we created a system to explore the symbiotic relationship between language and the expression of that language through sound.

However, notation was only one step in investigating a sound and language relationship and how sound is understood culturally. The majority of my students had come to know sound in language through hangul, the written Korean language. As introduced in Chapter Three, hangul is a phonetic alphabet and its script is a representation of vernacular sounds, a visual reminder of the positioning of the vocal organs during articulation (Hoyt 2000: 157). Embedded within hangul are understandings of eum-yang (yin-yang in Chinese). Significant cultural understandings of sound are embedded in hangul, which frame the ways my students approach their understanding of sound.

With an understanding of the relationship between vocal text and written text and of the way sound in language behaves phonetically in hangul, my students and I devised exercises that explored linguistic and paralinguistic meaning: the way sound had meaning as timbre itself or as part of sonic design and equally how non-language sounds, such as a laugh, carry meaning, particularly as a performative gesture helping indicate character intention or subtext within a communicative moment on-stage. Then, we began to integrate sound within language by introducing what I called "simple text"—simple vowel-consonant combinations that explored the vibrations within the vowels and consonants themselves. We first counted numbers because the students were less likely to give numbers interpretive meaning and connect the use of the voice with text interpretation. Then, the students replaced the numbers with words. At this point there was the opportunity for interpretive uses of the voice, but the vibrations from the vowels and consonants could still be felt. Even when speaking a series of words as a sentence, the students could always return to pure sound or counting to remind themselves of the vibrations in the sound and refocus on timbre—sound itself—as having meaning.

During ear training exercises, I asked them to collect sounds they felt represented their culture and could be used as part of the semiotics of their performance text. Following Oh T'ae Sok's approach, each student would bring different sounds to class that they felt were "Korean." I was not interested in a definitive list of cultural sounds and corresponding meanings but of using the diverse collection of sounds to discuss the cultural meaning of sound within their communities. With some sounds, the students would generally agree on meaning, but other sounds had meaning specific to the student, depending on gender, age, life experience, or geographical origin.

Adding to our adaptations of Oh's work and the students' personal investigations of how culture affects the sounds we make and how we interpret the sounds we hear, I introduced the students to the work of Korean phonetician Moon Seung-Jae, entitled "What You Hear is What You See?" In this article, he detailed the first part of a two-part study in which he explored "the relationship between voice and the image information carried with the voice" (Moon 2002: 31). Moon sought to determine whether the mental image that a listener associates with a particular voice is accurate: "Is there a relationship between the voice and the image triggered by the voice?" (What You Hear: 31) .

To answer this question, Moon took eight Korean males and eight Korean females and recorded their voices speaking Korean. He then took two photos of each speaker, one a full body photo and the other a head shot. He asked a Korean-speaking experiment group to listen to the voices and try to match each voice with the correct photograph. The majority of the group successfully matched the correct voice with the correct photo. However, "even in the mismatches, there was a strong tendency for participants to agree on which voice should correspond to which photo."

Moon then did the second part of the study in which he took the same experiment to the US and asked an American-English-speaking experiment group to match Korean voice recordings to photographs of the speakers. The study found that "the Americans demonstrated no accuracy in matching the foreign voices to photos, but they too were consistent in their errors" (Moon 2009).

Moon's conclusion to the first study suggests that voices conjure up particular images with which many people identify. As a result, "the psychological effect of voice is not just an illusion, but the result of a mechanism based on the physical and concrete properties of the voice" (Moon 2002: 41). But the second study with the Americans indicated otherwise. Moon commented, "As a phonetician, I had expected the results [to be] more or less similar. Voice is a voice after all. But I was wrong. It seems culture plays a certain, important role" (Moon 2003). Moon's comment that he once thought "voice is a voice after all" with Berry's assertion (refer Chapter One) that her work can cross cultures because "the voice is the voice" (Ellis 2010: 122), comes from a similar premise—the voice, or perhaps sound initiating from voice, is universal. Like Moon, I came to understand that voice/sound was not universal but culturally influenced.

Dr. Moon's research suggested to me that the Korean experiment group was hearing something in the Korean voices that the Americans could not hear. If the Americans had access to the same vocal identifying marks as the Koreans did, the

Americans should have been able to use sound clues to identify at least some of the basic information, such as age and gender, a voice provides. Other clues might be so closely intertwined with language, or the use of language, that the Americans without Korean language skills would not have been able to guess the speaker. It seemed then that the social training the Korean participants received from their culture enabled them to decode certain aural/oral messages. Moon's research suggested that social oral/aural training helped the listener "read" sound/voice.

Cultural ear-training: Field research at Namdaemun Market

We integrated Moon's research into our project and did field research at Namdaemun Market, a permanent open market in the heart of Seoul. During our initial visits, we listened to and recorded the sounds of the vendor cries. We analyzed the way calls were sonically designed to catch the ear of the passer-by. We listened to dialogues between vendors and customers and the way they both used non-language sounds to influence each other when haggling over prices. We listened to ambient environmental sounds that forced speakers to change vocal tactics in order to be heard or to communicate better.

During the training process, the students realized the training was encouraging them to think and talk about sound in a different way. This shift affected the way they approached building a character. Up to this point, we had worked with building character voices using Linklater's suggested approach to building character like forming "answers to questions such as 'Who am I?' . . . 'What do I want?'" (Linklater 1976: 204).

The voice training we were developing seemed to be asking different questions of the students. Instead of first asking "What do I want?" and using it as inspiration to generate a vocal response, the students were first listening to a sound, which generated a responsive question: "What do I sound like it want?" The difference between the two questions is significant because the question shapes the process of building a character. The question "Who am I?" constructs a relationship between the actor and the character during the rehearsal process, away from the audience. Although audience reception may be a factor in the actor's choices, in general, the actor builds the character through textual analysis, personal experience, and rehearsal. A tremendous part of character building is completed before introducing it to an audience. The question, "Who does it sound like I am?" constructs a relationship not only between actor and character but also includes the listening audience as performance participant. The actor-producer of sound asks the question to the audience-receiver of that sound. The actor and audience create the character together by answering the character-building question in the moment of the aural/oral performance. In this way, the audience response becomes integral to building the character; indeed, much more of the work of building a character is done in the presence of the audience. This process accomplishes two things: (1) it points to ways in which the actor's agency and culturally influenced voice training construct the "who"—the character—for the benefit of the listening audience, even as it

(2) creates an oral/aural relationship not found in the question, "Who am I?" While that question represents a self-reflective thought process, "Who does it sound like I am?" represents a performance process, an oral/aural engagement that places culturally influenced voice/sound in the center of building the character.

In our second series of visits to the market, students shifted their focus from listening to sound towards thinking about the particular ways the voice is trained by the marketplace environment. Both vendor and performer have the opportunity to develop certain vocal skills and adjust them according to the specifics of their jobs and the conditions of the outdoor space. If vendors and performers use their voices well to draw a crowd, they have the opportunity to be rewarded monetarily for their efforts. Economics, as well as space and discipline-specific tasks, shape the training of the voice. While collecting audio samples of vendor calls, my students and I asked vendors to explain the way the environment of Namdaemun shaped their voices. During the interviews we asked the following questions:

- How long have you been selling with your voice in Namdaemun Market?
- Who taught you how to use your voice to sell?
- In your opinion, what qualities in the voice work best to attract customers and sell your products? How do you use your voice to attract customers?
- Who has the best voice in Namdaemun, in your opinion, and why?
- Is the best voice also the one who sells the most?
- Have you lost your voice selling in the market? How do you get your voice back?
- Do you always use the same style of voice or do you change sounds to attract customers or sell something new?

Most of the street vendors I spoke with taught themselves vocal techniques, mostly through trial and error. Some vendors learned through mimetic training, mentoring with a more experienced vendor. They all also agreed that while good vocal techniques will attract listeners, the best voice did not always sell the most: sometimes the rain drove customers away or the product was unpopular with consumers for some unknown reason. One female vendor attributed her successful sales record, as well as the strength of her voice, to being a devout Christian. But most of the vendors attributed the strength of their voices to the many years practicing their craft in the challenging environment of the marketplace. With this information, students had a better understanding of the particular vocal culture within the market, what sounds are valued, whose voices are valued, and how vocal sounds shape one's experience of Namdaemun as being unique from the other open-air permanent markets in Seoul. Importantly, the students better understood how the sounds and voices of Namdaemun play a part in shaping one's experience of this site and suggest a soundscape that is "Korean."

From their previous training in other classes, the students understood the literal function of "site-specific" performance. Here we moved away from using more traditional notions of "site" as a geographical place to other notions of site and how site is built through aural/oral exchange. Sally Mackey, in her work with performing place, differentiates the terms site, place, environment, and location. For her, site is equal to location as a "geo-physical, chorographic, delineated area." Site can be used conceptually whereas location "nods at person-inhabitation – site need not have that nuance." Place is "the aura . . . of a location together with the location itself and one with which human being[s] build a personal relationship and interaction. Place is both known physical materiality and psychological construction" (Mackey 2007: 75). In applying Mackey's terminology to our project, were we investigating the site as location or investigating the way this site becomes a place through the building of a personal aural relationship and through aural/oral interaction? If Moon's assertion is correct and "the psychological effect of voice is not just an illusion, but the result of a mechanism based on the physical and concrete properties of the voice" (41), then could the physical materiality and psychological construction of Namdaemun Market be shaped, in part, through the cultural sign-systems that helped my students connect with the market and participate within its performative structure? In their subsequent visits, students also collected oral histories from vendors, which included personal stories about their experiences in the markets or described concerns about the changing, perhaps disappearing, culture of the open-air market in modern Korean society. We conducted Studs Terkel-style interviews, which we edited into monologues and pieced together to tell the larger story of the market.

The Terkel-style techniques I taught students were based on those documented by Rick Ayers in his book, *Studs Terkel's Working: A Teaching Guide* (2001) written in cooperation with Terkel. I will not reiterate the details that are already articulated in Ayers book, but will simply point out a few of the adaptations we made. For the interview process, Ayers suggests,

> In a Studs Terkel interview, you do not talk about yourself like the New Journalist would. You begin with a short introduction to set the scene, then you report the interview. But here is where the authorship, the view of the interviewer, comes in more strongly than the Q & A format: you edit, severely edit, the interview. You take out all, or almost all, of your own questions. You cut and edit the responses to create a coherent narrative from the interviewee—a monologue, if you will.
>
> *(Ayers 2001:9)*

Students in my class not only collected oral histories as narrative but also used the interview process for training the ear to listen to the market/street sounds and record what they heard through written text and sound notation, to be taught to fellow students later during student-led devising sessions. After recording the interview, the students wrote the narrative out verbatim (word for word exactly, including non-language additions often found during unrehearsed storytelling, such as "um," "err," coughing, laughing, side comments made to companions, and so forth.). This process also trained the ear to listen closely to vocalizations and word choice. Over the course of several weeks of devising and rehearsal, students continued to edit down the interview into a three-minute actor's monologue to be combined with other students' monologues in a larger devised, original performance project.

My students and I replaced the short introduction Ayers suggested in favor of vocal choices to set the scene and move the action from one interview/monologue to another. Sometimes we placed the monologues back-to-back, similar to the linear construction found in Terkel's books, or we interwove the monologues as if they were dialogues between characters. Additional adaptations included multimedia equipment used during performance, such as live-feed video and microphones. Students also performed soundscapes in front of the audience with noise-makers from a prop table. Students sometimes divided one monologue into a chorus of voices. They played with genres, combining vocal gestures that might be considered "realistic" with vocalizations that might be considered abstract or "surreal."

Creating original, devised performances: The culture-voice relationship as the center of the creative process

Students devised voice training exercises based on their experiences in the market. One exercise was nicknamed "Competing Voices." Two students would enter the playing space and use interview material and vendor calls to catch the attention of the rest of the group. Later, we relocated this exercise to a local park in front of the school and students performed for passersby and local street vendors who critiqued the students' ability to gain their attention. It seemed that the vocal tactics used in vendor calls were preferred not only because they best captured and sustained listener attention, but also because they appeared to be more socially acceptable or culturally familiar. As a vocal tactic, volume successfully grabbed the passerby but was unsuccessful in sustaining listener attention. The most successful tactics were humor and the familiar vocal inflection patterns used by local street vendors in the area. Students learned empirically how the marketplace environment affected vocal training and performance.

After a site visit, students took a short sample of a vocal performance, such as a sales call, and analyzed the vocal performance by breaking it down into rhythm and melodic progression. Students usually wrote down verbatim the vendor calls with sound notation to help them during student-led and peer teaching sessions. Students used their understanding of *p'ansori* performance structure to shape their final performance of marketplace monologues.

The result was a performance of a place through the sounds, voices, and narratives found in that place. The aural/oral training used in performance created an audience/performer relationship that foregrounded a culturally influenced sound sign-system, communicating sound as well as text to engage the listener-spectator. In this way, culture became one of the material conditions of training the voice and shaping performance. A different "way of working," or training, the voice was made possible by strategically rethinking certain principles of voice practice through the cultural and educational context at KNUA. By investigating the politics of training and production, my voice classroom became an environment that invited critical inquiry and reflection, which trained students for a different kind of theatre making.

Notes

1 Later in this chapter, I will discuss how other prominent theatre practitioners, specifically Brecht and Laban, also looked to the off-stage site of the streets as a performance space inspiring models for on-stage body/voice performance.

2 The traditional name for a *p'ansori* performer, usually used during *p'ansori*'s "heyday" in the 19th century.

3 Based on my conversations with street performers and theatre professionals in Seoul, I suspect that this might also be one motivation for certain performers and theatre companies. Political theatre is quite active in Seoul and has been for some time. Korean theatre was very engaged with politics during the 1980s student democratic movement, although some of my colleagues feel it has since become less politically influencial and more commercially driven. Although I continue to research this topic, it is beyond the scope of this chapter to discuss these issues in depth.

4 This statement is based on informal discussions with multiple street performers at Insadong and Daehangno in Seoul over the course of four years researching this topic.

5 For example, Rudolph Laban encouraged his British assistant Jean Newlove to visit the marketplace to listen to "a stall-holder hawk[ed] his wares" as a part of Laban's lesson on "the dance of life." He explained, "true dance had lost its way, becoming an artificial art form and a pale reflection of earlier times when it had fulfilled an important role in society" (Newlove 1993: 15–16), and Brecht notates the calls of newspaper vendors in his writing ("The Street Scene: A Basic Model for an Epic Theatre," in Willett 1964: 128). Both artists appear to use the marketplace to inspire their own work by treating the marketplace as a site for training and/or performance.

6 Brecht wrote, "Until one understands the novelty, unfamiliarity and direct challenge to the critical faculties of the suggestion that street-corner demonstration of this sort can serve as a satisfactory basic model of major theatre one cannot really understand what follows [i.e. Brecht's epic theatre]" (Brecht 1957, 1963, 1964: 121).

7 Terkel reprinted a Brecht poem "A Worker Reads History," from *Selected Poems of Bertolt Brecht*, trans. H.R. Hays, to introduce his book *Working*, a collection of oral histories. (Terkel 1972: 15).

8 *Division Street: America* released in 1967 was a collection of oral histories collected from 70 people interviewed in Chicago, USA, exploring race relations in America by using one downtown Chicago street, named Division, as a microcosm for the race issues many American cities and citizens were facing during the Civil Rights movement in the 1960s.

9 Ayers quotes Smith from "The Shades of Loss," "For sixteen years now, inspired in part by the work of the great chronicler of American life, Mr. Studs Terkel, I have been searching for American character by using the tools of the theater" (in *Stud's Terkel's Working: A Teaching Guide*, 2001: 67).

10 Here I am borrowing from Brian Edminston's use of Dorothy Heathcote's "Mantle of the Expert" approach. Refer Heathcote and Bolton (1995).

References

Aston, E., Savona, G. (1991). *Theatre as Sign-System: A Semiotics of Text and Performance*. London: Routledge.

Ayers, R. (2001). *Studs Terkel's Working: A Teaching Guide*. New York: New Press.

Berry, C. (1973). *Voice and the Actor*. New York: Collier.

Brecht, B. (1957, 1963, 1964). *Brecht on Theatre*. ed. & trans. John Willett. New York: Hill and Wang.

Burkman, O. (2002). *The Guardian*, 1 March 2002.

Carlson, M. (1989). *Places of Performance: The Semiotics of Theatre Architecture*. Ithica, London: Cornell University Press.

Ellis, S. (2010). "The Body in the Voice," an interview with Cicely Berry, in *American Theatre Magazine Special Issue: Pillars of Voicework*, January. New York: Theatre Communications Group. www.americantheatre.org/2010/01/01/the-body-in-the-voice/. Accessed 30 March 2017.

Heathcote, D., Bolton, G. (1995). *Drama for Learning: Dorothy Heathcote's Mantle of the Expert Approach to Education*. Portsmouth: Heinemann.

Houseman, B. (2002). *Finding Your Voice: A Complete Voice Training Manual for Actors*. London: Nick Hern.

Houseman, B. (2008). *Tackling Text [and Subtext]: A Step-by-Step Guide for Actors*. London: Nick Hern.

Hoyt, J. (2000). *Soaring Phoenixes and Prancing Dragons: A Historical Survey of Korean Classical Literature*. Korean Studies Ser. 20. Seoul: Jimoondang.

Kim, A. J., Graves, R. B. (1999). *The Metacultural Theater of Oh T'ae Sok: Five Plays from the Korean Avant-Garde*. Honolulu: University of Hawai'i.

Kim, S.K. (2003). "East and West: The Twain Shall Never Meet?" *Korea Herald*, 16 April 2003.

Knowles, R.P. (1996). "Shakespeare, Voice, and Ideology: Interrogating the Natural Voice," in Bulman, J.C. (ed.) *Shakespeare, Theory, and Performance*. London: Routledge, 92–113.

Lessac, A. (1968). *The Use and Training of the Human Voice: A Practical Approach to Speech and Vocal Dynamics*. 2nd revised ed. New York: Mayfield Publishing.

Linklater, K. (1976). *Freeing the Natural Voice*. New York: Drama.

Linklater, K. (2017). LinklaterVoice.com. www.linklatervoice.com/kristin-linklater-voice-centre-calendar/event/144-sound-movement-embodying-language. Accessed 27 March 2017.

Mackey, S. (2007). "Transient Root: Performance, Place and Exterritorials," *Performance Research*, 12 (2), 75–78.

McCallion, M. (1988). *The Voice Book*. London: Faber and Farber.

Mills, E. (1999). *Theatre Voice as Metaphor: The Advocacy of a Praxis Based on the Centrality of Voice to Performance*. Unpublished MA dissertation, Rhodes University, Grahamstown.

Moon, S.J. (2002). "What You Hear Is What You See?" *Journal of the Acoustical Society of Korea*, 21, 31–41.

Moon, S.J. (2003). Personal interview. Seoul, Korea, 28 January 203.

Moon, S.J. (2009). "Can You See What I'm Saying?" Attrib. Fenella Saunders, 27 October. http://madang.ajou.ac.kr/~moon/discover.html.

Nelson, J. (2015). *The Voice Exercise Book: A Guide to Healthy and Effective Voice Use*. London: National Theatre Publishing.

Newlove, J. (1993). *Laban for Actors and Dancers*. New York: Routledge.

Pihl, M. (1994). *The Korean Singer of Tales*. Cambridge: Harvard University Press.

Pavis, P. (1996). *The Intercultural Performance Reader*. London: Routledge.

Rodenburg, P. (1992). *The Right to Speak*. New York: Routledge.

Terkel, S. (1967). *Division Street America*. New York: New Press.

Terkel, S. (1972). *Working.* New York: New Press.

Werner, S. (2001). *Shakespeare and Feminist Performance.* London: Routledge, 2001.

Zarrilli, P. B. (2002). "Introduction to Part One," in Zarrilli, P.B. (ed.) *Acting (Re)Considered.* 2nd ed. London: Routledge, 7–21.

CONCLUSION

This monograph has asked how two vocal training traditions, situated within very different cultural contexts, might interweave at the level of technique in order to create a practical curriculum that could address the needs of my students at the Korean National University of Arts, and later, the Royal Central School of Speech and Drama and East 15 Acting School. However, in adapting techniques for my classrooms, I found I had to investigate the larger key principles that underpinned the practices. Eventually, an examination of principles and pratices necessitated a larger investigation of the worldviews that contexualized each training tradition, leading me to ask "What is a voice? What can/should it do? How can/should it do it?" What was once a context-specific curriculum design grew into Lo and Gilbert's "bigger picture," suggesting the possibility of an intercultural/interdisciplinary "way of working."

In creating an alternative paradigm for training the voice, I have also needed to (re)consider the relationship between training and performance, how they affect and are affected by each other. Performance demands shape voice training, but different approaches to training also suggest more performance possibilities. By training in several traditions simultaneously, the student has the opportunity to (re)consider vocal form and aesthetic function in new and different combinations.

A detailed analysis of technique, with comparisons between adapted *p'ansori* and adaptations of the "natural/free" voice approach, was the foundation from which to begin interweaving approaches in the voice studio. Beginning with an analysis of breath production, both *p'ansori* and "natural/free" voice techniques seemed to practice similar inhalation techniques but not exhalation techniques. When converting the exhaled breath into sound, the difference seemed to depend on the use of muscular contraction, resonating chambers, desirable pitch range, and culturally influenced, discipline-specific aesthetics.

Aesthetics in *p'ansori* produce the desirable "thick voice" or husky quality of *sŏngŭm*. During the process of training *sŏngŭm*, the cultivated vocal break is used to create sorrowful harmonics by playing with the space between chest and head voice. To a *p'ansori* artist, the alteration of the vocal folds during training is not "vocal abuse" but vocal strengthening that helps, not hinders, characterization and emotional vocal range. The beauty of the *sŏngŭm*, or "sound/voice," comes in part from the excess muscular contraction but for Linklater, tension "murders" the vibrations necessary to create a rich, resonating sound (1976: 41). As Park noted, "*Pansori* as a vocal art is not unique in the sense that its vocal techniques strive to interpret faithfully its distinct aesthetic, just as the Western classical singing strives to reveal its own aesthetics" (1995: 226).

The purpose of training switches if I am suggesting the student root the breath in the "I" of the voice, cultivating the actor's "self" (Berry 1973:22) or if I am helping the student overcome ego-identification to "form one body" (Leder 1990:171) with the audience.

Moving between different concepts of breath necessarily introduced movement between breath/*ki* in *p'ansori* and "energy" as understood in the "natural/free" voice approach.

An investigation into the role of breath in both training traditions led to questions about the role of "energy" and its perception as actor's "presence." Both *p'ansori* and the "natural/free" voice approach were interested in "energy," which suggested to me another point of overlap between the two training modes. But, *ki* and "energy" function differently in each practice. By focusing on "centering" and *dahnjeon* breathing as examples of practice, this monograph attempted to articulate how "energy" and *ki* might be generated by technique. During the transmission of technique, the idea of feedback loops seemed to suggest how an exchange of "energy" might happen between teacher and student, and then between performer and audience characterized as "flow," "comunitas," or "forming one body." When an actor, who has trained her voice by interweaving very different practices from multiple cultures, performs for an audience of attentive listeners from different cultures and/or discipline-specific knowledges ranging from novices to connoisseurs, what may result is varied perceptions of how "energy" functions within the dramaturgy and aesthetics of a performance, characterized as multiple "presences."

Next, this monograph progressed to an investigation of the relationship between voice/sound and text, characterized as "vocal text." The interaction between "vocal text" and "text" offered the possibility of placing voice/sound in the center of the creative process by adapting speaking/listening models from verbatim theatre. Aural/oral based performance structures, such as those found in *p'ansori*, storytelling, and oral history performance, offer the actor the opportunity to travel the voice/sound along a form/function continuum. The actor has the choice to move from the aesthetic objectives of realism by (re)considering the voice/sound as "text" within an aural/oral relationship. Indeed, the idea of "text" is understood almost entirely through aural/oral processes, such as a one-to-one interview, mimetic training, and vocal devising and performance.

This monograph also demonstrated the importance of site in influencing vocal training and performance. By returning to the marketplace, a traditional training and performance site of *p'ansori*, students were able to combine their developing "ear-training," attentive, detailed listening to sound and its proposed meaning, with stories told to them by marketplace vendors. The result was a performance of "place" through the sounds, voices and narratives found in the site. The aural/oral performance created an audience/performer relationship that relied on a culturally influenced sound sign system to communicate vocal text as well as text to engage the listener-spectator.

When interweaving key principles and practices of adapted *p'ansori* with adaptations of the "natural/free" voice approach into my classrooms, I am careful to keep techniques contextualized within their historical and cultural reference. When I teach "centering" and all that practice has to offer from an Anglo-American voice tradition, I use the English word "center." When I teach "*dahnjeon* breathing," working towards a deeper integration of bodymind and cultivating *ki* as "energy," I use the Korean word *dahnjeon*.

Technical exercises, their names and how they are framed for the student are important to the way the student understands and embraces technique. For instance, Bae Il-dong taught me how to "harvest" the sound. Techniques are developed from principles rooted in a philosophy of the body and voice. The materials of training (body, voice, breath, energy, "presence," sound, text, and so forth) are not universally accessible and understood "human" experiences but are a part of a "lived body" experience, heavily influenced by the socio-cultural understandings of "self" and the place of body as "self" within practice.

My pedagogical approach views different traditions along a continuum of training. As techniques mix within the environment of my students' bodies/voices, any emergent understandings of what a voice is, what it can/should do, and how voice can/should do "it," result from a polar relationship between traditions within this environment of transference. These interactions are sometimes intentionally constructed in studio and sometimes through accidental happenings when using "trial and error" as a teaching/learning method.

The benefit of training in two different traditions simultaneously means the student can call upon different training techniques depending on the performance task. The student can think and talk about the materials of training using different concepts and different vocabularies. In my experience, having multiple worldviews in the voice studio enriches the experience of training and designing interactions between worldviews helps address the many ways my students understand their bodies and voices and the potential of the voice as it is trained. This approach also offers the possibility of theorizing one understanding of these materials, which could benefit the ways voice trainers and scholars think, talk about, and train the actors' voices.

Throughout this monograph, embedded within each chapter, has been a sustained critique of my practice and profession. The comparisons between *p'ansori* and the "natural/free" voice put into sharp relief differences that had to be negotiated in order to interweave both traditions. This process has offered an opportunity for voice practitioners/trainers, like myself, to (re)consider fundamental assumptions made about voice within the pedagogy. What could "natural/free" voice training learn by reviewing its own principles of the voice, re-examining the potential of the voice by considering it through a very different discipline like *p'ansori*? The discoveries made here could also be fruitfully extrapolated and contribute to discussions in performance studies, ethnomusicology, voice studies, and those interested in intercultural theories and practices.

There is a growing trend in teaching Anglo-American voice pedagogy internationally, a trend that follows the larger intercultural theatre movement that has been evolving over the past 50 years. I suspect that as the invitations and means to travel and teach internationally become available to more voice trainers, this field will notice a rise in intercultural/interdisciplinary training techniques. Obviously, I am not the only teacher who has sent herself on a professional journey to find solutions for curriculum problems while teaching in countries, cultures, and languages not her own.

It is inevitable that this new direction in the field influences the way practitioners think and talk about the voice. It is appropriate that voice trainers reevaluate the language and ideas behind practice given the new contexts in which this practice is being taught. The basic questions raised in the Introduction about the nature of intercultural work are useful guideposts to direct discussions about overseas work and intercultural/interdisciplinary integrations in voice pedagogy.

How can intercultural training avoid reducing training traditions to "mere techniques"?

How does/can one address Berry's vision of a "true meeting of cultures"?

Who decides and how will they decide when this "true meeting" has occurred?

As Ong asks, who owns the work?

If one allows these questions to guide practical training, voice teachers will be exposing themselves to a new theoretic basis for teaching voice. By expanding into the field of intercultural training, voice practitioners must engage in theoretical discourse to responsibly shape the practice. Participating in ongoing discussions can provide the necessary foundation for teaching voice overseas and articulating the influences and integrations that can happen when two cultures meet and interact. I am suggesting here more than simply a code of ethical behavior. I am suggesting that the field of voice training embrace theory and practice together as the foundation for curriculum design.

As practitioners, like myself, struggle to articulate empirical knowledge through the limitations of language, scholars in the field of intercultural discourse will also need to cultivate new skills by which to evaluate the writings of practice. The writings of practice will always refer back to the studio work regardless of the absence of experience in a book medium. By embracing a "practice as research" model, scholars will have the skills to better evaluate the language and ideas behind the training techniques.

The intercultural/interdisciplinary approach I am detailing in this monograph is simply offered as one possibility. What is detailed here represents a point in an ongoing developmental process. I hope that this work adds to ongoing discussions for both practitioners and scholars, and proposes an alternative approach to training actors' voices.

References

Berry, C. (1973). *Voice and the Actor*. New York: Collier.
Leder, D. (1990). *The Absent Body*. Chicago: University of Chicago Press.
Linklater, K. (1976). *Freeing the Natural Voice*. New York: Drama.

INDEX